Catechism
of the
Catholic Church

Simplified Version

By:
Rev. Msgr. Vincent M. Walsh

Foreword by Cardinal Justin Rigali

Table of Contents

Table of Contents (continued)

Table of Contents (continued)

PART FOUR – CHRISTIAN PRAYER (2558-2865)

Foreword

Monsignor Vincent M. Walsh, J.C.D., a priest of the Archdiocese of Philadelphia, presents to the public his new work *Catechism of the Catholic Church - Simplified Version*. He endeavors to offer the rich content of the Church's catechetical teaching in an abbreviated form, which he hopes will be easily accessible and helpful to many people. It is my prayer that his pastoral effort will indeed bear much fruit in communicating "the inscrutable riches of Christ" (Eph.3:8).

Cardinal Justin Rigali
Archbishop of Philadelphia

Feast of St. Gregory the Great
September 3, 2004

I

Ecclesiastical Approval

This book had been submitted to the Archdiocese of Philadelphia Censor Librorum who has stated in writing that there is nothing in this book that is contrary to faith or morals.

Public Domain

The Catechism has been a blessing to the entire Church. Hopefully, this Simplified Version will also bless many. Therefore, from the very beginning this Simplified Version is in public domain. Any person can reproduce any part of this Catechism. Any publishing house can print and sell this Simplified Version. Anyone can translate and publish the text. All that is asked is that acknowledgement be given to:

Key of David Publications
204 Haverford Road
Wynnewood, PA 19096

Printed by: DigiPrint Solutions, LLC
Bensalem, PA 19020
215-604-0950

Explaining A Simplified Version

Previous Simplified Versions

Previous Simplified Versions include *Love and Responsibility, Theology of the Body and the Eucharistic Encyclical.* A Simplified Version places the text (paragraph by paragraph) into fewer words with an easier style, while remaining true to the original work.

Four Drafts

To accomplish this, the final text went through four separate drafts.

1. Extracting the main thoughts from each paragraph
2. Adding the secondary thoughts of each paragraph
3. Comparing the Simplified Version with the Catechism to assure accuracy
4. Placing the thoughts into an easy-to-read style

Getting a Final Product

The result is a simplified version (not a summary) in which the thoughts of every single paragraph are in the final draft. Also, every attempt was made to highlight the reasoning process that links the thoughts.

In Brief Paragraphs

After each section, the Catechism reviews its teachings in an "in brief" section. Since the whole Simplified Version is meant to be brief, these paragraphs are totally omitted.

Numbering of Paragraphs

The Catechism has 2865 numbered paragraphs. These numbers are very helpful and are retained after the headings of each section. The numbers of the "in brief" paragraphs are noted so the reader can see clearly the sequence.

Comments on the Catechism

The Catechism is a treasure house of the Church's teachings, containing the best theology expressed as succinctly as possible. However, the original can be difficult to read because it draws from so many sources.

Full Richness

Obviously, a Simplified Version cannot capture the full richness of the original Catechism. With the numbering of all the paragraphs, the reader can very easily find the corresponding paragraphs in the Catechism.

Table of Contents

The original Table of Contents was very complex. A totally new table was written and incorporated into the text.

Footnotes

The original Catechism has many footnotes. To help the reader, many of these footnotes have been made part of the text, (as the names of the saints or scriptural citations).

Since the Simplified Version is aimed primarily at a very wide audience, the name of the particular council (as "Second Vatican Council) is used instead of the document's title.

Quotes to Remember

This section has been added to the original according to the space available between chapters.

PROLOGUE

Three Truths (1-25)
Scripture gives three clear truths:
1. Eternal life is to know God and Jesus whom he sent (Jn.17:3);
2. God wills all to be saved and to know the truth (1Tim.2:3-4);
3. All are saved only in the name of Jesus. (Acts 4:12)

God Comes Close to Man in Jesus (1-3)
God created man to share in his blessings. God always comes close to man and calls man to seek him. To gather men (scattered by sin) God sent Jesus, his only Son. In Jesus he invites men to become his adopted children and heirs of eternal life.

Jesus sent his disciples to preach and to baptize, so everyone would know God's call. (Mt.28:18-20) The apostles "preached everywhere" and the Lord "confirmed the message by the signs that attended it." (Mk.16:20)

Those who heard must now proclaim this apostolic Good News, (faithfully preserved in the Church) and hand it on to each new generation.

Catechesis – The Making of Disciples (4-5)
Catechesis is the Church's efforts to make disciples and to instruct them. Catechesis must impart Christian teaching in a full and systematic way.

Catechesis builds upon other parts of Church life (missionary preaching, apologetics, Christian living, sacraments, etc) in gaining new members and in deepening their inner growth.

Previous Catechisms (6-10)
Renewal in the Church is always accompanied by intense Catechesis. Excellent catechetical works were written by St. Cyril of Jerusalem, St. John Chrysostom, St. Ambrose and St. Augustine (among others).

The Roman Catechism (Council of Trent) gave rise to the works of St. Charles Borromeo, St. Peter Canisius, and St. Robert Bellarmine.

After the second Vatican Council, the Extraordinary Synod of Bishops (1985) asked for a catechism of all Catholic doctrines.

Presenting An Organic Synthesis (11-12)

This catechism draws from the Scriptures, the Church Fathers, the liturgy and the Church's Magisterium, and presents an organic synthesis of fundamental Catholic doctrines. Hopefully, it will help the faithful and those responsible for catechesis.

The Four Pillars (13)

The great tradition of Catholic Catechesis is built upon four pillars:
1. the Creed,
2. the Sacraments,
3. the Commandments
4. the Our Father (The Lord's Prayer)

PART ONE: THE PROFESSION OF FAITH (14)

Part One has three chapters:
1. God the Father and Creator,
2. Christ as Lord and Savior
3. The Spirit as Sanctifier.

PART TWO: THE SACRAMENTS OF FAITH (15)

This explains how the salvation accomplished by Jesus Christ and the Spirit is made present in the liturgy and in the seven sacraments.

PART THREE: THE LIFE OF FAITH (16)

The third part shows how man can gain his final goal (heaven) by keeping the Ten Commandments.

PART FOUR: PRAYER IN THE LIFE OF FAITH

The fourth part shows the importance of prayer and explains the seven parts of the Our Father.

Practical Directions for Using This Simplified Version (18-22)

Each theme must be seen in relationship to others. The following changes have been made in this Simplified Version. Many of the footnotes in the original are now part of the text itself. The quotations (in smaller print in the original) are shortened and integrated into the main text. The "In Brief" sections are omitted. Only the numbers are cited so the reader is not confused.

Need for Adaptations (23-25)

The catechism does not try to adapt the message to various cultures or age groups. These indispensable adaptations are the task of the catechist. The goal of catechesis is charity. "Whatever is proposed for belief, for hope, or for action must be always directed to the love that never ends." (Roman Catechism)

Quotes to Remember

Catechesis is intimately bound up with the whole of the Church's life. (Second Vatican Council)

The plan of this catechism is inspired by the great traditions of catechisms which build upon the four pillars of the Creed, the sacraments, the commandments and prayer.

Periods of renewal in the Church are also intense moments of catechesis.

3

PART ONE
THE PROFESSION
OF FAITH
(26-1065)

1
MAN'S CAPACITY FOR GOD (26-49)

I Believe (26)
> Understanding what "<u>to believe</u>" means.
> 1. Man's search for God (Chapter One)
> 2. God coming to man by Revelation (Chapter Two)
> 3. Man responding in faith (Chapter Three)

Called to Search For God (27 – 28)
> God has placed a desire for himself in every person. He draws man to himself and facilitates man's search. Man is called to speak with God and be in communion with him. (Second Vatican Council)
> Historically, man's religious beliefs have been expressed in diverse ways. These religious expressions show that man is a "religious being." "God made all peoples that they would search for him." (Acts 17:26-27)

Inhibiting Factors (29 – 30)
> Many factors (ignorance, evil, desire for riches, bad example, teachings hostile to religion) lead man to reject his "vital bond to God." Out of fear, man hides himself. (cf Gn.3:8-10) God still calls man to seek him, and every person must search for God with his intellect, will and "an upright heart." "You have made us for

yourself, and our heart is restless until it rests in you." (St. Augustine)

Proofs for God's Existence (31 – 32)

Proofs for God's existence come from arguments which converge, convince and provide ways for man to know God. These proofs are found in the physical world and man's inner world.

Paul writes clearly "What can be known is evident to them (pagans) because God made it evident to them. He is perceived in what he has made." (Rom.1:19-20) Augustine states that all human beauty is a witness to God.

Proofs From Within the Person (33)

Man is endowed with a sense of moral goodness. By his conscience, man asks about God's existence. This shows that man has a spiritual soul (the seed of eternity) which comes directly from God.

So the world and the human person can begin to exist, they must participate in a Being Who has no origin and no end. The person must realize that the goal of human existence is God himself.

The Power of Reason (35)

Man can reason to the existence of a personal God. However, God has also chosen to reveal himself. Rational proofs can show that revealed truths are not opposed to reason.

Reason's Power and Limits (36 – 38)

Man, by reason alone, can know that God exists through the created world which God has made. (First Vatican Council) Therefore, man can accept God's revelation.

However, serious obstacles exist. First, religious truths cannot be seen. Second, religious truths demand self-sacrifice. Third, man experiences inner disordered appetites. Man is easily persuaded to consider as false what he does not want to acknowledge as true. (Pius XII – Humani Genesis) Therefore, man needs revealed truths, even those which man can grasp by reason (such as God's existence).

5

The Limits of Human Language (39-40)

The intellect (unaided by the Bible) can grasp some truths about God. Therefore, a dialogue with all peoples (atheists, philosophers, etc.) is possible. Yet, we are limited and can speak about God only with human language.

Describing God (41-43)

We begin to describe God according to his creatures (which reflect his goodness). We also "purify" our language because human words fall short in describing him. Although limited, our language can still attain to God, (sometimes expressing only what God is not).

In Brief - 44 - 49

Quotes to Remember

Indeed, he is not far from each one of us. For, in him we live and move and have our being. (Acts 17:28)

....

The dignity of man rests above all in the fact that he is called to communion with God. (Second Vatican Council)

....

Our heart is restless until it rests in you. (St. Augustine)

....

Man can reason to the existence of a personal God.

....

Out of fear, man still hides himself from God.

....

All human beauty is a witness to God

....

6

2
God Comes to Man (50 - 141)

Beyond Human Knowledge (50)
Fortunately, God has revealed his eternal plan by sending his Son, Jesus Christ, and the Holy Spirit (a mystery revealed only in this final age).

God Wants Man to Come Near in Jesus (51 –53)
God wants all men to have access to him through Christ and in the Holy Spirit. (cf Eph.1:9 and 2:18)   Although "dwelling in unapproachable light" (1 Tim.6:16), God wants to communicate his life to man. Man can share in God's nature and live beyond his natural capacity.

God's revelation culminated in the person and mission of Jesus Christ. "The Word of God became the Son of man in order to accustom man to perceive God and to accustom God to dwell in man." (St. Irenaeus)

Revelation not destroyed by sin (54 – 55)
God manifested himself to our first parents and clothed them with grace.   Even sin did not ruin God's plan because he immediately promised redemption. (Gen. 3:15) "Again and again you offered a covenant to man." (Eucharistic Prayer IV)

Salvation to People Groups (56 – 58)
Sin shattered man's unity. However, God said to Noah, "I am establishing my covenant with you and your descendants after you." (Gen. 9:9) God planned salvation according to groups, "each with its own language, by their families, in their nations." (Gen.10:5) This division into nations was cosmic, social and religious.   However, God's plan was always threatened by polytheism and idolatry.

This covenant with Noah remained in effect until the proclamation of the gospel and brought forth many holy people (the just Abel, the king priest Melchizedek, Noah, Daniel and Job).

Gathered Together in Abraham (59 – 61)

To gather scattered humanity, God chose Abram and named him Abraham, "the father of many nations." (Gen.17:5) His descendents (Israel) prepared for the Church and were the root onto which the Gentiles were grafted. (Rom. 11:17-24)

From Moses to the Prophets (62-64)

God freed his people from Egypt, made a covenant with them (through Moses on Mt. Sinai) and gave them his law. Israel is God's priestly people, the first to hear God's word.

Through the prophets, God proclaimed a radical redemption and told his people to await a new covenant. (Jer. 31:31-34) In the Old Testament, God used many women to keep Israel's hopes alive (Sarah, Rebecca, Judith, Esther, etc.). Among these, Mary is the purest figure

CHRIST JESUS – FULLNESS OF ALL REVELATION

God's Final and Complete Word (65-66)

In the last days, God "has spoken to us by a son." (Heb.1:1-2) In his own unsurpassable Word, God has said everything. There will be no other word. "In giving us his Son, he spoke everything to us. He has no more to say." (St. John of the Cross)

Because this plan of salvation will never pass away, there will be no new public revelation. (Second Vatican Council) However, much in Christian revelation is not yet completely explicit.

Private Revelations (67)

"Private revelations" (discerned and welcomed by the Church) do not complete Christ's definitive Revelation. Rather, they help believers in a certain historical period to live Christ's revelation more fully. The Church rejects those revelations (associated with non-Christian religions and recent sects) which claim to surpass or correct Christ's revelation.

In Brief – 68 - 73

Intact and Transmitted (74-75)

God wants everyone to be saved through Jesus Christ (1Tim.2:4), who must be proclaimed to all nations. Therefore,

God has kept this revelation intact to be transmitted to all ages. (Second Vatican Council)

Christ commanded his disciples to preach the gospel. (Mt. 28:19-20; Mk. 16:15)

Two Forms (76)

The gospel was transmitted in two ways:
1. Orally - (By their preaching, good example and establishing institutions the apostles passed on what they heard from Christ or were taught by the Spirit.
2. In writing - The apostles and others (under the Spirit's inspiration) put this message into writing.

The Bishops and Tradition (77-79)

The apostles established bishops as their successors with the authority to teach. This apostolic preaching, (especially as expressed in the inspired books), must be preserved through a continuous line of apostolic succession.

This living transmission is called Tradition, distinct from, yet closely united with, Sacred Scripture. God's revelation will always remain active and present in the Church because God still speaks to the Church, and the Spirit still leads believers into full truth.

Same Source and Goal (80)

Both Sacred Tradition and Sacred Scripture (which are bound closely together) flow from a common source and have the same goal. They make present the mystery of Christ who always remains with the Church.

Two Modes – Scripture and Tradition (81-82)

Sacred Scripture is God's speech written under the breath of the Holy Spirit. Tradition transmits, in its entirety, the Word of God to the apostles' successors. The Church does not derive her certainty about revealed truths from Scripture alone. Both Scripture and Tradition must be equally honored.

What the Apostles Learned (83)

This Tradition comes from what the apostles learned from Jesus and the Holy Spirit. The first generation Church had no written New Testament and the New Testament itself shows the process of a living Tradition. This Tradition must be distinguished from various types of traditions (liturgical, theological, etc.) which grew up in local churches and is subject to Church Magisterium.

INTERPRETATION OF THE FAITH HERITAGE

Faithful to the Teaching (84)
By adhering to this Tradition, the people remain faithful to the apostolic teaching. Thus, there should be a remarkable harmony between the bishops and the faithful.

An Authentic Interpretation (85-87)
Giving an authentic interpretation of God's Word (written or oral) belongs to the teaching office of the Church, that is, to the bishops in communion with the Pope, who exercise their authority in Jesus' name.

This Magisterium is not superior to God's Word, because the Church teaches what has been handed down by the Spirit, expounding God's Word from the single deposit of faith. By their docility to their pastors, the faithful hear the words of Christ. "He who hears you, hears me." (Lk.10:16)

Dogmas – Proposed Truths (88-90)
The Church proposes truths which are actually contained in or have a necessary connection with Divine Revelation. The faithful must adhere to these dogmas by faith.

Dogmas and the spiritual life are connected because dogma illuminates the path of holiness. The person should welcome this light.

All dogmas are connected and coherent. They have a "hierarchy", since they vary in their relationship to the Church's foundation.

Inability to Err (91-93)
All the faithful, anointed by the Spirit, can understand and hand on these truths.

When the bishops and the faithful, by their supernatural appreciation of faith (sensus fidei) manifest a universal consent in matters of faith or morals, the whole body of the faithful cannot err.

The People of God, guided by Church's Magisterium, can adhere to these truths and apply them in daily living.

Ways of Growing in Faith (94-95)

Faith grows by the study of believers, by theological research, by reading the scriptures and by preaching.

Sacred Tradition, Sacred Scripture and the Magisterium of the Church are so connected that one cannot stand without the others.

In Brief - 96 - 100

God Uses Words to Speak (101-104)

Just as the Lord Jesus took the nature of man, so God speaks to us in the words of men.

Throughout Sacred Scripture, God speaks one Word which expresses himself completely. "One and the same Word of God extends throughout Scripture. One and the same utterance resounds in the mouths of all the sacred writers. (St. Augustine)

Therefore, the Church venerates the scripture as she does the Lord's Body. She feeds all the faithful from the one table of God's Word and Christ's Body.

Written By God (105)

God is the author of Sacred Scripture because it has been written under the guidance of the Holy Spirit. The Church accepts as sacred and canonical all of the books of the Old and New Testament, whole and entire, with all their parts.

Who Used Human Authors (106-108)

God chose and inspired certain men who used their own powers in writing. The Spirit showed them what he wanted written and no more. They were still true authors.

Because all that the human author wrote was affirmed by the Spirit, these books teach faithfully and without error what God wanted to reveal for our salvation. Nevertheless, the Christian faith is not a "religion of the book" but of the living Word of God (Jesus).

11

Attentiveness and Study Needed (109-110)
The correct interpretation of scripture demands attentiveness to what the human author wanted to say and to what God wanted to reveal. Discovering the human author's intention demands a study of the culture, the modes of narrating and of the different forms of writing (history, poetry, prophecy, etc.).

Three Criteria (111-114)
Scripture must be interpreted in light of the Spirit who wrote the Scriptures. Correct interpretation requires that the reader:
1. Be attentive to the "content and unity of the whole Scripture." God's plan (in the Old and New Testament) has a unity in Christ. "Sacred Scripture, like the 'heart of Christ' was closed before the Passion. Since the passion the Scriptures have been opened." (St. Thomas Aquinas)
2. Read the scriptures within the Church's living tradition. "According to the spiritual meaning which the Spirit grants to the Church." (Origin)
3. Apply the "analogy of faith" (the coherence of all truths among themselves and within God's plan).

Three Spiritual Senses (115-119)
Scripture has both a literal sense (the words themselves) and three different spiritual senses:
1. <u>Allegorical</u> sense–recognizing events in the light of Christ (the parting of the Red Sea) as a sign of Baptism
2. <u>Moral</u> sense– using as a help to act justly
3. <u>Anagogical</u> sense– seeing the truths in light of eternal happiness

All interpretation is subject to the Church and exegetes must help the Church form a firmer judgment. "I believe in the gospel because of the authority of the Church." (St. Augustine)

THE CANON OF SCRIPTURE

Seventy-three Inspired Books (120)
Based upon the apostolic Tradition, the Church discerned 73 inspired books, (46 Old Testament books and 27 New Testament books). The list of these books is in the Appendix.

Permanent Value of Old Testament (121-123)

The Old Testament books are divinely inspired and have permanent value. The Old Testament was oriented to prepare for Christ and the books are a storehouse of sublime teaching and sound wisdom.

The Church always venerated the Old Testament books and condemned Marcionism, (a heresy claiming that the Old Testament was void.)

Gospels – The Heart of the New Testament (124 – 125)

The central object of the New Testament is the acts, passion and glorification of Jesus Christ and his Church's beginnings under the Spirit. The gospels are the heart of all the scriptures and the principle source of Christ's life and teachings.

Three Stages of Formation (126-127)

The gospel's formation had three stages:
1 What Jesus did while living among us.
2 What the Church, under the Spirit's power, taught orally about Jesus after his Ascension.
3 What the four authors selected to be written and which was shaped according to the situation of their churches.

The gospels have a unique place in the lives of the saints. "There is no doctrine which could be better than the text of the Gospel." (St. Caesarea the Younger) "Mainly the gospels occupy my mind. I am always finding fresh lights, hidden and enthralling meanings." (St. Therese of Lisieux)

Old and New – Light for Each Other (128-130)

The Church has shown the unity of God's plan by seeing Old Testament "types" which prefigure what Christ accomplished.

Because the Old Testament retains its own intrinsic value, the New Testament must be read in light of the Old (as the early Christians always did). "The New Testament lies hidden in the Old and the Old is unveiled in the New." (St. Augustine)

Old Testament events (such as the call of the Patriarchs and the Exodus) have value in God's plan even though they were intermediate stages.

Life in God's Word (131-133)

Everyone must have access to the Bible. The Word of God must be the soul of theology (in all its forms) and of the ministry of the word. Especially, the homily must be nourished by Scripture. By reading scripture, the faithful learn the "surpassing knowledge of Jesus Christ." "Ignorance of the scriptures is ignorance of Christ." (St. Jerome)

In Brief - 134 - 141

Quotes to Remember

God wants everyone to be saved through Jesus Christ, who must be proclaimed to all the nations so this revelation might reach the ends of the earth.

It pleased God to reveal himself and to make known the mystery of his will. (Second Vatican Council)

In the condescension of his goodness God speaks to us in human words.

God is the author of Sacred Scripture because it has been written under the guidance of the Holy Spirit.

The gospels are the heart of all the scriptures and the principle source of Christ's life and teachings.

Ignorance of the scriptures, is ignorance of Christ.
(St. Jerome)

3
Man's Response to God (142-184)

Faith and Obedience (142-144)

By revelation, God calls men. By faith, man responds to God's invitation. By this "obedience of faith" (Rom. 1:5) man submits his will and intellect to God, the Revealer, because God guarantees its truth. Abraham is the model of this obedience and Mary is the most perfect embodiment of this submission.

Abraham (145-146)

Abraham went as a pilgrim to a strange land, even when he did not know where he was going. After his wife Sarah conceived by faith, Abraham was willing in faith to sacrifice his son, Isaac. (Heb. 11:17) Being "strong in faith" Abraham became the "father of all who believe." (Rom. 4:11)

Jesus – the Perfecter (147)

Although Hebrews praises the many Old Testament persons who "received divine approval" the author says that "something better" awaits us, namely, Jesus the "perfecter of our faith." (Heb. 12:2)

Mary – the Purest Realization (148-149)

By the "obedience of faith" Mary welcomed the angel and gave her consent "Let it be done to me according to your word." (Lk. 1:37-38) Elizabeth praised her for believing that "The word spoken to you would be fulfilled." (1:45) Because of her faith, Mary is blessed by all generations to come. (1:48) Because Mary's faith never wavered, the Church venerates her as the purest realization of faith.

A Unique, Personal Adherence (150)

Faith is a personal adherence to God and a free assent to all that God has revealed. Because we entrust ourselves fully to God, it is different from any faith we place in a human person.

CHARACTERISTICS OF FAITH

To The Beloved Son (151)

For a Christian, believing in God must be joined to a faith in Jesus, who is God's "Beloved Son". Jesus himself commanded, "Believe in God and believe also in me." (Jn.14:1) We believe because Jesus is the "Word made flesh" (Jn.1:14) and "has seen the Father." (Jn.6:46)

And to the Spirit (152)

Only through the Holy Spirit can a person believe in Jesus. "No one can say 'Jesus is Lord', except by the Holy Spirit." (1Cor.12:3) The Spirit is God because "He searches the depths of God." (1Cor.2:10-11) Only God can know God completely.

A Free Gift (153)

Peter proclaimed that Jesus was the Christ, Jesus said that this knowledge was revealed by "My Father who is in heaven." (Mt.16:17) Therefore, faith is a free gift from God, which makes it easy to accept and believe the truth.

Intellect Assenting to Truth (154-155)

Faith is also an authentically human act which does not violate man's dignity. In human affairs we trust the word of others (as when a couple exchanges wedding vows). Therefore, man can certainly trust God, with whom he shares an interior communion. By faith, man's will (aided by God) commands his intellect to assent to a divine truth. (St. Thomas Aquinas)

God Supplies Motives (156)

Faith does not result from the truths appearing naturally intelligible but from the authority of God who cannot deceive. Certainly, God supplies external proofs to help our natural powers (such as Christ's miracles and the Church's growth). These motives of credibility show that faith is not "a blind impulse." These external helps aid the Spirit's internal promptings.

Greater Than Human Light (157)

Although revealed truths might be obscure, faith is more certain than human knowledge because it is based upon God's Word. "The certainty of divine light is greater than the light of natural reason." (St. Thomas Aquinas) "Ten thousand difficulties do not make one doubt." (Cardinal Newman)

Seeking to Understand (158)

Because "faith seeks understanding" the person should want a more penetrating knowledge of God's Revelation. Paul wants "the eyes of your hearts to be enlightened." (Eph.1:18) The believer should see the totality of God's plan and the union of revealed truths in Christ "I believe in order to understand, and I understand, the better to believe." (St. Augustine)

Faith and Science (159)

The truths of faith and of science cannot contradict one another because God is the source of all truth. True research done in a scientific manner will never contradict moral laws. Man's persevering investigation of creation is really led by God.

Freely Chosen Yet Required (160-161)

Because God wants man to respond freely, no one can be coerced to believe. Christ bore witness to the truth but never forced people into the kingdom.

Faith in Jesus (and in the Father who sent Him) is absolutely required to attain eternal life. The person must persevere in this faith to the end of life. "Without faith it is impossible to please God." (Heb.11:6)

Can Be Lost (162)

In order not to lose faith the believer must be nourished by the Word of God. Paul wrote that "Certain persons have made shipwreck of their faith." (1Tim.1:18-19) Final perseverance requires a faith "working through charity." (Gal.5:6)

Will Be Tested (163-165)

By faith we can "taste in advance" the joys of seeing God face to face. "It is as if we already possessed the wonderful things our faith assures us of." (St. Basil)

Unfortunately, faith is often tested. During earthly trials, heaven seems far away. When experiences of evil shake our faith, we must "walk by faith, not by sight." (2Cor.5:7) We must turn especially to Mary who experienced a "night of faith" at the cross.

Receiving Faith From Others (166-167)
Although faith is a personal act, the believer does not act in isolation. Having received human life from others, the believer also receives faith from others, and passes it on to others.

The Apostles Creed begins with "I believe" (the act of the individual believer). The Nicene Creed begins with "We believe", the faith of the Church, expressed by all at Mass.

The Church's Faith (168-169)
First, the Church believes and professes the Lord. Later, the person (won over by the Church) can say, "I believe." "What do you ask of God's Church?" asks the baptismal liturgy. The answer is "faith" which offers "eternal life."

The Church is not the author of salvation. This comes from God alone. We do not believe in the Church as if she is the author of our salvation. We believe that through the Church we receive our salvation.

The Need for Formulas (170-171)
Also, we do not believe in the formulas of the Creeds but in the realities expressed by these formulas. However, the formulations help us to approach these realities, to live the faith.

The Church guards Christ's own words, hands on the apostolic confessions of faith and teaches her children the "language of faith".

Transmitting the One Faith (172-175)
Through all these centuries and cultures, the Church has transmitted one faith, believing that all people have "one Lord, one faith, one Baptism." (Eph.4:4)

Having received faith from the apostles, the Church hands on this faith with a unanimous voice. Though languages differ throughout the world, the content of the Tradition is one and the same. One and the same way of salvation appears throughout the whole world. (St. Irenaeus)

"We guard with care this faith because this deposit of a great price causes the very vessel that contains it to be renewed." (St. Irenaeus)

Quotes to Remember

The invisible God addresses men as his friends and receives them into his own company. (Second Vatican Council)

By faith man completely submits his intellect and his will to God.

Believing is possible only by grace.

Faith is a personal act – man's free response to God's invitation.

We do not believe in formulas, but in the realities which formulas express.

The truths of faith and the truths of science cannot contradict one another because God Is the source of all truth.

4
The Creeds (185-197)

The Apostles Creed

I believe in God, the Father Almighty, creator of heaven and earth. I believe in Jesus Christ his only Son, our Lord. He was conceived by the power of the Holy Spirit and born of the Virgin Mary. He suffered under Pontius Pilate, was crucified, died and was buried. He descended into hell. On the third day he rose again. He ascended into heaven, and is seated at the right hand of the Father. He will come again to judge the living and the dead. I believe in the Holy Spirit, the holy catholic Church, the communion of saints, the forgiveness of sins, the resurrection of the body and life everlasting. Amen

The Nicene Creed

We believe in one God, the Father, the Almighty, maker of heaven and earth, of all that is seen and unseen. We believe in one Lord, Jesus Christ, the only Son of God, eternally begotten of the Father, God from God, Light from Light, true God from true God, begotten not made, one in Being with the Father. Through him all things were made. For us men and for our salvation he came down from heaven: by the power of the Holy Spirit he was born of the Virgin Mary, and became man. For our sake he was crucified under Pontius Pilate; he suffered, died, and was buried. On the third day he rose again in fulfillment of the Scriptures; he ascended into heaven and is seated at the right hand of the Father. He will come again in glory to judge the living and the dead, and his kingdom will have no end. We believe in the Holy Spirit, the Lord, the giver of life, who proceeds from the Father and the Son. With the Father and the Son he is worshiped and glorified. He has spoken through the Prophets. We believe in one holy catholic and apostolic Church. We acknowledge one baptism for the forgiveness of sins. We look for the resurrection of the dead and the life of the world to come. Amen

20

The Need for Creeds (185-186)

A communion in faith requires a common language. Therefore, whoever says, "I believe" pledges himself to what others believe.

Especially for baptismal candidates, the Church wanted summaries which expressed all the essential elements." This summary of faith encompassed in a few words the whole knowledge of the true religion contained in the Old and New Testaments." (St. Cyril of Jerusalem)

Various Names (187-190)

These syntheses have various names:

1. Profession of faith – what the believer must profess
2. Creed – from "Credo" meaning I believe
3. Symbol of faith

The Greek word "symbol" means the broken half of an object which, when pieced together with the other half, verifies the communion of the believers.

This creed has three parts – of the Father and creation, of the Son and redemption and of the Spirit and sanctification. "These are the three chapters of our baptismal seal." (St. Irenaeus)

Articles of Faith (191)

Church Fathers called these truths the "articles of faith", joined together as members of a body. An early tradition speaks of the Creed containing twelve articles, symbolizing the number of the apostles.

Numerous Creeds (192-193)

There have been numerous Church Creeds which respond to special needs, such as the Athenasian Creed, the symbol of the Council of Trent and the Credo of the People of God. (Pope Paul VI)

Although no creed is ever superseded or irrelevant, two creeds have a special place in the Church.

The Two Special Creeds (194-197)

The Apostles Creed is the ancient baptismal symbol of the Church of Rome. The Nicene Creed has its authority from the first two ecumenical councils (Nicea, 325 and Constantinople, 381).

This catechism will follow the Apostles Creed, but will refer frequently to the often more explicit Nicene Creed. "This Creed is the treasure of our soul." (St. Ambrose)

Quotes to Remember

A communion in faith requires a common language.

....

Especially for baptismal candidates, the Church wanted summaries which explained all the essential truths.

....

From the beginning, the apostolic church handed on her faith in brief formulas for all.

....

Through the centuries, many professions of faith have been articulated to respond to the needs of different eras.

....

No creed is ever superseded or irrelevant.

....

This catechism will follow the Apostles Creed but Will refer frequently to the Nicene Creed.

....

5
God the Father Almighty (198-278)

God – Father – Creation (198)
The Creed begins with God (the beginning and end of all creation); with the Father (the first Divine Person); and with creation (the first of God's works).

First Truth – God (199)
"I believe in God" is the most fundamental affirmation, because the whole Creed speaks of God and man's relationship to him.

God is One (200-201)
"I believe in one God". The Nicene Creed shows that belief in God's oneness and God's existence are inseparable and fundamental. "The Lord our God is one Lord." (Dt.6:4) "God is one in nature, substance and essence." (Roman Catechism)

The prophets called Israel to fidelity. "Hear O Israel for I am God and there is no other." (Dt.6:4-5) They call us to adore one God. "To me every knee shall bow and every tongue shall swear." (Is.45:22-24)

No Division (202)
Jesus says there is "one Lord" (Mk.12:29-30) and yet Jesus says that he is "the Lord." (Mk.12:35-37) Therefore, Christian faith confesses that Jesus is Lord and the Holy Spirit is "the Lord and giver of life." Yet there is no division in God. "There is only one true God, eternal, infinite and unchangeable, the Father and the Son and the Holy Spirit; three persons but one essence." (Fourth Lateran Council IV)

The Name Revealed (203-204)
In the Old Testament, God revealed his name. By doing this, God made himself more accessible and invited us to know Him better.

Although God revealed many names to Israel, the name he used when speaking with Moses was "Yahweh" – "I am who am." (Ec.3:13-15)

23

The God of History (205)

God identified himself to Moses as the God who guided the Patriarchs (Abraham, Isaac and Jacob). God keeps his promises that he would act within human history.

The Mysterious Name (206-207)

Moses said, "If the people of Israel ask me 'What is his name?' What shall I say to them?" God said to Moses, "I am who am" and "Say to this people of Israel, 'I am has sent me to you'." (Ex.3:13-15)   Although clearly revealed, this name shows that God is hidden yet always close to men. His name shows faithfulness because he was there in the past (the God of your fathers) and he will always be there. "I will be with you." (Ex.3:6,12)

Awe and Respect (208-209)

In God's mysterious presence, Moses saw his own insignificance. Others, like Isaiah ("Woe is me! I am lost" -6:5) and Peter ("Depart from me, O Lord, I am a sinful man" - Lk.5:8) had the same experience of awe in God's presence.

Out of respect, Israel did not pronounce the word, "Yahweh" but used instead "Adonai", meaning "Lord." Christians used this word "Lord" to affirm Jesus' divinity. "Jesus Christ is Lord." (Ph. 2:11)

God – Forgiving and Merciful (210-211)

After Israel sinned, God agreed to remain with them. (Ex.32-33) He even showed that he was a forgiving God, "A God merciful and gracious." (Ex.34:6)

God's name ("I Am") shows his faithfulness. By sending his Son, God is "rich in mercy." (Eph.2:4) Jesus had the same divine name, "Then you will realize that 'I Am'." (Jn.8:28)

No Beginning or End (212-213)

Over the centuries, Israel realized that God had no end, "Your years have no end." (Ps. 102:26-27) James writes that in the Father, there is "no variation or shadow due to by change." (1:17)

"I am" means that God alone "is." He has no beginning and no end and from him all creatures receive their existence.

"HE WHO IS"

God is Love (214)
God revealed himself as "abounding in steadfast love and faithfulness". (Ex. 34:6) Israel thanked God for this steadfast love and faithfulness. (Ps. 138:2) John says "God is love." (1Jn.1:5 and 4:8)

God is Truth (215-217)
"You are God, and your words are true." (2Sam.7:28) Because he is truth, we must abandon ourselves to God's word. Our first parents committed sin because they were led into doubt about God's word.

God alone can give us true knowledge about all creation. He is also truthful in revealing himself because he sent Jesus "to bear witness to the truth." (Jn.18:37)

God's Motive is Love (218-221)
Through the prophets, Israel discovered that love was God's only motive in revealing himself. (Is. 43: 1-7 and Hos. 2) God's love is as a father's love. His love is stronger than a mother's love for her children or a bridegroom's love for the bride. Even when the world sinned, "God so loved the world that he gave his only begotten son." (Jn.3:16)

God's love is "everlasting" and will never be removed. (Is.54:8) "I have continued my faithfulness to you."(Jer.31:3) John reveals God's innermost secret, "God is love." (1Jn.4:8), his inner being is an eternal exchange of love between Father, Son and Spirit.

Our Duties (222-227)
Believing in one God has enormous consequences. "We must serve God first." (Joan of Arc) We must live in thanksgiving. We must recognize the dignity of every human person. We must use created things according to God's plan and we must trust in God in every circumstance. "God alone is enough." (St. Teresa of Jesus)

Faith in the Trinity (232-233)

Christians are baptized "in the name of the Father, and of the Son and of the Holy Spirit." They are not baptized "in the names" of the Father, Son and Spirit because there is only one God, the Most Holy Trinity. The Baptismal confession of faith has three parts because "the faith of all Christians rests on the Trinity." (St. Caesarilus of Arles)

The Central Mystery (234)

The Trinity is the central mystery of Christian life, the source of all the other mysteries, and the most fundamental mystery in "the hierarchy of the truths of faith." The whole history of salvation is identical with the way God revealed himself as Father, Son and Spirit.

Three Aspects (235)

This section will explain three aspects:
1. how the Trinity was revealed
2. how the Church has articulated the mystery
3. how God the Father fulfilled his plan by sending the Son and the Spirit

Inner Life and Exterior Work (236-237)

"Theology" refers to God's inner life and "economy" refers to God revealing and communicating his life to us. By God's actions in history (economy), he reveals his inner life (theology). Knowing God's inner life enlightens our understanding of his plan.

The Trinity is a mystery which would not be known unless revealed. The mystery is inaccessible both to reason alone and to Israel before the sending of Jesus and the sending of the Holy Spirit.

REVEALED AS TRINITY

Two Meanings of Father (238-239)

Many religions call God "Father" meaning "creator of the world." God was also "Father" as the giver of the covenant and of the law to Israel, "his first-born son." (Ex.4:22)   He was "father to the king" and "father of the poor."

God as Father means two things.   He created everything and has loving care for all.   In the Bible, motherhood also expresses God's tenderness.   Although God uses the image of human parents, God is neither man nor woman.   No one is father as God is Father.

Jesus' Unique Revealing (240-242)

Jesus further revealed God as Father not just as Creator but as eternally Father to Jesus, the only-begotten Son.   "No one knows the Son except the Father and no one knows the Father except the Son and anyone to whom the Son chooses to reveal him." (Mt.11:27)   Jesus is the "Word" who was "in the beginning with God" and "was God." (Jn.1:1)   He is "the image of the invisible God. (Col.1:15)

The Church declared that Jesus was "consubstantial" with the Father. (Nicea 325)   Jesus is "the only begotten Son of God, eternally begotten of the Father, light from light, true God from true God, begotten not made, consubstantial with the Father." (Constantinople 381)

The Revealing of the Spirit (243-245)

Jesus said he would send "another Paraclete" (Jn.14:17, 26; 16-13), and revealed the Spirit as a third person together with the Father and Son.   When the Spirit was sent to the Church in person by the Father and the Son (after Jesus' glorification) the mystery of the Trinity was revealed in its fullness.

"We believe in the Holy Spirit, the Lord and giver of life, who proceeds from the Father." (Constantinople 381)

The Sixth Council of Toledo (638) said that the Father is "the source and origin of the whole divinity."   The eternal origin of the Spirit is connected with the Son's origin.   "Yet he is not called the Spirit of the Father alone, but the Spirit of both the Father and the Son." (Toledo XI 675)   "With the Father and the Son, he is worshipped and glorified." (Nicene Creed)

Relationship to Father and Son (246)

The Nicene Creed says the "Spirit proceeds from the Father and the Son."   The Council of Florence (1439) says, "The Spirit

27

has his nature and subsistence at the same time (simul) from the Father and the Son. He proceeds eternally from both as from one principle and through one spiration."

Different Formulas (247-248)
The Latin liturgy between 700 and 1200 began to say, "the Holy Spirit who proceeds from the Father and the Son." The earlier Council of Constantinople (381) had used a different formula, "the Holy Spirit proceeded from the Father through the Son." Unfortunately, these different expressions of the same truth have constituted a point of disagreement with the Orthodox Churches.

The Orthodox formula ("through the Son") stresses the Father as the first origin of the Spirit. The Latin formula ("and the Son") stresses the oneness of the Father and the Son. This Latin formula is valid. The Father and the Son are the single principle from which the Spirit proceeds.

TEACHING OF THE FAITH

Root of Faith (249)
The Trinity has always been the very root of the Church's faith (expressed in the baptismal liturgy). Paul summarized this apostolic faith, "The grace of the Lord Jesus Christ and the love of God and the fellowship of the Holy Spirit be with all of you." (2Cor.13:13)

Three Important Terms (250-252)
In the early Ecumenical Councils the Church clarified its understanding of the Trinity in order to respond to heresies. The Church developed three important terms:

Substance, (also called essence or nature) which designates the divine being in its unity.

Person, which designates the Father, Son and Spirit in the real distinction among them.

Relation, which designates that their distinction lies in the relationship of each to the others.

One God (253)

The Trinity is <u>one</u>. The Church does not believe in three Gods but in one God in three persons (the "consubstantial Trinity)." The divine persons do not share the one divinity among themselves. Each of them is God, whole and entire. "Each of the persons is that supreme reality, namely, the divine substance, essence or nature." (Fourth Lateran Council)

Distinct Persons (254)

Father, Son and Spirit are not just three names for three modalities of the one God. They are really distinct from one another in their relations of origin. "It is the Father who generates, the Son who is begotten and the Holy Spirit who proceeds." (Fourth Lateran Council - 1215)

Based On Relationships (255-256)

The real distinction of each Person lies in their relationship to one another. "In the relational names of the persons, the Father is related to the Son, the Son to the Father and the Spirit to both."(Eleventh Council of Toledo-675) The Father is wholly in the Son and in the Spirit. The Son is wholly in the Father and the Spirit. The Spirit is wholly in the Father and the Son. (Council of Florence - 1442)

"I entrust to you today the profession of faith in the Father and the Son and the Holy Spirit. Each person considered in himself is entirely God." (St. Gregory of Nazeanzus)

THE TRINITARIAN MISSIONS

God's Plan Unfolds (257)

The Father "destined us in love to be his sons" through "the spirit of sonship." (Eph.1:4-5,9) This plan comes from the Trinity and unfolds in creation in the missions of the Son and the Spirit, and in the mission of the Church.

The Work of All Three (258)

This divine plan is the common work of the three divine persons. However, each person does the work according to his unique personal qualities. "One God and Father <u>from whom</u> all things are and one Lord Jesus Christ, <u>through whom</u> all things are,

29

and one Holy Spirit in whom all things are. (Council of Constantinople II – 553) The qualities of the three divine persons are revealed in the missions of Jesus and the Spirit.

Revealing Each Person (259)

God's work in history reveals the Trinity (what is proper to each divine person and what is proper to their one divine nature). The Christian life is a communion with all three persons. Whoever glorifies the Father glorifies also the Son and Spirit.

Inviting All (260)

God wants every creature to enter into the unity of the Trinity. Jesus promised, "If a man loves me, he will keep my word, and my Father will love him, and we will come to him, and make our home with him." (Jn.14:23)

"O my God, Trinity, help me to forget myself entirely so to establish myself in you, unmovable and peaceful as if my soul were already in eternity." (St. Elizabeth of the Trinity)

In Brief - 261 –267

ALMIGHTY

His Almighty Power (268-269)

Of all God's attributes, the Creed speaks only of his almighty power. This power is universal (creating and ruling everything) loving and mysterious (known only by faith).

God is the "Mighty One of Jacob". (Gen. 49:24) "Whatever God wills is done." (Ps.115:3) He can do everything in heaven and earth. He is the Lord of the universe governing all events by his will.

A Fatherly Care (270-271)

God's almighty power is also fatherly. "I will be a father to you, and you shall be my sons and daughters." (2Cor.6:18) God's power is not arbitrary. "Nothing can be in God's power which could not be in his just will or his wise intellect." (St. Thomas Aquinas)

God's Mysterious Ways (272-274)

In our trials God does seem to be absent and powerless. However. God's power is fully revealed in the death and resurrection of Jesus. "For the foolishness of God is wiser than men, and the weakness of God is stronger than men." (1Cor.1:24-25) In Jesus' death and resurrection, God has revealed the "immeasurable greatness of his power in us who believe." (Eph.1:19-22)

Only faith can embrace these mysterious ways of God's power. Mary believed the angel's words that "Nothing will be impossible with God" (Lk.1:37) and she proclaimed that "he who is mighty has done great things for me." (Lk.1:49)

Knowing that nothing is impossible for God, we can accept everything in the Creed without any hesitation.

In Brief 275 – 278

Quotes to Remember

"I believe in God" is the first and most fundamental affirmation of the Apostles Creed.

"I am who am" is a mysterious name just as God is mystery.

By revealing his name, God also reveals his everlasting faithfulness.

John goes further, affirming "God is love" (1Jn.4:8; 16)

6
Creation of Heaven and Earth (279-354)

The First Act of Creation (279-281)

"In the beginning God created the heavens and the earth." (Gen.1:1) The Church says that God is the "Creator of heaven and earth" and "of all that is seen and unseen."

God's saving plan begins with creation and culminates in Christ who reveals God's plan the glory of a new creation in Christ. (cf Rom.8:18-23)

CATECHESIS ON CREATION

Finding Our Origins (282-283)

A catechesis on creation lays the foundation for all catechesis by answering the questions, "Where do we come from?" and "Where are we going?" These questions are decisive for life's meaning.

Certainly scientific studies have enriched our knowledge of the cosmos. These discoveries should lead us to thank God for revealing this wisdom.

Questions Beyond Science (284)

However, some questions go beyond these scientific studies and try to discover the meaning of all creation. Is the universe governed by fate or by an intelligent and good Being called God? Why is there evil and where does it come from?

Challenges to Faith (285)

The Christian faith faces a challenge from those philosophers who say that the world is God (Pantheism); from those who say the world comes from two sources, good and evil (Dualists and Manicheists); from those who say the world comes from evil (Gnostics); from those who think God created but has no continued interest in the world (Deists); and from those who say there is only the material universe (Materialists).

Responses (286)

To these questions, human intelligence can give some response. Man can know God's existence with certainty even if this knowing is obscured by error. However, a full understanding comes when reason is helped by faith. "By faith we understand that the world was created by the word of God." (Heb.11:3)

Need for Revelation (287-288)

God progressively revealed the mystery of creation in his revelation to Israel. God formed Israel and revealed himself as the Creator. "I am the Lord, who made all things." (Is.44:24)

This revelation about creation and about God's Covenant with Israel are inseparable because creation is God's first step toward the Covenant. The Jewish prophets, liturgy and wisdom sayings express this witness of God's creation.

First Three Chapters (289)

The first three chapters of Genesis express the truths of creation, its origin, order and goodness. Genesis shows man's vocation, the drama of sin and the hope of salvation. These texts are the prime source of catechesis about the beginning mysteries (the creation, the fall and the promise of salvation).

THE WORK OF THE TRINITY

Three Truths (290)

"In the beginning God created the heavens and the earth." (Gen.1:1) This sentence shows three truths. First, God gave a beginning to all that exists. Second, he alone is Creator. Third, everything depends on God.

The Work of Three Persons (291-292)

John's gospel says that all things were made through God's word "and without him nothing was made." (1:1-3) The Church also confesses the Holy Spirit's creative action. He is "the giver of life." The Old Testament suggests and the New Testament reveals this creative activity of both the Son and the Spirit.

This creative cooperation of the three Persons is confirmed by the Church's rule of faith. "He made all things by himself, that is, by his Word and by his Wisdom, by the Son and the Spirit" who are "the Father's hands." (St. Irenaeus)

Manifesting and Communicating the Glory (293-294)

The world was made for the glory of God, "not to increase it but to show it forth and communicate it." (St. Bonaventure) Love is the only reason God created. "God created to manifest his goodness." (First Vatican Council)

God's glory is the communicating of his goodness to us. "The glory of God is man fully alive" and man's life is the "vision of God." (St. Irenaeus) Creation exists "so God can bring about his own glory and our happiness.

THE MYSTERY OF CREATION

Freely Willed by God (295)

The created world did not happen by necessity, nor by blind chance. God freely willed to create so that every creature would share in his life and goodness. "By your will they existed and were created." (Rev.4:15)

Starting From Nothing (296-297)

No created thing "pre-existed" nor did creation just emanate from God. "God shows his power by starting from nothing to make all he wants." (St. Theophilus of Antioch)

By creating from nothing, God gives us hope that there is more than a material world. At their martyrdom, the valiant mother told her seven sons, "Look at the heaven and the earth and see everything that is in them, and recognize that God did not make them out of things that existed." (2Mac.7:28)

Beyond Bodily Life (298)

Because God created out of nothing, he can give spiritual life to sinners and bodily life to the dead through the Resurrection. God "gives life to the dead and calls into existence those things that do not exist." (Rom.4:17)

Sharing in God's Goodness (299)

Through wisdom, God ordered the universe, especially human persons who are called into a personal relationship with Him."

34

(Col. 1:15) The human intellect can grasp what God's tells us through material creation, but only with great effort. Creation is God's gift to man and shares in his goodness.

Above Yet Present (300)

Although God's greatness is unsearchable (Ps. 145:3), he is always present to his creation. "In him, we live and move and have our being." (Acts 17:28) God is "more inward than my most innermost self." (St. Augustine)

Bringing to Completion (301)

God always sustains the whole world and will bring human history to its final goal. Recognizing this total dependence on God is the source of wisdom. "How would anything have endured if you did not will it?" (St. Augustine)

DIVINE PROVIDENCE

Creation's Destiny (302-305)

God did not make creation "complete from the beginning", but willed "a state of journeying." God always guides all creation toward its ultimate perfection by Divine Providence. "By his providence God protects and governs all things which he has made." (First Vatican Council)

God's care for every creature (from least to greatest) is concrete and immediate. God does "whatever he pleases." (Ps.115:3) Christ opens and no one shuts, shuts and no one opens." (Rev.3:7) "The purpose of the Lord will be established." (Prov.19:21)

Scripture, in attributing actions to God without mentioning any other causes is not using a "primitive mode of speech", but is professing a faith in God's lordship over all history. Jesus tells us not to be anxious, "Your heavenly Father knows what you need. "Seek first his kingdom and all these things shall be yours as well." (Mt.6:31-33)

Inviting Us to Cooperate (306-308)

God uses our cooperation. In his goodness, He gives us our existence and by our free will the opportunity to cooperate in his plan.

God even invites us to "subdue the earth and have dominion over it. (Gen.1:26-28) He invites us to complete his work of creation. As knowing collaborators, we are "God's fellow workers." (1Cor.3:9)

We believe that God, the Creator (the first Cause) is always at work in us (the second cause). "For God is at work in you." (Phil.2:13) We can do nothing without God, especially gain eternal life. "Without a Creator, the creature vanishes." (Second Vatican Council)

Why Is There Evil? (309)

Why does evil exist? This unavoidable and painful question can be adequately responded to only by the entire story of Christian faith, which includes the goodness of creation, the drama of sin, God's covenants, the sendings of Jesus and the Spirit, and the founding of the Church. It includes the sacraments and the invitation to eternal life (which mysteriously can be rejected by anyone). Every aspect of Christian life is part of the answer to this question of evil.

A World "in a State of Journeying" (310)

God did not create a perfect world. In fact, God could have created a better world. (St. Thomas Aquinas) God created this world "in a state of journeying." The more perfect exists alongside the less perfect. Nature has both constructive and destructive forces. Physical good will always be mixed with physical evil until creation reaches perfection.

Moral Evil (311)

Angels and men can freely choose to go astray. God never causes moral evil, either directly or indirectly. He permits moral evil because he respects man's freedom and knows how to draw good out of evil. "We know that in everything, God works for good for those who love him." (Rom.8:28) "God would never allow any evil if he could not cause good to emerge from it." (St. Augustine)

Good From Evil (312-314)

It takes time to see how God draws good from a moral evil. After being sold into slavery, Joseph told his brothers, "It was not you who sent me here, but God. You meant evil, but God meant it for good." (Gen.45:8 and 50:20) God used Jesus' death (the greatest moral evil) for our redemption. Nevertheless, evil never becomes a good.

The saints witness to God drawing good out of evil. "Some rebel against what happens to them but God does nothing without the salvation of man in mind." (St. Catherine of Siena) "Nothing can come but that God wills." (St. Thomas More) "The Lord showed me that all manner of things shall be well." (Julian of Norwich)

Because we have only partial knowledge, many aspects of God's providence are hidden from us.

In Brief - 315 - 324

Heaven and Earth (325-327)

God is the "Creator of heaven and earth." (Apostles Creed) He created "all that is, seen and unseen." (Nicene Creed)

"Heaven and earth" means creation in its entirety. It shows the <u>bond</u> and the <u>distinction</u> between earth and heaven. "Earth" is the world of men. "Heaven" designates either the firmament, God's place of final glory, or the place where saints and angels live.

"From the beginning God made at once, out of nothing, both the spiritual (angels) and corporeal (earth) and, after that, God made the human creature who shares in both orders of spirit and body. (Fourth Lateran Council)

Angels (328 - 330)

Scripture and Tradition teach the existence of spiritual, non-corporeal beings (angels). <u>Angel</u> is the name of their office (what they do), and <u>spirit</u> is the name of their nature (what they are). While seeing the face of God, they also are his messengers who "hearken to the voice of his word." (St. Augustine) Angels are personal, immortal, spiritual beings who have intelligence and will. By their glory, they surpass all visible creatures.

With Christ (331)

Christ is the center of the angelic world because "in him all things were created in heaven and on earth, visible and invisible."

(Col.1:16) The angels are messengers of his saving plan. "Are they not all ministers sent forth to serve?" (Heb.1:14)

Activity in Scripture (332-333)

Angels have been active from the beginning. In Genesis, they closed the earthly paradise (3:24), saved Hagar and her son (21:17), and kept Abraham from killing Isaac. (22:11) Later in scripture, they led God's people, announced births, and assisted the prophets.

The angel Gabriel announced the birth of John the Baptist and the birth of Jesus. (Lk.1:11-26) Angels announced Jesus' birth to shepherds (Lk.2:14), protected him in infancy (Mt.1:20; 2:13), served him in the desert (Mk.1:13), and strengthened him in the garden. (Lk.22:43) Angels witnessed to Christ at the tomb and at his Ascension. They will also announce Jesus' return to judge mankind. (Mt.24:31)

Their Work Now (334-336)

The Church benefits from the help of angels. At funerals, the angels are asked to lead the deceased into Paradise. All believers have a guardian angel who watches them from conception to death. Angels surround all human life with their care.

THE VISIBLE WORLD

Six Days of Work (337-338)

Symbolically, scripture pictures God working for six days and "resting" on the seventh. These texts teach us the truths we need to know for our salvation. All creation owes its existence to God and is rooted in the primordial event of God drawing the world out of nothingness and having time begin.

Because God saw his creation as "good", every creature has its own truth and goodness. Therefore, man must respect God's creation and avoid any action which would have disastrous consequences for the human race and its environment.

Dependent and Diverse (339-341)

All God's creatures are interdependent. No creature is self-sufficient and all must depend upon and serve each other. This diversity brings about the universe's beauty.

Progressively, man discovers the universe's beauty and the laws of nature which call forth admiration and should lead man to submit to his Creator.

Man at the Summit (342-343)

The "six days" of creation (from the less perfect to the more perfect) show a "hierarchy" of creatures. God, however, takes care even of the lowly sparrow. (Lk.12:6-7)

Scripture shows that man is at the summit of creation and clearly distinguishes his creation from all others. (Gen.1:26) Created by God and ordered to his glory, all creatures have a solidarity. "May you be praised, O Lord, in all your creatures." (St. Francis of Assisi)

Day of Rest (344-348)

"Since on the seventh day God was finished with the work he had been doing, he rested on the seventh day." (Gen.2:1) These inspired words contain much instruction:

God has placed in nature a foundation of his laws which man must respect.

God's work looked forward to the Sabbath. Therefore, worship of God is inscribed in creation.

Keeping the Sabbath corresponds to God's wisdom and law.

Eighth Day (349)

The seventh day completed the first creation, but the eighth day (Christ's Resurrection) begins a new creation which culminates in the greater work of redemption. This second creation surpasses the first in splendor.

In Brief - 350 - 354

Quotes to Remember

We firmly believe that God is the master of the world and of history.

7
Man in God's Image (355-421)

The Four Aspects of Man (355)
"God created man in his own image, in the image of God he created him, male and female he created them." (Gen.1:27) The following paragraphs will examine these four aspects of man:
1. He is in the image of God.
2. He unites in his nature both the spiritual and material worlds.
3. He is male and female.
4. He enjoys a friendship with God.

The Dignity of God's Image – the Human Person (356-357)
In material creation only man can know and love God. He was willed by God for his own sake and he is called to share in God's own life. "What made you establish man in so great a dignity? You are taken with love for him." (Saint Catherine of Siena)

Being in God's image makes the individual a person, a "someone" and not a "something." He is capable of self-knowledge and of having friendship with other persons. He is called into a covenant with God and can make a response of love not known by any other creature.

All For Man (358)
God created everything for man. "For man is more precious in God's eyes than all other creatures. For him the heavens and the earth exist. God did not spare his own Son for the sake of man. Nor does he ever cease to work until he has made him sit at his right hand." (St. John Chrysostom)

United in Christ (359-361)
This mystery of man becomes clear only in the mystery of Christ. "That is why Christ took on himself the role and the name of the first Adam, in order that he might not lose what he had made in his own image." (St. Peter Chrysologus)

The human race has a unity. "From one ancestor, God made all nations to inhabit the whole earth." (Acts 17:26) "The human race has unity in its origin (God), in its nature (body and soul), in its dwelling place (earth), in its supernatural goal (heaven), and in the means to heaven (Christ's redemption)." (Pope Pius XII) All men are truly brothers.

BODY AND SOUL – TRULY ONE

Man - Body and Soul (362-363)

Using symbolic language, the Bible says that God willed man to be both corporeal and spiritual. "Then the Lord God formed man of dust from the ground, and breathed into his nostrils the breath of life and man became a living being." (Gen.2:7)

In scripture, "soul" can mean human life or the entire human person. Soul especially means man's spiritual principle.

In God's Image (364)

Animated by a spiritual soul, the human body shares in the dignity of "God's image." The human person, body and soul, is meant to become a temple of the Spirit. In man, the material world can freely raise its voice in praise of the Creator. (Second Vatican Council)

Only One Nature (365-368)

The spiritual soul is the "form" of the body. Man is not the union of two natures. In man spirit and matter form one nature. God creates every spiritual soul immediately. It is not "produced" by the parents and does not perish at death. It is reunited with the body at the final resurrection.

When Paul prays writes about "spirit, soul and body" (1Thes.5:23), he used the word "Spirit" to mean that the soul has a supernatural goal of union with God. The biblical word "heart" also means the place where the person decides for or against God.

MALE AND FEMALE

Equality of Man and Woman (369-370)

God willed that man and woman would have perfect equality as human persons. "Being man or being woman" is a good and each possesses an inalienable dignity.

God is neither man nor woman. He is pure spirit. The different perfections of man and woman (as mother, father, husband, wife) reflect God's infinite perfections.

Made for Each Other (371-373)

Man and woman were created for each other. Because man was alone, God created a "helper fit for him." (Gen.2:19-20) When God fashioned the woman, the man cried out in wonder, "This at last is bone of my bones and flesh of my flesh" (Gen.2:23), acknowledging that woman shares his humanity.

God did not make man and woman incomplete, but he created them as a "helpmate" for each other. In marriage, by becoming "one flesh", they can transmit human life and cooperate with God in creating.

Although called to "subdue the earth" (Gen.1:28), man and woman must not destroy creation.

Created in Original Harmony (374-376)

Man was created in friendship with his Creator, in harmony with himself and with all creation, and in a state surpassed only by the new creation in Christ.

Our first parents, Adam and Eve, enjoyed an original "state of holiness and justice" by which they shared in divine life. While remaining in this divine intimacy, they would not suffer or die. They also possessed a personal inner harmony and a harmony with each other, and with creation. This was called "original justice."

In Control and In the Garden (377-379)

This divine gift of "mastery" was realized within man himself. He was free from the triple concupiscence that now subjects all men to sensual pleasure, to covetousness of earthly goods, and to false self-assertion. These three evils are "sensual lust, enticement for the eyes and a pretentious life." (1Jn.2:16)

In the garden work was not yet a burden but a collaboration with God. Unfortunately, our first parents lost this entire harmony by their sin.

In Brief - 380 - 384

The Source of Evil (385)

Man rightly asks "Where does evil come from?" "I sought to know where evil comes from and there was no solution." (St. Augustine) For Augustine, the mystery was clarified only by his religious conversion. We, too, examine this question of evil with our eyes upon Christ, who alone is its conqueror.

SIN AND GRACE

Understanding Sin (386-387)

Human history is filled with sin. By understanding the profound relationship of man to God the evil of sin is unmasked.

Without the clarity of the Bible we would explain sin as a weakness, a mistake or a necessary consequence of a poor social structure. By knowing God's plan, we can see that sin is really man's abuse of his freedom.

Adam and Christ (388-389)

Israel could never grasp the ultimate meaning of the story of Adam and Eve. They knew Adam (the source of sin) but not Christ (the source of grace). Only the Holy Spirit would "convict the world in regard to sin and righteousness and condemnation." (Jn.16:8)

This doctrine of original sin is the "reverse side" of the Good News. Jesus is our Savior because all men need to be saved. Tampering with the doctrine of original sin will undermine the mystery of Christ.

Human History and the Fall (390)

Although using figurative language, the story of Adam's sin does describe an event which took place at the beginning of human history. All human history is marked by that fall of our first parents.

A Prior Fall – Satan (391)

Man's fall contains a "seductive voice", the voice of a fallen angel, called "Satan" or the "devil." The Church teaches that Satan and other demons were created "good by God but they became evil by their own doing." (Fourth Lateran Council)

A Free Irrevocable Choice (392-393)

These demons made a free irrevocable choice to reject God. This rebellion is reflected in the tempter's words, "You will be like God." (Gen.3:5) Having sinned from the beginning, the devil is now "the father of lies." (Jn.8:44)

God's mercy toward these fallen angels is useless. Their sin is unforgivable because their choice is irrevocable. "There is no repentance for the angels, just as there is no repentance for men after death." (St. John Damascene)

Disastrous Influence (394-395)

Because of the devil's disastrous influence, Jesus came to earth "to destroy the works of the devil" (1Jn.3:8), especially his power to seduce man to disobedience.

Satan's power is not infinite and he cannot prevent the building up of God's kingdom. Although Satan can cause grave injuries (both spiritual and physical) God still guides all human history. Why God permits demonic activity is a mystery. We know that "in everything God works for good with those who love him." (Rom. 8:28)

ORIGINAL SIN

Man's Need to be Tested (396)

Man had to freely accept God's friendship. God's command to Adam (not to eat of the tree of knowledge of good and evil) shows symbolically that man had to acknowledge his limits as a creature and submit his behavior to God's laws.

The First Sin (397)

By sin, man set aside his trust in God and disobeyed. All subsequent sin would be disobedience and lack of trust. By sin, man rebelled against his status as a creature. Man chose to be like God "without God and not in accordance with God." (St. Maximus)

What They Lost (398-399)

Our first parents lost original holiness and became afraid of God, whom they now falsely thought was jealous of his prerogatives. The soul's control over the body's powers was shattered. The union of man with woman became subject to tensions and their sexual relationship was marked by lust and domination. (Gen.3:5-16)

Creation became hostile to man and death made its entrance into human history. "Sin entered the world and through sin, death ..." .(Rom.5:12)

A History of Sin (400-401)

Sin inundated human history and even entered God's Covenant with Israel. Even after Christ's death, sin was present in the Christian community. There is a universality of sin.

This is confirmed by our own experience. Often refusing to acknowledge God, man has broken the right order that should reign within himself and with other creatures." (Second Vatican Council)

Everyone Affected (402 - 403)

All are implicated in sin. "Death spread to all men because all men sinned." (Rom.5:12) However, all are offered salvation in Jesus Christ. "One man's act of righteousness leads to acquittal and life for all men." (Rom.5:18)

This overwhelming misery which oppresses is connected with the fact that Adam's sin has been transmitted to all at birth. This sin is the "death of the soul." Therefore, the Church baptizes even tiny infants "for the remission of sins." (Council of Trent)

Transmission of Effects (404)

We do not exactly know how this "original sin" is transmitted. Adam and Eve were supposed to transmit original holiness and justice to everyone. In their "fallen state" they could only pass on a human nature deprived of original holiness and justice. Therefore, original sin differs from other sins. It is contracted (a state) not committed (an act).

Deprived of Our Heritage (405)

By original sin we are deprived of original holiness and justice. Human nature is not totally corrupted, but is wounded in its natural powers. It is subject to ignorance, sin and death, and has an inclination to evil (called "concupiscence"). Baptism erases original sin and turns the person back to Christ. However, the inclination to sin that persists requires that man be in a constant, spiritual battle.

Two Errors (406)
Pelagius (5th century) reduced the influence of Adam's fault to bad example and taught that man could lead a good life without God's help. In contrast, the first Protestant teachers (16th century) taught that original sin had radically permeated man and man's tendency to evil was insurmountable. The Church taught against Pelagius at the Council of Orange (529) and against Protestant teachers at the Council of Trent (1546).

Today's Battle (407)
Original sin provides great insight into man's activity in the world. Although remaining free, man has come under "the devil, who has the power of death." (Council of Trent) Man is ignorant of his own inclination to evil and makes serious errors in education, politics and social action.

A Battlefield Due to Sin (408-409)
Original sin and all personal sins place the world in a sinful condition. This "sin of the world." (Jn.1:29) refers also to the negative influences exerted by sinful social structures. A dramatic situation exists in which "the whole world is in the power of the evil one." (1Jn.5:19) Man is on a battlefield and only by God's aid does he succeed in achieving his own inner integrity. (Second Vatican Council)

A Promised Victory (410-411)
After original sin, God still called man and even promised a victory. He announced that there would be a Messiah and Redeemer, a battle between the serpent and the Woman, and the final victory for her descendents, "I will put an enmity between you and the woman and between your offspring and hers, he will strike at your head while you strike at his heel." (Gen.3:15)

This passage announces Christ as the "New Adam" who superabundantly makes amends for Adam's sin. Many church Fathers see Mary as the "new Eve", the first to benefit from Christ's redemption by her Immaculate Conception and freedom from all personal sins.

Why Was Sin Permitted? (412)

Many Christian writers answered that question. "Christ gave us better blessings than the devil took away." (Leo the Great) "There is nothing to prevent human nature from being raised up to something greater, even after sin." (Thomas Aquinas) "O happy fault, ... which gained for us so great a Redeemer." (Easter Vigil Exsultet)

In Brief - 413 - 421

Quotes to Remember

"Heaven and earth" means all that exists – creation in its entirety.

God wills the interdependence of creatures.

Christ is the center of the angelic world.

"Angel" is the name of their office not of their nature. (St. Augustine)

Every spiritual soul is created directly by God.

Sin is present in human history. Any attempt to ignore it would be futile.

For us a new day has dawned: the day of Christ's resurrection. This eighth day begins the new creation.

8
Jesus Christ, His Only Son Born of Mary
(422-483)

Jesus – God's Gift in Time's Fullness (422-424)

"But when the fullness of time had come, God sent forth his Son, born of a woman ... (Gal.4-5). This is "the gospel of Jesus Christ, the Son of God" (Mk.1:1) by which God has acted for us beyond all expectation.

We believe that Jesus of Nazareth, born of Mary at Bethlehem, who died on the cross in Jerusalem under Pontius Pilate is the eternal son of God made man. He "came from God" (Jn.13:3), "descended from heaven" (Jn.3:13), and is the "Word made flesh who dwelt among us. We have seen his glory as of the only Son from the Father" and from his fullness we have all received grace upon grace. (Jn.1:14-16)

Jesus made Peter the rock of his Church because he confessed, "You are the Christ the Son of the living God." (Mt.16:16)

Preached by Eyewitnesses (425)

The early disciples were eager to "speak of what we have seen and heard" (Acts 4:20) and they invited people into their unity in Christ. "That which was from the beginning, ... we proclaim also to you, so that you may have fellowship with us." (Jn.1:1-4)

Seeing God's Plan in Christ (426-428)

Catechesis must "reveal the whole purpose of God's design in the Person of Christ. Catechesis must put people in union with Christ, who alone "can lead us to the love of the Father in the Spirit." (Second Vatican Council)

Everything in catechesis must be taught in reference to Christ. The catechist must say. "My teaching is not mine, but his who sent me." (Jn.7:16) The catechist must seek "the surpassing worth of knowing Jesus Christ". (Phil.3:8)

Four Parts (429)

This faith in Jesus Christ will be explained according to four parts:

      1.   the titles of Christ

2. his Incarnation
3. his Paschal Mystery
4. his Glorification

HIS ONLY SON – OUR LORD

The Name Jesus (430-431)
Jesus (in Hebrew) means "God saves." The angel Gabriel told Mary "You shall name him Jesus." (Lk.1:31) The angel told Joseph to name the child "Jesus, because he will save his people from their sins." (Mt.1:21) Besides delivering Israel from Egypt, God made them aware of their sins so they would invoke him as their Redeemer.

Invoking the Name (432-433)
Jesus means "God saves" and all can invoke his name. "There is no other name under heaven by which we must be saved." (Acts 4:12)

Once a year, the high priest sprinkled sacrificial blood and invoked the name of the Savior God in atonement for Israel's sins. Paul writes that God put forward Jesus "as an expiation by his blood" (Rom.3:25) and "reconciled the world to himself." (2Cor.5:19)

The Power of the Name (434-435)
After the resurrection, Jesus is the "name which is above every other name." (Phil.2:10) Devils feared this name. Disciples performed miracles in this name, and the Father granted all petitions in Jesus' name.

Liturgical prayers end with the words "through our Lord, Jesus Christ." The high point of the Hail Mary is Jesus' name. Many Christians, such as St. Joan of Arc, died with Jesus' name on their lips.

The Name "Christ" (436 - 437)
This Greek word translates the Hebrew word "Messiah", "Anointed" consecrated for God's mission. Jesus, the Messiah who would inaugurate God's Kingdom, had to be anointed by the Spirit.

49

The angels announced to the shepherds a "Savior who is Christ the Lord." (Lk.2:11) Jesus is "the one whom the Father consecrated and sent to the whole world." (Jn.10:36) God told Joseph to take Mary as his wife so that Jesus would be of the messianic lineage of David. (Mt.1:20)

The Anointed Messiah (438-440)

Because the Father anointed him with the Holy Spirit (who is the anointing) Jesus is the Christ (the anointed one). This eternal messianic consecration was revealed years later when Jesus was baptized by John and later explained by Peter. "God anointed Jesus of Nazareth with the Holy Spirit that he might be revealed to Israel." (Acts 10:38)

Many people called Jesus the Messiah. Because of political connotations, Jesus accepted this only with reserve. However, when Peter professed him as Messiah (Mt.16: 16-23) Jesus revealed his messianic kingship. Jesus is the "Son of Man who came down from heaven" (Jn.3:13) who is called "to give his life as a ransom for many." (Mt.20-28) After Jesus' resurrection, Peter said "God has made him both Lord and Christ." (Acts 2:36)

ONLY SON OF GOD

"Son of God" – A Human Title (441)

In the Old Testament, the title "son of God" (denoting an intimacy with God) was given to angels, the children of Israel and to kings. Therefore, those who called Jesus "son of God" were not implying that Jesus was more than human.

A Divine Sonship (442-443)

Peter said, "You are the Christ, the Son of the living God" (Mt.16:16), Jesus said that this was revealed by his heavenly Father. (Mt.16:16-17) Paul said that God "was pleased to reveal his Son to me" (Gal.1:15-16), and Paul proclaimed in the synagogues that Jesus "is the Son of God". In these instances, Peter and Paul were speaking of Christ's divine sonship, the very center of apostolic faith.

Earlier, when Jesus was asked by the Sanhedrin "Are you the Son of God?" he answered "You say that I am." (Lk.22:70) Also, Jesus said he was "the Son" who knew the Father in a unique way. (Mt.11:27)

Jesus clearly distinguished his sonship from others. He always said "my Father" and only in prayer taught the disciples to say "Our Father." After his resurrection he emphasized his when he said to Mary Magdalene, "my Father and your Father." (Jn.20:17)

The Father's Voice (444-445)
At Jesus' Baptism and Transfiguration the Father designated Jesus as his "beloved Son." (cf Mt.3:17 and 17:5) When Jesus called himself the "only son of God" (Jn.3:16) he affirmed his eternal preexistence. The Centurion's words "Truly this man was the Son of God" is a Christian profession of faith. Only after the resurrection can the believer give "Son of God" its full meaning.

By his resurrection Jesus was "designated Son of God in power". (Rom.1:3) The apostles confessed "We have beheld his glory, as of the only Son from the Father." (Jn.1:14)

The Name "Lord" (446)
In the Old Testament, Kyrios (the Greek word meaning "Lord'") indicated the divinity of Israel's God. This word Kyrios ("Lord") is used in the New Testament for the Father and for Jesus, thereby recognizing Jesus as God.

During His Lifetime (447)
David wrote, "The Lord said to my Lord." (Mt.22:41-46) Jesus used this sentence to proclaim his divinity to the apostles. (Mt.22:41-46) Jesus showed his divine sovereignty by his power over illness, death and Satan. When people gave Jesus the title "Lord", they recognized a divine mystery of Jesus.

The Post-Resurrection Meaning (448-451)
Thomas said, "My Lord and my God" (Jn.20:28), a title of adoration. The disciples said, "It is the Lord" (Jn.20: 28 and 21:7), a title of affection. By calling Jesus "Lord", the New Testament affirms that the honor due to the Father is also due to Jesus because he "was in the form of God." (Phil.2:6)

Believing in Christ's unique lordship, Christians refused to submit totally to any earthly power. Caesar was not "the Lord" because "the kingdom of the world now belongs to our Lord and to his anointed." (Rev.11:15) The purpose of all human history is Jesus, the world's Lord and Master.

Christian prayer is filled with the title "Lord". Scripture concludes in hope, "Amen. Come, Lord Jesus." (Rev.22:20)

In Brief - 452 - 455

Why Did Jesus Come? (456-459)
Jesus was made man "for our salvation." The Word became flesh to reconcile us with the Father. (4:14) "As captives, we awaited a Savior; as prisoners, help; as slaves, a liberator. Did not these things move God to descend to human nature?" (St. Gregory of Nyssa) God sent his Son "so we might live through him" (1Jn.4:9), and so we "should not perish but have eternal life." (Jn.3:16)

Jesus is our model. He said "Learn from me." (Mt.11:29) The Father commanded us to "Listen to him." (Mk.9:7) Jesus told us to "Love one another as I have loved you." (Jn.15:12)

Our Gift (460)
By becoming flesh, Jesus made us "partakers of the divine nature." (2Pt.1:4) "The Word became man so that man might become a son of God." (St. Irenaeus) "For the Son of God became man so that we might become God." (St. Athanasius) Jesus "assumed our nature, so that he, made man, might make men gods." (St. Thomas Aquinas)

Becoming Flesh – The Incarnation (461-462)
The Church calls Jesus' assuming a human nature, the Incarnation. Jesus "took the form of a servant, being born in the likeness of men." (Phil.2:7) "A body have you prepared for me … then I said, 'Lo, I have come to do your will, O God'." (Heb.10:5-7)

The Unique Christian Belief (463)
The distinctive sign of the Christian faith is belief in the Incarnation. God's Spirit reveals to the believer "that Jesus Christ has come in the flesh." (1Jn.4:2) God "was manifested in the flesh." (1Tim.3:16)

True God and True Man

Heresies About Jesus (464)

Jesus Christ is not part God and part man, nor is he a confused mixture of the divine and the human. The Church fought these heresies by clarifying the truth that Jesus Christ is true God and true man.

Gnostic Docetism (465)

The first heresies (Gnostic Docetism) denied Jesus' true humanity. However, the Church taught that God's Son had truly "come in the flesh." Jesus is Son of God by nature and not by adoption. (Council of Antioch) Later, Arius said that Jesus was "from another substance" than that of the Father. Against Arius, the Church declared that Jesus is "begotten, not made, of the same substance as the Father." (Nicea, 325)

Jesus is Not a Human Person (466)

The Nestorian heresy said that Jesus is a human person who is joined to the divine person of God's Son. Against Nestorius, the Church said that in Christ there was only one person, the Divine Person who became man by "uniting to himself in his person the flesh animated by a rational soul." Mary was proclaimed "the mother of God" because from her the Word received his body, animated by a rational soul. Therefore, "The Word is said to be born according to the flesh." (Ephesus 431)

Jesus Had a True Human Nature (467)

Another heresy (Monophysitism) claimed that Jesus' human nature ceased to exist when assumed by the divine person. However, the Church declared that Jesus "was begotten from the Father before all ages as to his divinity and in these last days, ... was born as to his humanity of the Virgin Mary, the Mother of God." In Christ, there are "two natures without confusion, change, division or separation. The distinction between the natures was never abolished by their union." (Council of Chalcedon, 451)

Overstressing His Humanity (468 - 469)

Later heresies overstressed Christ's humanity and made it a personal subject. In contrast, the Church said that everything in Christ's human nature is attributed to his divine person as its proper subject, even his sufferings and death. "Jesus Christ is true God, Lord of glory and one of the Trinity" (Council of Constantinople 553)

Jesus is inseparably true God and true man. "What he was, he remained and what he was not he assumed. (Roman Liturgy) "O, only-begotten Son and Word of God, you ... without change became man and were crucified." (Liturgy of St. John Chrysostom)

SON OF GOD – YET MAN

How Did Jesus Become Man? (470)

Jesus' "human nature was assumed, not absorbed". Therefore, the Church teaches the full reality of Christ's human body and human soul (with intellect and will). Yet, Christ's human nature belongs to the Son of God. Christ's actions in his human nature derive from "one of the Trinity." Jesus communicates to his human nature his own personal mode of existence in the Trinity. "The Son of God acted with a human will and loved with a human heart." (Second Vatican Council)

Jesus' Human Knowledge (471-472)

The heretic Apollinarius taught that Jesus had no human soul because it was replaced by the Word. Therefore, the Church declared that the Son assumed a rational, human soul which has true human knowledge. This human knowledge is limited and was used in an historical context. Jesus could "increase in wisdom" and could learn from human experiences because he took "the form of a slave." (Phil.2:7)

Knowing God's Plan (473-474)

By union with the Word, Jesus knew what pertains to God, especially in his immediate knowledge of the Father (Mk.14:36) and in his divine penetration into men's secrets. (Mk.2:8)

Christ enjoyed a full understanding of the eternal plan, which he came to reveal. He didn't know what he was not sent to reveal, e.g. the time of restoring the Kingdom to Israel. (Acts 1:7)

Having Two Wills (475)

Christ possessed two wills, divine and human. These are not opposed to each other. They cooperate so that the Word made flesh willed humanly all that he had already decided divinely with the Father and the Holy Spirit. Christ's human will "submits to his divine and almighty will." (Third Council of Constantinople - 681)

Seeing God Through Jesus' Body (476-477)

Christ's body, being truly human, was finite. Therefore, his human face can be portrayed in images. (Second Council of Nicaea II 787) Through Jesus' body "we see our God made visible and are caught up with love of the God we cannot see." (Christmas Preface) The believer "who venerates the icon, is venerating in it the person depicted." (Second Council of Nicaea)

Importance of the Sacred Heart (478)

"The Son of Man knew me and gave himself for me." (Gal.2:20) Because Jesus loved every person with a human heart, the Sacred Heart of Jesus is rightly considered the chief sign of his love for all human beings. (Pius XII - Encyclical on the Sacred Heart)

In Brief - 479 - 483

Quotes to Remember

When the fullness of time had come, God sent forth his Son, born of a woman. (Gal.4:4)

We believe and confess that Jesus of Nazareth is the eternal Son of God made man.

9
Conceived by the Holy Spirit (484-570)

Mary Conceives by the Spirit (484-486)

The Annunciation begins "the fullness of time." (Gal.4:4) Mary conceived Jesus in whom the "whole fullness of deity" dwells "bodily". (Col.2:9) To Mary's question of "How can this be, since I do not know man?" the angel replied, "The Holy Spirit will come upon you." (Lk.1:34-35) By the Spirit, Mary conceived the eternal Son of the Father in a humanity drawn from her own.

This Son of the Father is the Christ, anointed by the Spirit from the beginning. This anointing was progressively revealed because his whole life manifested how "God anointed Jesus of Nazareth with the Holy Spirit and with power." (Acts 10:38)

MARY'S PREROGATIVES

Mary and Jesus (487 - 488)

The Church's teaching about Mary illumines our faith about Christ. In preparing a body for Jesus (Heb.10:5), God wanted a creature's free cooperation. He chose Mary (a daughter of Israel and a virgin betrothed to Joseph) to be his Son's mother. A woman (Eve) had shared in the coming of death, so a woman should share in the coming of life (Second Vatican Council).

Holy Women (489)

Many holy women prepared for Mary. Eve received the promise of a posterity who will win the victory over the evil one. She is called "the mother of all the living." (Gen.3:15, 20) Sarah and Hannah conceived children in their old age. Among all women, Mary "stands out among the poor and the humble" and "the new plan of salvation is established in her." (Second Vatican Council)

Conceived Without Sin (490-491)

Mary was enriched with gifts appropriate to her call. She was "full of grace." (Lk.1:20)

Over the centuries, the Church realized that this "full of grace" meant that Mary was redeemed from the first moment, her

Immaculate Conception. Mary, "from the first moment of her conception by the merits of Jesus Christ, was preserved immune from all stain of original sin." (Pope Pius IX – 1854)

Redeemed by Christ's Merits (492-493)

By Christ's merits, Mary "is redeemed in a more exalted fashion." (Second Vatican Council) The Father blessed Mary "in Christ with every spiritual blessing" and chose her "In Christ before the foundation of the world, to be holy and blameless." (Eph.1:3-4)

The Eastern Church calls Mary "The All-Holy" and says that she is "free from any stain of sin ... formed as a new creature." By God's grace, Mary remained free of personal sin throughout her life.

Total Gift of Self (494)

Mary responded with the obedience of faith. "Behold, I am the handmaid of the Lord, let it be done to me according to your word." (Lk.1:28-38) She gave herself entirely to the person and work of her Son. Church writers, call Mary "The Mother of the living". "Death came through Eve but life through Mary."

Truly – the Mother of God (495)

She is seen as "the mother of Jesus." However, Elizabeth, moved by the Spirit, rightly calls Mary "the mother of my Lord" (Lk.1:43) because she conceived the second person of the Holy Trinity. The Church proclaimed that Mary is truly Mother of God, "Theotokos." (Council of Ephesus, 431)

Conceiving Yet Remaining a Virgin (496-498)

The Church has always taught that Jesus was conceived "by the Holy Spirit without human seed" .(Lateran Council 649) This virginal conception was the sign that Jesus was truly the Son of God. He is, "truly of the race of David according to the flesh, Son of God according to the will and power of God, truly born of a virgin." (St. Ignatius of Antioch)

This virginal conception is beyond human understanding. Joseph had to be told "That which is conceived in her is of the Holy Spirit." (Mt.1:20. Isaiah had prophesied "Behold, a virgin shall conceive and bear a son." (7:14)

Faith in Jesus' virginal conception met with lively opposition from Jews, unbelievers and pagans. (St. Justin – 150) This opposition shows that the virginal conception was not some adaptation of a first century belief. Mary's virginity, her giving birth to Jesus and the Lord's death are three mysteries which were "accomplished in God's silence." (St. Ignatius – 107)

Always a Virgin (499-501)

In giving birth, Mary's real and perpetual virginity was not diminished but was sanctified. (Second Vatican Council)

Sometimes the Bible mentions brothers and sisters of Jesus. The Church has always seen these "brothers and sisters" as not being other children of Mary. In fact, Matthew speaks of "his brothers James, Joseph", who are actually the sons of "the other Mary." (cf 13:55 and 28:1)

GOD'S PLAN FOR MARY

Why Born of a Virgin? (502-504)

The virgin birth highlights Christ's person and his redemptive mission. Mary's virginity shows God's absolute initiative in the Incarnation. Because Jesus has only God as Father, he is properly Son of the Father in both natures." (Council of Friuli 796)

Jesus is conceived by the Holy Spirit because he is the new Adam, "a life-giving spirit". He is the "man from heaven". From his conception, God gave to Jesus' humanity "the Spirit without measure" (Jn.3:34) so that "From his fullness, we can all receive." (Jn.1:16)

A New Era Begins (505-507)

By his virginal conception Jesus begins a new era, namely, the birth of children adopted by the Holy Spirit through faith. This new life comes not from "the will of the flesh nor the will of man, but of God." (Jn.1:16) Accepting this new life is virginal, a gift from the Spirit.

Mary's virginity is a sign of her own faith. As both virgin and mother, Mary is a perfect symbol for the Church who receives God's Word in faith and brings forth children in the Spirit.

In Brief - 508- 511

MYSTERIES OF CHRIST'S LIFE

The Stories (512-513)

The Creed says nothing explicitly about Jesus' hidden or public life. Because all that Jesus did and taught is important, catechesis uses the gospel stories.

We study three things:
1. elements common to all the stories
2. a sketch of Jesus' hidden life
3. a sketch of Jesus' public life

Stories That Reveal the Mystery (514 – 515)

The gospels do not record every event of Jesus' life (even of his public ministry). The stories were written so we "may believe that Jesus is the Christ, the Son of God" and, therefore, "have life in his name. (Jn.20:31)

The four evangelists had faith in Jesus and wanted to share their faith. They recorded Jesus' deeds, miracles and words to reveal that in him "the whole fullness of deity dwells bodily." (Col.2:9) His humanity was a "sacrament", a sign and instrument of our salvation. His earthly life led to the invisible mystery of his divine sonship and redemptive mission.

The Mystery at Work in the Stories (516-518)

All of Jesus' words and deeds are a revelation of his Father. "Whoever has seen me has seen the Father." (Jn.14:9) Jesus always did his Father's will, and his life shows "God's love among us." (Jn.4:9)

Christ's whole life is a mystery of redemption, which comes primarily through his death on the cross. This mystery is at work in his poor birth, his hidden life of obedience, his purifying word, his miracles and exorcisms and in his Resurrection.

In all his words and deeds, Jesus aimed at restoring fallen man to his original vocation. "When Christ became incarnate, he procured for us a 'short cut' to salvation. What we lost in Adam, we might recover in Christ Jesus." (St. Irenaeus)

We Share His Riches (519-521)

Christ's riches are for everyone. He lived and died "for us men and for our salvation." (cf 1Cor.15:3) He is still "our advocate before the Father" (1Jn.1:1) for he "lives to make intercession for us." (Heb.7:25) Jesus invites us to be his disciples and to follow him.

By becoming a man, Christ enables us to live in him. "We must continue to accomplish in ourselves the stages of Jesus' life." (St. John Eudes)

JESUS' INFANCY AND HIDDEN LIFE

The Prophets and John the Baptist (522-524)

God prepared the world for his Son's coming. God had the prophets announce Jesus. God even awakened expectation in pagan hearts.

John the Baptist, surpassed "all the prophets, of which he was the last." Even in his mother's womb, he announced Christ's presence. Later, he rejoiced as the "friend of the bridegroom" (Jn.3:29), and went before Jesus "in the spirit and power of Elijah." (Lk.1:17)

The Advent liturgy highlights John's martyrdom and instills in us his words, "He must increase, but I must decrease." (Jn.3:30)

Our Christmas Mystery (525-526)

In the poverty of Jesus' birth (witnessed first by shepherds) heaven's glory was manifested. "The virgin today brings into the world the Eternal and the earth offers a cave to the Inaccessible." (Romanus the Melodist)

Becoming a child (the condition for entering the Kingdom) demands being "born from above." (Jn.3:7) Christmas is fulfilled when Christ is formed in us. "We have been made sharers in the divinity of Christ who humbles himself to share our humanity." (Antiphon for January 1)

The Circumcision (527)

Jesus' circumcision on the eighth day (Lk.2:21) is the sign of his submission to the law and his future participation in Israel's worship. This sign prefigures Baptism (the "Circumcision of Christ").

The Three Wise Men (528)

The Epiphany event (which includes the wise men, Jesus' baptism and the wedding feast of Cana) manifests Jesus as Israel's Messiah, the Son of God and Savior of the world. The Magi represent the pagan nations who will welcome the gospel. By their coming to Jerusalem, they correctly seek in Israel the king of the nations. Only by turning toward the Jews can the pagans discover Jesus. All the nations are part of the "family of the patriarchs" and "worthy of the heritage of Israel." (St. Leo the Great)

Encounter in the Temple (529)

By his presentation in the Temple, Jesus is manifested as the first born who belongs to the Lord. His "encounter" (the name used in Byzantine tradition) with Simeon and Anna symbolizes the recognition of Jesus as "light of the nations" and "the glory of Israel." Mary's sorrow prefigures Christ's death which will be a salvation "for all the peoples." (Lk.2:22-39)

Fleeing to Egypt (530)

The massacre of the innocents causes Jesus' flight into Egypt and shows the opposition of darkness to the light. "His own people received him not." (Jn.1:11) His return from Egypt recalls the Exodus and shows Jesus as the definitive liberator of God's people. (Mt.2:15)

Thirty Years of Obedience (531 – 533)

For thirty years, Jesus engaged in manual labor and lived as a Jew obedient to God's law. He was "obedient" to his parents and "grew in wisdom and in stature and in favor with God and man." (Lk.2:51-52.

Jesus' obedience was an image of his obedience to his heavenly Father and anticipated his obedience in the Garden. By obedience, he restored what Adam's disobedience had destroyed. (cf.Rom.5:19)

By our daily ordinary actions, we enter into fellowship with Jesus. "Jesus' home in Nazareth is a school, teaching us the value of silence, family life and the redeeming law of human work." (Pope Paul VI - 1964)

Consecrated to the Father (534)

Jesus' staying behind in the Temple (the only recorded event of his hidden life) showed his total consecration to his divine mission. His parents did not fully understand Jesus' reply, "Did you not know that I must be about my Father's work?" (Lk.2:41-52)

JESUS' PUBLIC LIFE

Getting Baptized (535)

Jesus' public life began while John was preaching a "baptism of repentance." Suddenly, Jesus appears and wants to be baptized. When Jesus receives John's baptism, the Father says, "This is my beloved Son" (Mt.3:17), and the Spirit, in the form of a dove, comes upon Jesus. This manifests Jesus as both Messiah of Israel and Son of God.

Anointed For His Mission (536)

By this baptism, Jesus accepts his mission as God's suffering servant. He is the "Lamb of God" and his baptism anticipates his bloody death which will take away the sin of the world. (Jn.1:29) The Father delights in his Son, and the Spirit (already fully possessed by Jesus) comes to "rest on him" (Jn.1:32-33), showing that Jesus will be the source of the Spirit. The heavens (closed by Adam's sin) "were opened" (Mt.3:16) and the water was sanctified (a prelude to the new creation).

Buried With Him (537)

By descending into the baptismal water, Christians enter into this mystery of Christ's death and become the Father's beloved son. "Let us be buried with Christ by Baptism to rise with him." (St. Gregory of Nazranzus) "After the bath of water, the Holy Spirit swoops down upon us and we become sons of God." (St. Hilary of Poitiers)

Faithful in the Desert (538-540)

Immediately, the Spirit leads Jesus into a forty day fast in the desert. This period concludes with three diabolical temptations which recapitulate the temptations of Adam in Paradise and of Israel in the desert. Jesus rebuffs these attacks and does not compromise his filial attitude toward the Father.

62

These events reveal Jesus as the new Adam. He also fulfills the vocation of Israel (who was not faithful during forty years in the desert). In these forty days, Jesus anticipates the full victory of his passion when he will conquer the devil, bind him and take back his plunder. (Mk.3:27)

Jesus does not accept Satan's proposed definition of his Messiahship. By overcoming these temptations, he is able "to sympathize with our weaknesses", like us "in everything but sin." (Heb.4:15)

Preaching The Kingdom (541-542)

After John is arrested, Jesus takes up his message "The time is fulfilled. The Kingdom of God is at hand. Repent, and believe in the gospel." (Mk.1:15) Jesus inaugurates the Kingdom of God which will culminate when he is "lifted up from the earth". (Jn.12:32) Jesus, stands at the heart of God's plan to gather the human race into his Church.

Everyone's Kingdom – Especially For the Poor and Sinful (543-545)

This Kingdom is for everyone. God's word is a seed which exerts its full power within the believer. (Second Vatican Council)

This kingdom belongs especially to the poor, because Jesus "preaches the good news to the poor." (Lk.4:18) This includes the "little ones" with whom the Father is pleased. (Mt.11:25) By experiencing hunger and privation, Jesus shared in poverty. He identified himself with the poor, and made love for the poor a condition for entering the kingdom.

Jesus invites all sinners. He shows the Father's boundless mercy and the vast joy in heaven "over one sinner who repents." (Lk.15:7)

Need For a Choice (546)

Through his parables, Jesus invites his hearers to enter the kingdom. He asks them to make a radical choice. ("He sells all that he has and buys that field" - Mt.13:44) The kingdom requires deeds and the use of God's talents. (Mt.13:3-9) The parables contain the secrets of the kingdom. Only a person inside the Kingdom can understand their message.

Miracle Power (547-548)

Jesus' words are accompanied by miracles which manifest the Kingdom. These miracles show that he was sent by the Father, they invite people to believe in him as the Son of God. In spite of miracles, some people reject Jesus. Others claim that his power comes from Satan. (Mk.3:22)

Setting People Free (549-550)

In freeing people from illness, hunger and death, Jesus performed messianic signs. His primary task, however, was to free men from sin (the greatest slavery) which causes all forms of human bondage. (Jn.8:34-36) Jesus' Kingdom means Satan's defeat. Driving demons out of some people (exorcisms) anticipates Jesus' full victory on the cross over the "ruler of this world" (Jn.12:31).

FORMING THE APOSTLES

Choosing the Twelve (551)

Jesus chose twelve apostles, shared his authority with them and "sent them out to preach the Kingdom of God and to heal." (Lk.9:2) They will always be associated with his kingdom because through them Jesus directs his Church. Jesus promised them that they would "sit on thrones judging the twelve tribes of Israel." (Lk.22:30)

Placing Peter at the Head (552-553)

After Peter proclaimed "You are the Christ, the Son of the living God." (Mt.16:16) Jesus bestowed special authority upon him, "You are Peter, and on this rock I will build my Church and the gates of Hell will not prevail against it." (16:18) Peter will always remain the unshakeable rock of the Church who strengthens his brothers. (Lk.22:32)

Jesus gave Peter special authority. "I will give you the keys of the Kingdom of heaven, and whatever you bind on earth shall be bound in heaven, and whatever you loose on earth will be loosed in heaven. (Mt.16:19) "To bind" and "to loose" mean authority to forgive sin, to define doctrines and to make disciplinary decisions in the Church. Jesus entrusted this authority to the Church through the apostles (Mt.18:18) and in particular, through Peter, to whom he specifically entrusted the keys of the kingdom.

Transfigured Before Them (554)

Jesus said he would suffer "be killed and on the third day be raised." (Mt.16:21) The apostles did not understand these words. Therefore, Jesus chose Peter, James and John to come to a high mountain, to see his face and clothes become dazzling with light. They saw Jesus speak with Moses and Elijah, and heard the Father say, "This is my Son, my Chosen; listen to him." (Lk.9:35)

Disclosing His Glory (555-556)

By this action, Jesus disclosed his divine glory and revealed his death in Jerusalem. He showed that he fulfilled the law (symbolized by Moses) and the prophets (symbolized by Elijah). "The Trinity was present: the Father as the voice; the Son in a man; the Spirit in a shining cloud." (St. Thomas Aquinas) "Your disciples saw your glory, so they would understand that your passion was voluntary." (Byzantine Transfiguration Liturgy)

Jesus' Baptism proclaimed our own Baptism. His transfiguration proclaimed our resurrection when Christ "will change our lowly body to be like his glorious body." (Phil.3:21)

Unfortunately, Peter's desire to remain on the mountain shows he still did not see the need for death before entering the kingdom. (St. Augustine)

Toward Death in Jerusalem (557-558)

After that, Jesus "set his face to go to Jerusalem" (Lk.9:51), knowing that a prophet should not "perish away from Jerusalem." (Lk.13:33)

Jesus still loved Jerusalem and would gather her children "as a hen gathers her brood beneath her wings." (Mt.23:37) He even wept over Jerusalem, wishing that the city, "knew the things that make for peace!." (Lk.19:41-42)

Entering Jerusalem (559 – 560)

Jesus carefully chose the time and the details of his entrance into Jerusalem. By "riding on an ass", he fulfilled the prophecy. (Zech.9:9) By his humility, he conquered the Daughter of Zion (a figure of the Church). The poor and children, like the angels at his birth, acclaim "Blessed is he who comes in the name of the Lord."

In Brief - 561-570

Quotes to Remember

The most Blessed Virgin Mary, from the first moment of her conception, was preserved immune from all stain of original sin. (Pope Pius IX)

....

The Annunciation to Mary inaugurates the fullness of time.

....

Jesus is conceived by the Holy Spirit in Mary's womb because he is the new Adam.

....

Christ's whole life is a revelation of the Father.

....

Jesus' religious life was that of a Jew obedient to God's law.

....

The Baptism of Jesus inaugurates his mission.

....

The gospel stories are written so we might believe and by believing "have life in his name".

....

Christ stands at the heart of the gathering of men into the family of God.

....

10
Suffered, Crucified, Died and Buried (571-630)

Accomplishing God's Plan (571-573)
Jesus' death and resurrection accomplished God's "once for all." (Heb.9:26) This is the very center of the "good news" proclaimed by the apostles. The Church faithfully proclaims Jesus' interpretation that he "should suffer these things and enter into his glory." (Lk.24:26-27)

Jesus was "rejected by the elders, the chief priests and the scribes" and was "handed over to the Gentiles to be mocked and scourged and crucified." (Mk.8:31, Mt.20:19) Faith examines the circumstances of Jesus' death (from the gospels and other historical sources) to understand better the meaning of redemption.

Reasons For the Accusations (574 - 575)
From the very beginning, certain groups agreed to destroy Jesus. (Mk.3:6 and 13:1) Because Jesus expelled demons, forgave sins, healed on the Sabbath, gave novel interpretations to the law, and was friendly with public sinners, some ill-intentioned persons thought Jesus was possessed by the demon. (Mk.3:22) He was accused of blasphemy, false prophecy and religious crimes (which Jewish law punishes by stoning).

Jesus' deeds were a "sign of contradiction", especially for Jerusalem's religious authorities (whom John calls "the Jews"). In contrast, Jesus' relationship with the Pharisees was not always polemical. He endorsed some of their teachings (resurrection from the dead, almsgiving, fasting, addressing God as Father, the centrality of love) and, on occasion, dined with them.

The Four Objections (576)
Four objections arose against Jesus' ministry:
1. Jesus seemed to be acting against some essential institutions of Israel.
2. He did not submit to the whole written law or the Pharisaic interpretation.
3. He did not accept the centrality of the Temple as God's holy dwelling place.
4. He claimed a share in God's glory which is given to no man.

Fulfilling the Law (577)

At the very beginning, Jesus presented the law given on Sinai in light of the New Covenant. Jesus said, "Do not think I have come to abolish the law or the prophets. I have come not to abolish but to fulfill." (Mt.5:17) Anyone who breaks the least law and teaches others "will be called least in the kingdom of heaven." (Mt.5:17-19)

Keeping the Law (578 - 580)

As Israel's Messiah, Jesus kept the law in its all-embracing detail, to "the least of these commandments." (Mt.5: 17-19) The Jews admitted that they could not observe the Law and had an annual Day of Atonement.

The Pharisees had a zeal for the Law but unfortunately they lapsed into a hypocritical casuistry. Otherwise, they could have prepared for God's intervention in Jesus.

Only Jesus, the Divine Legislator, "born of a woman, born under the law" could perfectly fulfill this law. (Gal.4:4) Jesus had the Law engraved on his heart. He took upon himself "the curse of the Law", so he could redeem men "from the transgressions under the first covenant." (Gal.3:13)

Offending Some Teachers (581-582)

Jesus (seen by the people as a rabbi) offended the Jewish teachers because he refused to put his teachings alongside of theirs (as just another opinion). He spoke "as one who had authority and not as their scribes." (Mt.7:28-29) "You have heard it said ... but I say to you." (Mt.5:33-34) He also rejected the Pharisees' human traditions which made "void the word of God." (Mk.7:13)

Concerning dietary laws, Jesus brought out their real meaning, showing that only what comes from the heart can defile a man. (Mk.7:18-21) The other teachers did not accept Jesus even though his preaching was accompanied by miracles. They especially rejected his teaching that someone could help his neighbor on the Sabbath.

Respect for the Temple (583 – 584)

Jesus showed the deepest respect for the Temple, going there every year of his hidden life. (Lk.2:41) When twelve years old, Jesus remained in the Temple to remind his parents that he must be about his Father's business. (2:46-49) In John's gospel, he patterned his public ministry according to his pilgrimages to Jerusalem.

For Jesus, the Temple was a house for prayer and he was angered when its outer court was used for commerce (Mt.21:18) After the resurrection, the apostles continued to revere the Temple. (Acts 2:46)

The Temple's Destruction (585-586)

Jesus predicted the Temple's destruction. Not one stone would remain "upon another." (Mt.24:1-2) This prophecy was distorted at his trial (Mk.14:57-58) and used as an insult on the cross. (Mt.27:39-40)

Jesus willingly paid the Temple tax for himself and Peter. He identified himself with the Temple by claiming to be God's definitive dwelling among men. His death presaged the destruction of the Temple and began a new age when man "will worship the Father neither on this mountain nor in Jerusalem." (Jn.4:21)

THE CLAIMS OF JESUS

The Real Stumbling Block – Forgiving Sins (587 – 589)

The real stumbling block for Israel's religious authorities was Jesus' role in the redemption of sins.

Jesus scandalized the Pharisees by eating with sinners. (Lk.5:30) He had not come "to call the righteous, but sinners to repentance." (Lk.5:37) He said that sin is universal and that anyone is blind who claims not to need forgiveness. (Jn.8:33-36)

Jesus gave scandal by saying that God the Father was also merciful (Mt.9:13) and by hinting that he (Jesus) could admit sinners to the messianic banquet. (Lk.15:1-2) However, the great dilemma was caused by Jesus' forgiving of the sins of the paralytic. The authorities correctly asked "Who can forgive sins but God alone?." (Mk.2:7) By forgiving sins Jesus was either blaspheming (making himself equal to God) or he was speaking the truth.

Believing His Claims (590-591)

Jesus said that a person "greater than Jonah, greater than Solomon, greater than the temple is present." (Mt.12:41-42) These words are justified only if Jesus is God. This is true also of Jesus' other claims "Before Abraham was, I am" (Jn.8:58) and "I and the Father are one." (Jn.10: 30)

Jesus asked the authorities to believe because he did the works of God. (Jn.10:38) Such a demand for belief throws light upon the Sanhedrin's misunderstanding of Jesus. They condemned him as a "blasphemer" (Mt.26:64-66) due to ignorance and "hardness of unbelief." (Lk.23:34)

In Brief - 592 - 594

THE TRIAL

Varied Jewish Opinions (595-596)

Besides Nicodemus and Joseph of Aramathea (both secretly disciples of Jesus), "many, even among the authorities, believed in him." (Jn.12:42) After Pentecost, many priests and even some Pharisees became believers. (Acts 6:7 and 15:5) Years later, James told Paul that thousands who were zealous for the Law had become believers. (Acts 21:20)

The authorities were not unanimous in their stance toward Jesus. The Pharisees wanted to excommunicate Jesus' followers. (Jn.9:22) Caiaphas, the high priest, thought that Jesus should die "that the whole nation should not perish" .(Jn.11:4-50) In asking Pilate to condemn Jesus, the Sanhedrin used the charge of "political revolt."

Jews Are Not Collectively Responsible for Jesus' Death (597)

Jesus' trial is historically complex and we cannot place responsibility upon the Jews in Jerusalem. Jesus forgave them from the cross, and, after the resurrection, Peter says that the Jews and their leaders acted in "ignorance." (Acts 3:17) "Jews today cannot be charged with the crimes committed during Jesus'

passion. They should not be spoken of as rejected or accursed."
(Second Vatican Council)

We Sinners Are Responsible (598)

Really, "sinners were the authors and ministers" of all Jesus'
suffering. (Roman Catechism) Because of our sins, the Church
places responsibility primarily upon Christians (a responsibility
often given only to Jews).

"We must regard as guilty all those who relapse into their
sins. Our crime in this case is greater in us than in the Jews.
Because we profess to know him, when we deny him, we lay
violent hands on him." (Roman Catechism) "Nor did the demons
crucify him. You crucify him when you delight in your vices and
sins." (St. Francis of Assisi)

Not a Coincidence (599-600)

Jesus didn't die from an unfortunate coincidence of
circumstances. St. Peter said that he died "according to the
definite plan and foreknowledge of God." (Acts 2:33) The people
involved were merely passive players in a script written by God.

God's "predestination" includes each person's free response to
grace. The Bible says that they "gathered together against your
holy servant Jesus to do what your plan had predestined to take
place." (Acts 4:27-28) God permitted their acts of blindness to
accomplish his plan of salvation.

Foretold By Scripture (601)

Scriptures foretold Jesus' death as a ransom "to free men from
the slavery of sin." (Is. 53:11) Christians professed that "Christ
died for our sins in accordance with the scriptures." (1Cor.15:13)
After the resurrection, Jesus explained that his death was needed
so he could enter into glory. (Lk. C 24)

Jesus in Solidarity With Sinners (602 – 603)

Christ was always destined to shed his blood, even though our
ransom was only manifested "at the end of the times." (1Pet.
1:18-20) Jesus was made "to be sin" so we "might become the
righteousness of God." (2Cor.5:21)

Jesus did not experience reprobation as if he himself sinned
(Jn.8:46) but he assumed our state of sinful waywardness. God

placed Jesus in solidarity with us sinners. He "did not spare his own Son" (Rom.8:32) so we might be "reconciled to God by the death of his son." (Rom.5:10)

God's Initiative in Christ (604 – 605)

Prior to any response on our part, "God sent us his Son to be the expiation for our sins." (1Jn.4:10) "While we were yet sinners, Christ died for us." (Rom.5:8)

The Father wants none "of these little ones to perish." (Mt.18:14) The Church teaches that "there is not, never has been, and never will be a single human being for whom Christ did not suffer." (Council of Quiercy – 853)

FOR OUR SINS

Jesus Embraced Plan of Salvation (606-607)

Christ always embraced the Father's will. "My food is to do the will of him who sent me, and to accomplish his work." (Jn.4:34) His death was in loving union with the Father. "The Father loves me, because I lay down my life." (Jn.10:17)

Jesus' accepted the Father's plan of redemption. Foreseeing his death, Jesus said, "For this purpose I have come to this hour." (Jn.12:27) From the cross, he said "It is finished." (Jn.19:30)

The Suffering Lamb (608-609)

Jesus is the "Lamb of God who takes away the sin of the world." (Jn.1:29) Jesus is the Suffering Servant. He is the new Paschal Lamb allowing himself to be led to slaughter. Jesus came "to give his life as a ransom for many." (Mk.10:45) Jesus was totally free in this decision. "I lay it down of my own accord." (Jn.10:18)

Perpetuating His Sacrifice (610 – 611)

"On the night he was betrayed", Jesus transformed the Last Supper into a memorial of his voluntary offering to the Father. He spoke of his body "given for you" and of his blood already being "poured out for the forgiveness of sins." (Lk.22:19) Jesus told his apostles to perpetuate this memorial of his sacrifice. In doing so, he made them priests of the New Covenant.

72

Accepting the Cup (612)

In Gethsemane, Jesus accepted this cup of the New Covenant from his Father. He was "obedient even to death", saying "not as I will but as you will." (Mt.26:39) Although the human nature was assumed by the "Author of life", Jesus accepted death as part of our redemption.

Surpassing All Other Sacrifices (613–615)

Christ's death accomplishes man's redemption and restores man to God through the blood of the Covenant (Mt.26:28). Christ's unique sacrifice completes and surpasses all other sacrifices. It is a gift from the Father (who handed over his Son) and a gift from the Son (who freely accepted death).

As prophesied by Isaiah, Jesus actually substituted himself for us. As the Suffering Servant, he bore "the sin of many" so the many would "be accounted righteous." (Is.53:10-12)

Becoming the Source of Salvation (616-617)

Jesus gave the value of redemption and atonement to his sacrifice. Not even the holiest man can take upon himself the sins of others and offer himself as a sacrifice. However, because the divine person of the Son exists in Christ, this sacrifice is a redemption for all. Christ's sacrifice was unique. Jesus is "the source of eternal salvation" and "merited justification for us." (Council of Trent)

Invited to Drink His Cup (618)

Christ can make us partners in his death in a way known only to God. He invites all to "take up their cross and follow him." (Mt.16:24) James and John were invited to drink the same cup (Mk.10:39) and Mary, his mother, was intimately involved in the cross. "Apart from the cross there is no other ladder by which we may get to heaven." (St. Rose of Lima)

In Brief - 619 - 623

A TRUE DEATH

Mystery of the Tomb (624)
Jesus had the full experience of death, namely his soul separated from his body. This state of the dead Christ is the mystery of the tomb and his descent into hell. It is the mystery of Holy Saturday (God's Sabbath rest) after Jesus fulfilled man's salvation.

The Link Between Mortal and Immortal State (625–626)
Jesus' stay in the tomb links his passable state (before Easter) with his glorious and risen state today. "I died, and behold I am alive for evermore." (Rev.1:18) "Because Jesus allowed death to separate his soul from his body and then reunited them in the resurrection, he is the meeting point for death and life, arresting in himself the decomposition of nature and becoming the source of the reunion for the separated soul and body." (St. Gregory of Nyssa)

During this time in the tomb, the divine person continued to possess both the human soul and the human body. "Although separated from each other, both remained with one and the same person of the Word." (St. John Damascene)

A Unique Corpse (627)
Christ's death ended his earthly human existence. However, his mortal corpse was not like others because "divine power preserved Christ's body from corruption." (St. Thomas Aquinas) His bodily resurrection on the third day was proof because bodily decay is thought to begin on the fourth day.

Our Burial In Baptism (628)
Baptism efficaciously signifies the believer's descent into the tomb. "We were buried with him by baptism into death." As Christ was raised from the dead so we too might "walk in newness of life." (Rom.6:4)

In Brief - 629 – 630

11
Descended into Hell and Rose on the Third Day (631-682)

Descent and Ascent (631-632)

Christ "descended" and also "ascended far above all the heavens" (Eph.4:9-10) The Creed teaches both his descent into hell and his resurrection, "Christ, that Morning Star, who came back from the dead." (Easter Vigil Exsultet) The apostles taught that Jesus, like all men, joined everyone else in the realm of death. However, he descended there as Savior "to preach to the spirits in person." (1Pt.3:19)

Declaring the Just (633-634)

This abode of the dead is called "hell" because the souls are deprived of the vision of God. Jesus delivered only the "holy souls." He did not descend into hell to deliver the damned or to destroy the hell of damnation. Rather, he freed the just who had gone before him. (Council of Rome, 745)

When Jesus "preached even to the dead" (1Pet.4:6) he completely fulfilled his mission. This act shows that Christ's redemptive act has spread to all men of all times.

Preaching to the Dead (635)

Jesus said that "the dead will hear the voice of the Son of God, and those who hear will live." (Jn.5:25) By dying, Jesus destroyed the devil (who has the power of death) and delivered those who "through fear of death were subject to lifelong bondage." (Heb.2:14-15) "Today a great silence reigns on earth. The King has gone to free from sorrow Adam in his bonds and Eve captive with him." (Ancient Holy Saturday Homily)

In Brief - 636 – 637

The Crowning Truth – He Is Risen (638)

God fulfilled his promises "by raising Jesus." (Acts 13:32-33) The Resurrection is the crowning truth of faith, believed by the first Christian community, handed on by Tradition and established by the New Testament documents. "Christ is risen from the dead. To the dead, he has given life." (Byzantine liturgy)

HISTORICAL AND TRANSCENDENT

A Real Event (639)
Christ's resurrection is a real event, historically verified in the New Testament. Around 56 A.D., St. Paul wrote that Christ "was buried"; that he was raised on the third day in accordance with the scriptures." (1Cor.15:3-4)   Paul also listed various witnesses (Cephas, the Twelve, etc.) to whom Jesus appeared.

Discovering the Tomb Empty (640)
The empty tomb is the first element of the Easter story. Obviously, an empty tomb is not a direct proof of Christ's Resurrection because the absence of his body could be explained in other ways. However, the empty tomb is an essential first. The disciples' discovery of the Resurrection began with the holy women, with Peter and especially with the disciple "whom Jesus loved." This Beloved Disciple "saw and believed." He was the first to realize that the absence of the body did not result from human means nor that Jesus merely returned to earthly life like Lazarus had done. (Jn.20:5-7)

Appearing to the Disciples (641)
Mary Magdalene and the holy women were the first to encounter the Risen One. (Mk.16:1)   They became the first messengers of the Resurrection to Peter and the twelve. Later, based on Peter's witness, the community exclaimed, "The Lord has risen indeed, and has appeared to Simon." (Lk.24:34)

Making Them Witnesses (642)
These visions made the apostles witnesses to the Resurrection and foundation stones of Jesus' Church. The faith of the Early Church was based upon the testimony of men who were known and who were still living. Besides Peter and the Twelve (the primary witnesses), Paul mentioned other witnesses and "more than five hundred brothers at once, most of whom are still living." (1Cor.15:6)

76

Experiencing the Risen Jesus (643-644)

Because of these witnesses, we realize that the Resurrection is a historical fact, not something outside the physical order. The disciples did not experience some mystical exaltation. Really, the passion had shocked them and they refused to believe the good news. The Risen Jesus had to "upbraid them for their unbelief and hardness of heart." (Mk.16:14)

While actually seeing Jesus, they "thought they were seeing a ghost." (Lk.24:37) Jesus said "A ghost does not have flesh and bones as you can see I have." (24:39) Thomas doubted and demanded a sign. (Jn.20:24-27) Even during Jesus' final appearance, "some doubted." (Matt.28:17) Their belief in the Resurrection did not come from their credulity but from a direct experience of the Risen Jesus.

Having a Real Body (645)

The Risen Jesus invited the disciples to touch him and to share a meal. They could see that he was truly risen and that he had the very same body, marked by the wounds of his passion. This authentic, real body had the qualities of a glorious body (not limited by space and time) able to be present how and when Christ willed. Jesus' body was no longer confined to earth, but belonged to the heavenly realm. Jesus could appear to his disciples (as a gardener or in other forms familiar to the disciples) so that their faith would be awakened.

A Life Beyond Time and Space (646)

Jesus had miraculously raised three people from the dead (Jairus' daughter, the widow's son and Lazarus). These three returned to ordinary, earthly life and would eventually die again. Jesus' Resurrection is essentially different. He has passed from a state of death to another life, beyond time and space. Sharing in divine life, Jesus' body is filled with the Spirit. He is now "the man of heaven." (1Cor.15:45-50)

A Historical Event Surpassing History (647)

No one saw Jesus rise from the dead. No gospel describes the event and no one can say how it came about physically. Although the Resurrection is an historical event (verified by the empty tomb and Jesus' appearances to his disciples) the Resurrection transcends history. Therefore, Jesus did not reveal himself to the whole world, but "to those who came up with him from Galilee to Jerusalem who are now his witnesses." (Acts 13:31)

A Work of Three Persons (648 – 649)

Because God has intervened in history, the Resurrection is an object of faith. All three Divine Persons participated in this event. By his power, the Father raised up his Son and introduced his Son's humanity into the Trinity. By the Resurrection, Jesus was revealed as the "Son of God in power." (Rom.1:3-4) This manifestation came through the Spirit who gave life to Jesus' dead humanity. (cf Rom. 6:4) As for the Son, he effected his own resurrection by his divine power. "I have power to lay down my life and I have power to take it up again." (Jn.10:17-18)

Body and Soul United to Divine Person (650)

The Resurrection happened because the divine person remained united to both the separated body and to the separated soul. "By the unity of the divine nature, which remains present in each of these two components of man, these are reunited." (St. Gregory of Nyssa)

THE MEANING AND SAVING SIGNIFICANCE

Confirming His Own Teaching and Promise (651-653)

"If Christ has not been raised, then our preaching is in vain and your faith is in vain." (1Cor.15:14) The Resurrection confirms Christ's teachings (even those not accessible to human reason). By rising, Christ has given definitive proof of his divine authority.

Christ fulfilled the Old Testament prophecies and all of his own promises. The Resurrection proves the divinity of Christ, showing that he is truly "I am", the Son of God and God himself.

Our Freeing and Our Receiving (654-655)

The Paschal mystery has two aspects, first, our liberation from sin (by Christ's death) and, second, our receiving new life (by his Resurrection). This new life (justification) is victory over death and a new participation in grace. After the resurrection, Jesus called us brothers, "Go and tell my brethren." (Mt.28:10) We are not brothers by nature but by adoptive grace.

The Risen Christ is the source of our own future resurrection. "In Christ all shall be made alive." (1Cor.15:22) We have been swept up in Christ and "have tasted ... the powers of the age to come." (Heb.6:5) "We live no longer for ourselves but for him." (2Cor.5:15)

In Brief - 656 - 658

The Ascension - His Irreversible Entry Into Glory (659 - 661)

Christ's body was glorified at the very moment of the Resurrection (as shown by the new powers he enjoyed). Yet, for forty days he appeared to his disciples while his glory remained veiled under the appearance of an ordinary humanity.

In his final apparition, Jesus "was taken up into heaven and sat down at the right hand of God." (Mk.16:19) His Ascension is the irreversible entry of his humanity into divine glory. After his Ascension, Jesus did appear to Paul "as to one untimely born." (Gal.1:16)

Jesus spoke to Mary Magdalene of another stage of his glory, "I have not yet ascended to the Father." (Jn.20:17) Therefore, Christ's glory shown to the disciples is quite different from the glory of Christ exalted at God's right hand. The Ascension is an historical event marking a transition from risen glory to exalted glory.

His Descending and Ascending (662-663)

The two events (Christ's coming down from heaven and his ascending up to heaven) are closely linked. Jesus said, "No one has ascended into heaven but he who descended from heaven, the Son of Man." (Jn.3:13) Human nature does not have "access to the Father's house." Only Christ can give us such access and give us confidence that we will be with him.

Jesus said he would "be lifted up from the earth." (Jn.12:32) This mystery (begun with the cross) is completed by the Ascension when Jesus entered "into heaven itself." In heaven, Jesus "makes intercession" for "those who draw near to God through him." (Heb.7:25)

Seated in Glory (664)

Now seated at the Father's right hand means that Jesus Christ has the glory of his divinity which he had before all ages. Because his flesh is glorified, he now is seated bodily. This "being seated" signifies the inauguration of the messianic kingdom. "His dominion is an everlasting dominion, which shall not pass away." (Dan.7:14) After the Ascension, the apostles became witnesses that Christ's kingdom "will have no end." (Nicene Creed)

In Brief - 665 - 667

COMING IN GLORY

All Power in Heaven and Earth (668-669)

By his Ascension Christ's humanity participates in God's power and authority. He is "Lord both of the living and the dead." (Rom.14:9) He possesses all authority. All creation is fulfilled in him. Although taken up to heaven, Christ dwells on earth in his Church and has authority in the Spirit over the Church (the Kingdom of Christ already present in mystery).

The Last Hour (670)

In Christ, we have entered into "the last hour." (1Jn.21:8) The renewal of the world is irrevocably under way. The Church (endowed with a real but imperfect holiness) anticipates this renewal when Christ's Kingdom is manifested through miraculous signs that accompany the gospel's proclamation.

Waiting for the King (671-672)

Jesus' reign will be perfectly fulfilled when he returns as King. "They will see the Son of Man coming in a cloud with power and great glory." (Lk.21:27) Although Christ's victory is definitive, his reign still suffers attack by evil powers. Someday there will be "new heavens and a new earth." Until then, the Church, (with sacraments and institutions) groans and travails. That is why Christians pray "Come, Lord Jesus." (Rev.22:20)

Jesus said that the hour of the glorious messianic kingdom had not yet come. (Acts.1: 6-7) Therefore, the present age (a time of the Spirit and of witness) is also a time of distress, of evil, of waiting and watching.

Awaiting Israel's Conversion (673-674)

We do not know the time of Christ's coming "which the Father has fixed by his own authority." (Acts 1:7) It could happen at any moment or it could be "delayed."

His coming is suspended until he is recognized by "all Israel." Peter said that heaven had to receive Jesus "until the time of universal restoration". (Acts 3:21) Paul said that Israel's heart was hardened until "the full number of Gentiles comes in." (Rom.11:20-26) Finally, there will be Israel's "full inclusion" (Rom.11:12) and God will be "all in all." (Eph.4:13)

The Final Deception – The Antichrist (675-676)

Before Christ comes, the Church will pass through a final trial which will shake the faith of many (cf Lk.18:8). This "mystery of inequity" will be a religious deception offering men a solution to all problems at the price of apostasy from the truth. The supreme deception will be the Antichrist, a pseudo-Messianism by which man glorifies himself in place of God.

This deception always happens when people claim to gain messianic hope within history, when really it can only come from "beyond history" and through the final judgment. The Church has rejected both millenarianism and its political form, secular messianism.

Triumph After Trials (677)

The Church will enter her final glory only by following her Lord in his death and resurrection. This will not be an historic triumph of Church ascendancy, but a victory of God. A final unleashing of evil will cause Christ's Bride to come down from heaven. After worldwide cosmic upheavals, God will triumph over evil by the Last Judgment. (Rev.20: 12)

Then – All Gathered For Judgment (678-679)

Jesus announced the Final Judgment which will reveal the conduct of every person. Our attitude toward our neighbor will disclose our acceptance or rejection of God's grace. Jesus will say, "As you did it to one of the least of these my brethren, you did it to me." (Mt.25:40)

By his death, Jesus acquired the right to pass definitive judgment on all mankind. The Father gave "all judgment to the

Son." (Jn.5:22)   The Son came "to save and to give life." (cf Jn.3:17)   However, by rejecting Christ's gift, a person can condemn himself for all eternity.

In Brief - 680 – 682

Quotes to Remember

The Resurrection of Jesus is the crowning
truth of our faith in Christ.

I order you, O sleeper, to awake. Rise from the dead,
for I am the life of the dead. (Ancient Homily)

The Risen Christ himself is the source
of our future resurrection.

We are already at "the last hour". The final
age of the world is with us.

Christ, as Lord of eternal life, has full right
to pass judgment on every man.

12
The Holy Spirit (683-747)

Saying "Jesus is Lord" (683)
Only through the Holy Spirit, can a person be in touch with Christ. (1Cor.12:3) By Baptism, the Spirit gives us the life of the Father which is offered in the Son. "Those who bear God's Spirit are led to the Son, and the Son presents them to the Father who confers incorruptibility on them." (St. Irenaeus)

The Spirit – The Last Person Revealed (684)
Although the Spirit is the first to communicate new life, the Spirit was the last of the persons to be revealed. St. Gregory of Nazianzus explained this pedagogy of divine "condescension" when he wrote that the Father was revealed in the Old Testament and the Son in the New. It was not prudent to reveal the Son's divinity until the Father's divinity was confessed. So, also, the Spirit's divinity was withheld until the Son's divinity was believed.

The Spirit Works in Our Midst (685-686)
The Nicene Creed teaches that the Holy Spirit is a person of the Trinity, of one substance with the Father and the Son. This section will study how the Spirit does his works (the divine "economy").

In this "final age" (ushered in by Christ's redeeming Incarnation), the divine plan is accomplished by the outpouring of the Spirit. He brings about the Church, the communion of saints, the forgiveness of sins, the resurrection of the body and life everlasting.

BELIEVING IN THE SPIRIT

Hidden – Yet Known By His Works (687-688)
Although the Spirit reveals Christ and makes us hear the Father's word, we do not hear the Spirit himself because he "will not speak on his own." (Jn.16:13) Because of this "divine self-effacement", the world "cannot receive him because it neither sees him nor knows him." Believers, however, know the Spirit because he dwells in them. (Jn.14:17)

The Spirit inspired the Scriptures, gave us Tradition, assists the Church's Magisterium, gives us communion with Christ through the sacraments, intercedes in prayer, bestows charisms and ministries, inspires missionary life and witnesses through the saints.

The Son and Spirit Working Together (689-690)
The Spirit is truly God consubstantial and inseparable from the Father and the Son, (both in their inner life and in their work). When the Father sends his Son, he also sends his Breath. Distinct but inseparable, both have a joint mission. The Son is seen and the Spirit reveals the Son.

When Christ was glorified, he could send the Spirit (Jn.7:19) and give his glory to believers. This joint mission (of Christ and the Spirit) is manifested in the children adopted by the Father who are united to Christ by the Spirit.

"Just as there is no distance between the body and the anointing oil, so there is no distance nor intermediary between the Son and the Spirit. Contact with the Son requires contact with the oil because every part is covered with the Spirit's anointing." (St. Gregory of Nyssa)

NAME, TITLES AND SYMBOLS

Both Spirit and Holy (691)
The name "Holy Spirit" was given by Christ. (Mt. 28:19) "Spirit" and "Holy" are two attributes common to all three divine persons. By joining these two words, the Church designates clearly this inexpressible person, the Holy Spirit.

Seven Other Names (692-693)
On four occasions, Jesus also calls the Holy Spirit "Paraclete" (Jn.14:16-26; 15:26 and 16:7), meaning "advocate" and "consoler." Jesus also calls him "the Spirit of truth." (Jn.16:13)

St. Paul calls him "the Spirit of the promise" (Gal.3:14), "the Spirit of adoption" (Rom.8:15), "the Spirit of Christ" (Rom.8:9), "the Spirit of the Lord" (1Cor.3:17) and "the Spirit of God." (Rom.8:14)

Eight Symbols of the Holy Spirit (694-701)

1. <u>Water</u> signifies the Spirit's action in Baptism. Our first birth took place in water, so the baptismal water signifies our divine birth.

2. <u>Anointing</u> is the sacramental sign of Confirmation (called "Chrismation" in the East). Jesus is God's anointed in a unique way because the Spirit established him as the Christ at his conception. Now, the glorified Jesus pours out the Holy Spirit until the saints constitute "the whole Christ" (St. Augustine).

3. <u>Fire</u> symbolizes the transforming energy of the Spirit. John the Baptist proclaimed that Jesus would "baptize with the Holy Spirit and with fire" (Lk.3:16). Jesus came "to cast fire on the earth" (Lk.12:40) and on Pentecost, the Spirit came in the form of tongues "as of fire" (Acts 2:3-4). Paul uses the image saying, "Do not quench the Spirit" (1Thes.5:19).

4. <u>Cloud and Light</u> - In the New Testament, the Spirit "overshadowed" the Virgin Mary and during the Transfiguration the Spirit came in a "cloud and overshadowed everyone. (Lk.9:34-35). At the Ascension, the cloud took Jesus from the disciples' sight. (Acts 1:9)

5. <u>The Seal</u> is very similar to <u>anointing</u>. "The Father has set his seal" on Christ. (Jn.6:27) This seal indicates the indelible effect of the Spirit in Baptism, Confirmation and Holy Orders.

6. The <u>hand</u> - In the Acts, the apostles bestow the Spirit by laying hands. The Church has kept this sign of the Spirit's power in the sacramental epiclesis.

7. The <u>finger</u> – The Spirit, "the finger of the Father's right hand," writes "on the tablets of human hearts." (2Cor.3:3)

8. The <u>dove</u> – When Christ came up from his baptismal bath, the Spirit in the form of a dove remained upon him. .

THE TIME OF THE PROMISES

The Spirit's Words About Christ (702)

Until Christ's coming (the "fullness of time"), the joint mission of the Son and the Spirit remained hidden. Both the Son and the Spirit were to be watched for. Therefore, the Church searches the Old Testament for what the Spirit, by inspiring the authors, tells us about Christ.

Creation – Both at Work (703-704)

God's Word and God's Breath are present at the origin of every creature. The Spirit "preserves creation in the Father through the Son." (Byzantine liturgy)

"God fashioned man with his two hands (the Son and the Spirit) so that even what was visible would bear the divine form." (St. Irenaeus)

The Promised Progeny (705 – 706)

God's promise to Abraham began the work of salvation which culminated in the Son, who assumed human nature, restored it to the Father's likeness and gave it God's Glory, the Spirit.

God promised Abraham a progeny in which all the nations would be blessed. This progeny is Christ himself. (Gal.3:16) God promised to give both his Son and Holy Spirit, "the guarantee of our inheritance." (Eph.1:13-14)

The Spirit Revealing Yet Concealing (707-708)

In the Old Testament manifestations, Christian tradition saw that the Word allowed himself to be seen and heard, while the cloud of the Spirit both revealed God and concealed him.

God gave the Law as a teacher to lead people to Christ. Although man found the law powerless to save, his growing awareness of sin enkindled a desire for the Holy Spirit.

God Amidst Israel's Infidelity (709-710)

God's Law should have governed Israel. Unfortunately, Israel gave in to the temptation to become a kingdom like the other nations.

Because of their infidelity, Israel was led into the exile (seemingly the failure of the promises). However, God began the restoration of his people and the purified remnant of exiles prefigured the Church.

The Spirit Prophesying the Messiah (711-713)

Two prophetic lines developed among this purified remnant. One led to an expectation of a Messiah and the other to the expectation of the Spirit.

In his "Book of Emmanuel", Isaiah prophesied that the Messiah would come from "the stump of Jesse", saying that "the Spirit of the Lord shall rest upon him." (Is.11:1-2) Isaiah's Servant Song (C 42, 49 and 50) prophesied that the Messiah would pour out the Holy Spirit."

The Spirit and Jesus (714-716)

Jesus quoted Isaiah "The Spirit of the Lord God is upon me because the Lord has anointed me." (61:1-2) Peter proclaimed that the prophecies about God sending the Spirit had been fulfilled at Pentecost. These prophecies describe a time when God's Spirit would renew men's hearts, reconcile peoples and transform creation.

Before Jesus returns, the Spirit would bring about "a people prepared for the Lord." (Lk.1:17) These "people of the poor" would rely on God's plans and would not seek the justice of men, but of the Messiah.

THE TIME OF FULFILLMENT

John - Elijah in the Power of the Spirit (717-720)

When Mary visited Elizabeth, John was "filled with the Holy Spirit even from his mother's womb." (Lk,1:15, 41) John completed the Spirit's work of forming "a people prepared for the Lord." (Lk.1:17)

Jesus called him "more than a prophet." (Lk.7:26) John prefigured the Holy Spirit as "a voice" who bore "witness to the light." (Jn.1:7) John actually saw the Spirit descend on Jesus and he could bear witness that Jesus is "the Lamb of God." (Jn.1:33-36) Through John, the Spirit could begin his work of restoring man.

Mary – The Spirit's Masterpiece (721-723)

Mary is the masterwork of the joint mission of the Son and the Spirit. She was a worthy dwelling place where the Son and Spirit could dwell among men. She is the "Seat of Wisdom." In her, the Spirit's wonders began to be manifest.

She was "full of grace" so she could carry Jesus "in whom the fullness of the deity dwells bodily." (Col.2:9) Conceived without sin, she was capable of welcoming this inexpressible gift of the Almighty. In Mary, the Spirit fulfilled the Father's plan, making her virginity uniquely fruitful in the birth of the Son.

The Spirit Uniting Others in Mary (724-726)

Jesus was made known first to the shepherds (representing the poor) and to the Magi (representing the Gentiles). Through Mary, the Spirit brought others into communion with Christ (Simeon and Anna, the bride and groom at Cana and the first disciples).

Through the Spirit, Mary became the woman, the New Eve (mother of the living), the mother of the "whole Christ" (represented by John at the cross). At Pentecost (the dawn of the end time) she was with the disciples when the Spirit inaugurated the Church.

Jesus – Anointed by the Spirit (727)

The entire mission of the Son and the Spirit is contained in this – that the Son is anointed with the Spirit from the first moment of his conception. Although Christ's whole work is a joint mission of Son and Spirit, we focus here on Jesus' promise of his sending of the Spirit.

Revealing the Spirit (728 -729)

Jesus alluded often to the Spirit. He spoke of the Spirit to Nicodemus (Jn.3:5-8), to the Samaritan woman (Jn.3:5-8) and to his disciples, concerning their prayer and concerning their witnessing. (Lk.11:13 and Mt.10:19-20) At the hour of his death, Jesus promised that the Spirit would be given by the Father (in answer to Jesus' prayer) and by Jesus (at the side of the Father).

The Spirit would come and teach us everything. He would remind us of Jesus' teachings and help us to bear witness to Jesus. The Spirit would also prove that the world is wrong about sin, righteousness and judgment.

Giving the Spirit (730)

Immediately after his resurrection, Jesus gave the Holy Spirit to his apostles by breathing on them. (Jn.20:22) At this moment, the mission of Christ and the Spirit became the mission of the Church. "As the Father has sent me, even so I send you." (Jn.20:21)

THE FINAL DAYS

Pentecost – The Spirit's Continual Coming (731-732)

On Pentecost, Christ's Passover was fulfilled by the outpouring of the Spirit who is manifested as a divine person and the Trinity is fully revealed. Those who believe in Christ come in the flesh and share in the communion of the Trinity. The Holy Spirit brings the world into "the last days", the time of the Church and of the kingdom.

Forgiving Sins and Bearing Fruit (733-736)

The first effect of the Spirit is the forgiveness of sins. Then, the Spirit gives us the very life of the Trinity which is to love "as God has loved us." (1Jn.4:11-12)

By his power, we can "bear the fruit of the Spirit (love, joy, peace, patience, kindness, goodness, faithfulness, gentleness, self-control". "Through the Spirit we are restored to paradise, led back to the kingdom of heaven, adopted as children and given confidence to call God Father." (St. Basil)

Bringing All Into God's Communion (737)

This joint mission of Son and Spirit is completed in the Church bringing the faithful into Christ's communion with the Father in the Spirit. By grace, the Spirit makes present the mystery of Christ (most of all in the Eucharist) to bring men into communion with God.

Sending the Church (738)

The Church's mission is not an addition to the joint mission of Son and Spirit but is its sacrament. The Church announces and makes present the mystery of the communion of the Holy Trinity. "Just as the power of Christ's sacred flesh unites those who receive into one body, so the undivided Spirit leads all into spiritual unity." (St. Cyril of Alexandria)

Three Other Parts of This Catechism (739-741)

Christ, the head of the Church, pours out the anointing of the Spirit. This leads to three other parts of this catechism:

Part Two: The sacraments, through which Christ communicates the Spirit to his members.

Part Three: The fruit of new life, which comes from these sacraments.

Part Four: The prayer given by the Spirit to the Church

In Brief - 742-747

Quotes to Remember

No one comprehends the thought of God, except the Spirit of God. (1Cor.2:11)

With John the Baptist, the Spirit began the restoration to man of the divine likeness.

There is no distance between the Son and the Spirit. (St. Gregory of Nyssa)

The Mission of Christ and the Spirit is brought to completion in the Church.

13
The Catholic Church (748 – 810)

The Spirit and the Church (748-750)
"Christ is the light of the nations. By proclaiming the gospel, we hope that this light will shine out visibly from the Church." (Second Vatican Council) Just as the moon has only the light of the sun, the Church has only the light of Christ.

The Church depends totally on the Spirit, because the Spirit "has endowed the Church with holiness" (Roman Catechism), and the Church is the place "where the Spirit flourishes." (St. Hippolytus) Belief that the Church is one, holy, catholic and apostolic is inseparable from belief in the Trinity. We do not believe in the Church but in God who bestowed his gifts on the Church.

GOD'S PLAN FOR THE CHURCH

The Church - Names and Images (751)
"Church" designates assemblies of people (usually for religious purposes). Ecclesia means the Chosen People, (above all, the assembly on Mt. Sinai where God established his holy people). When the Christian believers called themselves "Church", they saw themselves as the heirs to Israel. The English word "church" means "what belongs to the Lord."

Three Meanings (752)
In Christian usage, church has three inseparable meanings:
1. the liturgical assembly
2. the local community
3. the universal community

God gathers his people from all over the world into local communities which are especially made real in the liturgical Eucharistic assembly.

The Symbols of Church (753-757)
Scripture provides a host of images. Many Old Testament images come from the common theme of People of God. The New Testament images center upon Christ, the head of his body.

Other images (grouped around Christ) are based upon a shepherd, farming, building, family life and marriage.

1. The Church is the "sheepfold". Christ is the sole gate and the main shepherd.
2. The Church is the cultivated field or the olive tree in whom Jew and Gentile are reconciled. Christ is the true vine without whom we can do nothing.
3. The Church is God's building, founded on Christ as the cornerstone, built upon the apostles as the foundation and made up of believers (the living stones).
4. The Church is the heavenly Jerusalem, "our mother", the spotless spouse for whom Christ "delivered himself up so that he might sanctify her." (Eph.5:25-26)

ORIGIN – FOUNDATION - MISSION

The Trinity's Plan For the Church (758)

We study here the Trinity's plan for the Church and her progressive realization in history.

The Father's Family (759)

The eternal Father chose to create the whole universe and to create men to share his own life. He determined to call into his holy Church those who believed in Christ. This "family of God" took shape in history according to the Father's plan. Present in figure from the beginning, the Church was prepared for by Israel and was established by the Spirit in this last age. She will be gloriously completed at the end of time.

The Goal of Creation (760)

"The world was created for the sake of the Church." (First Century -Shepherd of Hermas) God created man to have communion with him. This is the Church (God's convocation). God permitted the angels' fall and man's sin to show his love. "God's will is creation and is called 'the world' and God's intention to save us is called 'the Church'." (St. Clement of Alexandria)

Preparing For the Church (761-762)

As soon as man sinned, God began gathering mankind into communion. This reunification takes place in the hearts of anyone "who fears him and does what is right." (Acts 10:35)

The Church's remote preparation began with the call of Abraham to be the "father of many nations." (Gen.12:2 and 15:5-6) The immediate preparation for the Church was God's election of Israel. However, the prophets accused Israel of breaking the covenant and prophesied the new and eternal covenant (Jn.31:31-34) instituted by Christ.

Jesus Ushers in the Kingdom (763-764)

By his preaching of the Reign of God, Jesus inaugurated the Church and ushered in the kingdom of heaven on earth. The Church is "the reign of Christ already present in mystery." (Second Vatican Council)

This kingdom shines out in Jesus' word. To welcome his word is to welcome the kingdom. The beginning of the kingdom is the little flock, whom Jesus gathered as their shepherd. They formed the "true family" of Jesus who taught them a new "way of acting" and their own prayer (the Our Father).

Gives the Church a Structure (765 - 766)

By choosing the twelve apostles, Jesus gave this community a structure which will last until the end of time. These twelve represent the twelve tribes of Israel and are the foundation stones of the New Jerusalem. (Rev.21:12-14) The apostles and disciples share in Jesus' power, mission and suffering.

The Church is born from Christ's total self-giving. The blood and water flowing from Christ's side symbolize the origin and the growth of the Church. Just as Eve came from the side of Adam, so the Church came from the side of Christ.

The Spirit Displays the Church (767 - 768)

After completing his work, Jesus sent the Spirit on Pentecost to sanctify the Church. The Church was openly displayed to the crowds and spread to the nations by preaching.

The Spirit gives the Church hierarchical and charismatic gifts. Endowed with these powers, the Church receives the mission to proclaim and establish the Kingdom of God among all peoples.

On Pilgrimage Until the Glory (769-770)

Until Christ returns and bestows his full glory, "the Church will make her pilgrimage in the midst of the world's persecutions and God's consolations." (St. Augustine) The Church is in exile and will be perfected by great trials until all the just are gathered in the Father's presence. Only by faith can someone see that the Church exists in history (her visible reality) and yet transcends history (her spiritual reality) bringing divine life.

Visible and Spiritual (771)

Christ established and sustains the Church as a visible organization through which he communicates truth and grace to all. The Church is:
1. a society with hierarchical structure
2. Christ's mystical body
3. a visible society and a spiritual community
4. an earthly Church endowed with heavenly riches
5. "one complex reality" with human and divine elements.

"The Church is so constructed that the human is subordinated to the divine, the visible to the invisible and this present world to the city yet to come." (Second Vatican Council) "Even if the pain of her long exile may have discolored her, yet heaven's beauty has adorned her." (St. Bernard)

Where God and Man Are One (772 – 773)

This nuptial of Christ with his Church is "the great mystery" and the Church, by union with Christ her bridegroom, becomes "the hope of glory." (1Cor.13:8)

The Church's whole purpose is to unite men with God. Her structure is totally ordered to holiness and measured by how well the Bride responds to the Bridegroom. Because Mary precedes all of us in holiness, the Marian dimension of the Church precedes the Petrine dimension. (Pope John Paul II)

A Visible Sign of Salvation (774)

Mystery (in Greek) is sometimes translated "sacrament." Later, "sacrament" emphasized the visible sign of salvation. Christ himself is this sacrament (mystery) "For there is no other mystery of God, except Christ." (St. Augustine) Christ's actions are revealed in the seven sacraments. In an analogical sense, the Church herself is a sacrament, containing and communicating this invisible grace.

Sign of Man's Unity (775-776)

The Church is the sacrament of man's inner union with God. She is also the sacrament of the unity of the human race because man's unity is rooted in God. At the end of time, she will gather men "from all tribes and peoples and tongues." (Rev.7:9) In her present state, she is a sign of a unity yet to come. She is "the visible plan of the love of God who desires that the whole human race become one People of God." (Pope Paul VI)

In Brief   777-780

THE PEOPLE OF GOD

Jew and Gentile Formed by the Spirit (781)

God wants to join individuals together to serve him in holiness. Therefore, he chose the Israelites as his own people and made a covenant with them. This prepared for the New Covenant in Christ's blood, in which God called Jew and Gentile into a race formed by the Spirit not by the flesh." (Second Vatican Council)

Seven Characteristics of God's People (782)

Definite characteristics distinguish this People of God from every other group in history:

1. The People of God are not the property of any one people group.
2. Membership comes from faith in Christ and Baptism, not from physical birth.
3. This people is messianic. Christ shares with them his anointing of the Spirit.
4. Their dignity is to be children of God because God's Spirit dwells within.
5. Their law is to love others as Christ loved them. (Jn.13:34)
6. Their mission is to be the "light of the world", a hope for the whole human race.
7. Their destiny is the Kingdom of God, in time and eternity.

95

The Three Offices of Christ (783 – 786)

Since Christ was anointed <u>priest,</u> <u>prophet,</u> and <u>king</u>, every member has these three offices and carries their responsibilities.

By Baptism believers are consecrated into a "holy priesthood." (Heb.5:1-5)

They share in Christ's <u>prophetic office</u> by adhering unfailingly to the truths given to the saints. They share in Christ's <u>royal office</u> by serving the poor and the suffering. "The sign of the cross makes <u>kings</u> of all those reborn in Christ and the anointing of the Spirit consecrates them as <u>priests</u>." (Pope Leo the Great)

THE BODY OF CHRIST

Abiding in Jesus' Body (787-788)

In sharing his mission, Jesus spoke of a more intimate communion, "Abide in me and I in you. I am the vine, you are the branches." (Jn.15:4-5) He announced a real communion between his body and ours. "He who eats my flesh and drinks my blood abides in me and I in him." (Jn.6:56)

After the Ascension, Jesus remained with them and even sent his Spirit. By his Spirit, Christ constitutes his mystical body, made up of people called from every nation. (Second Vatican Council)

Three Qualities (789)

The Church as Christ's Body has three specific qualities:
1. She is one body.
2. She has Christ as her head
3. She is Christ's bride.

Unity and Diversity in the Church (790-791)

In the Church, Christ gives his own life to believers through the sacraments. This is especially true of Baptism and Eucharist (which brings the believer into communion with Christ and with others).

Within the Church's unity, there is a diversity of the Spirit's gifts. This unity stimulates charity ("If one member suffers anything, all the members suffer with him.") and triumphs over all division. ("There is neither Jew nor Greek, slave or free, male or female for you are all one in Christ Jesus.")

Growth in Christ (792-794)

Through the Church, Christ, the head extends his reign over all things. In the Church, Christ provides the needed helps for our growth in him and for mutual assistance toward salvation.

The Whole Christ (795)

The saints are acutely aware that Christ and his Church make up the "whole Christ": "Let us rejoice that we have become Christ, for the fullness of Christ is the head and the members." (St. Augustine)

"Our redeemer has shown himself to be one person with the holy Church." (Pope St. Gregory the Great)

"Head and members form the same mystical person." (Saint Thomas Aquinas)

At her trial, St. Joan of Arc replied, "About Jesus Christ and the Church, I simply know they are just one thing and we shouldn't complicate the matter."

Bride and Bridegroom (796)

This unity between Christ and his is best expressed in the image of bridegroom and bride. John the Baptist called himself, "the friend of the Bridegroom." (Jn.3:29) Jesus called himself the bridegroom. (Mk.2:19) The Church is the spotless bride. (Rev.22:17) The Church and each believer is a bride "betrothed" to Christ and Christ always cares "for his own body" (Eph.5:29), "As head he calls himself the bridegroom, as body, he calls himself bride." (St. Augustine)

The Temple of the Spirit (797 –798)

"What the soul is to the human body, the Holy Spirit is to the Body of Christ, the Church." (St. Augustine) By the Spirit, all the parts of the body are joined. "The whole Spirit is in the head (Christ) and in each of the members." (Pope Pius XII) "In the Church there has been deposited the Holy Spirit. Where the Church is, there also is God's Spirit. Where the Spirit is, there is the Church and every grace." (St. Irenaeus)

The Holy Spirit is the principle of the Church's saving action. He works by God's Word, by the sacraments, by the grace of the apostles, by virtues and by charisms.

The Spirit's Gifts For the Church (799-801)

All charisms, extraordinary or simple, are graces of the Spirit which directly or indirectly benefit the Church. Charisms must be accepted with thanksgiving and used for Church's apostolic vitality. These must be genuine gifts of the Spirit and used with charity (the measure of all charisms).

All charisms must be discerned by the Church's shepherds who have the duty to test all things, "so that all charisms work for the common good." (1Cor.12:7)

In Brief - 802 - 810

Quotes to Remember

To believe the Church is one, holy catholic and apostolic
is inseparable from belief in God,
Father, Son and Holy Spirit.

The world was created for the sake of the Church.
(Shepherd of Hermas)

God willed to make men holy by gathering
them into a people.

Christ and his Church make up the "whole Christ".

14
The Church is One, Holy, Catholic and Apostolic   (811 – 870)

The Four Essential Features (811-812)

One, holy, catholic, and apostolic are the four essential features of the Church. They do not belong to the Church but to Christ, who makes the Church one, holy, Catholic and apostolic.

Although faith alone recognizes their divine source, their historical manifestations speak clearly to human reason. The Church's "marvelous propagation, eminent holiness, Catholic unity and invincible stability give an irrefutable witness of her divine mission." (First Vatican Council)

THE CHURCH IS ONE

Unity From the Trinity (813)

The Church's unity comes from the undivided Trinity. Christ "reconciled all men to God by his cross" and restored the unity of all people. She is one because her soul is the Holy Spirit. "The Holy Spirit brings about the wonderful communion of the faithful." (Second Vatican Council) "There is one Father of the universe, one Lord of the universe, and also one Holy Spirit. There is also one virgin become mother, and I should like to call her 'Church'." (St. Clement of Alexandria)

Diversity Within the Unity (814)

The Church also has a diversity of peoples, cultures, gifts and offices and particular Churches with their own traditions. This rich diversity does not oppose Church unity. Yet, sin always threatens this oneness. Paul wrote, "Maintain the unity of the Spirit in the bond of peace." (Eph.4:3)

Three Bonds of Unity (815)

Besides charity, the Church has three important visible bonds of communion:
1. the profession of one faith
2. the common celebration of worship (especially through the sacraments)

3. apostolic succession through Holy Orders

Entrusted to Peter and the Apostles (816)
This sole Church of Christ was entrusted to Peter and the other apostles. "This Church, constituted and organized as a society in the present world, <u>subsists in</u> the Catholic Church which is governed by the successor of Peter and by the bishops in communion with him." (Second Vatican Council) Only in the Catholic Church can the fullness of the means of salvation be obtained. To the apostolic college alone (with Peter as its head), did Our Lord entrust all the blessings of the New Covenant. All who belong to the People of God should be fully incorporated into this one Body of Christ. (Second Vatican Council)

Ruptures of Unity (817-818)
St. Paul had to censure certain rifts and divisions. Centuries later, more serious dissensions caused large communities to separate from full communion with the Catholic Church. The blame lies with both sides because these ruptures (heresy, apostasy and schism) are due to human sin. "Where there are sins, there are divisions. Where there is charity, there is unity." (Origen) Those living today cannot be charged with these sins of separation. The Catholic Church accepts as brothers those who have faith in Christ and have been baptized. They have a right to be called Christians and be accepted as brothers. (Second Vatican Council)

Outside the Church (819)
Outside of the Catholic Church there are many elements of sanctification (God's word, interior virtues, gifts of the Spirit and some visible elements). Christ's Spirit uses these Churches and ecclesial communities as means of salvation. Their power derives from the fullness that Christ gave to the Catholic Church. All these blessings lead to Christ and are calls to "Catholic unity." (Second Vatican Council)

Recovering Our Lost Unity (820 -822)
This unity given by Christ "subsists in the Catholic Church as something she can never lose." However, the Church must work and pray to maintain that unity. Jesus prayed "that they may all be one ... so that the world may know that you have sent me."

(Jn.17:21) The desire to recover our lost unity is a true call from the Holy Spirit which requires:

1. a permanent renewal of the Church in her fidelity to her vocation
2. a conversion of heart by the faithful
3. Common prayer (the soul of the ecumenical movement)

Also needed are <u>fraternal knowledge</u>, <u>ecumenical formation</u>, <u>dialogue</u> among theologians and <u>collaboration</u> in services to mankind.

The whole Church must be involved in this reconciliation of all Christians. Our hope lies in Christ's prayer because this gift is beyond human powers.

THE CHURCH IS HOLY

Made Holy By the Bridegroom (823-824)

The Church is unfailingly holy because Christ loved the Church as his Bride. He gave himself up for her and has given her the Holy Spirit. Because she is holy, the New Testament frequently calls her members "saints."

Sanctified by Christ, the Church herself becomes sanctifying and directs all her activities to the sanctification of the human race.

All Called to Be Holy (825-826)

Because the Church is endowed with a real (yet still imperfect) sanctity, all her members are called to the perfection of sanctity by which the Father himself is perfect.

Charity is the soul of holiness. "I realized that love enables the other members of the Church to act. Love is the vocation which includes all others; it is a universe of its own, comprising all time and space – it is eternal." (St. Therese of Lisieux)

Gathering Up Sinners (827)

Christ came to expiate sins. The Church clasps sinners to her bosom and follows the path of penance and renewal. All Church members, even her ministers, must acknowledge that they are sinners. "Though having sinners in her midst, the Church offers them the life of grace. If they live her life, her members are sanctified. When they move away from her, they fall into sins. (Pope Paul VI)

Canonizing Saints (828-829)

By canonizing saints, the Church recognizes the Spirit's power of holiness within her. "The saints have always been the true source of renewal in the most difficult moments in the Church's history." (Pope John Paul I) Their holiness is the hidden source of apostolic zeal.

In Mary, the Church has already reached a holiness that is without stain or wrinkle. Let all eyes turn to Mary, in whom the Church is "all holy."

THE CHURCH IS CATHOLIC

Catholic (Universal) in Means and in Mission (830-831)

The Church is Catholic (meaning "universal") in two ways. First, the Church is universal because Christ is present in her. She receives from him "the fullness of the means of salvation." In this fundamental sense, the Church was Catholic on the day of Pentecost and will be so until Christ returns.

Second, the Church is Catholic because she has a mission to the whole world. The new People of God (while remaining one) must spread throughout the world. God made human nature one and now he decrees that all the scattered people be gathered together. By its gift of universality, the church seeks the return of all humanity under Christ the Head. (Second Vatican Council)

Catholic Even When Local (832-833)

The Church is really present in all legitimately organized local groups of the faithful united to their pastors (called "Churches" in the New Testament). These communities might be small and poor. Yet, in these particular churches Christ is present and the One, Holy, Catholic and Apostolic Church is constituted. (Second Vatican Council)

The diocese (or eparchy) is a community of faithful headed by a bishop ordained in apostolic succession. These particular churches are modeled after the universal Church. In them the one and unique Catholic Church exists.

Unity in Rome (834)

Particular Churches are fully Catholic by their unity with Rome "which presides in charity." (St. Ignatius of Antioch) "For

102

with this Church (Rome), by reason of its pre-eminence, the whole Church must necessarily be in accord." (St. Irenaeus) "All Christian Churches have held the great Church of Rome as their basis and foundation since, the gates of hell have never prevailed against her." (St. Maximus the Confessor)

In A Variety of Cultures (835)
The universal Church is not just a federation of different particular Churches. The universal Church is rooted in a variety of cultures and takes on different external expressions. The rich variety shows forth the Catholicity of the undivided Church. (Pope Paul VI)

All Are Called (836)
All men are certainly called to this Catholic unity. The Catholic faithful, others who believe in Christ, and all mankind belong to or are ordered to Catholic unity.

Some Are Incorporated (837 - 838)
The fully incorporated are those who accept all the Church's means of salvation and who, by profession of faith, the sacraments, church government and communion, are united in the visible structure of the Church. However, a Church member who does not persevere in charity is not saved. He is in the Church's bosom, but "in body" not "in heart." (Second Vatican Council)

Others, who are baptized and are called "Christian" but who do not profess the Catholic faith are still joined to the Catholic Church in many ways. They enjoy a certain, although imperfect, communion with the Catholic Church. The unity with the Orthodox Church is so profound that it lacks little to attain the fullness to permit a common celebration of Eucharist. (Pope Paul VI)

The Jews – Awaiting An Unknown Messiah (839-840)
Those who have not heard the gospel are related to the People of God in various ways.

The Jewish People were the first to hear the word of God, and their faith is already a response to God's revelation. To them "belong the sonship, the glory, the covenants, the giving of the law, the worship and the promises" (Rom.9:4-5) and "this call of God is irrevocable." (Rom. 11:29)

The People of God of the Old Covenant and new People of God expect the coming (or the return) of the Messiah. However, the People of the New Covenant await the return of a risen Messiah. The People of the Old Covenant await the coming of a still unknown Messiah, because they do not know or they misunderstand Christ Jesus.

Muslims (841)

God's plan of salvation includes those who acknowledge the Creator. Among these, in the first place, are the Muslims who profess the faith of Abraham and believe in one merciful God as mankind's judge on the last day.

A Common Origin (842)

The Church's bond with non-Christian religions is the common origin and goal of the human race. "All nations stem from one stock and all share a common destiny, namely, God. His providence extends to all." (Second Vatican Council)

Other Religions (843)

The Church recognizes that in other religions there is a search for a God. Any goodness or truth in these religions is a "preparation for the gospel." (Second Vatican Council)

Possible Mistakes in Religious Behavior (844)

In his religious behavior, man can make mistakes. "Deceived by the Evil One, men have exchanged the truth of God for a lie and served the creature rather than the Creator. Without God, they are exposed to ultimate despair." (Second Vatican Council)

The Church As Noah's Ark (845)

The Father wants to reunite all humanity into his Son's Church. According to St. Augustine and St. Ambrose, the Church was prefigured by Noah's ark, which alone saved the world from the flood.

"Outside the Church There is No Salvation" (846)

How do we understand this saying from the Church Fathers? All salvation comes from Christ through his Body, the Church which is necessary for salvation because Christ is present in his Church.

Jesus said, "The man who believes and accepts Baptism will be saved; the man who refuses to believe in it will be condemned." (Mk.16:16) By these words Jesus also affirmed the necessity of the Church, because Baptism is its door to the Church.

Refusing to Enter (847)

Someone who knows the Catholic Church was founded as necessary by God and refuses to enter or remain in it, cannot be saved.

Just Not Knowing (848)

However, those, who through no fault of their own do not know either the gospel of Christ or his Church, can achieve salvation by seeking God with a sincere heart and by trying to do God's will. (Second Vatican Council) Although God can lead all people to salvation, the Church still has the duty to evangelize all men.

THE CHURCH ON MISSION

Sent to the Whole World (849-850)

Because of Jesus' command to make disciples of all nations, the Church has been divinely sent as "the universal sacrament of salvation" and must preach the gospel to everyone.

The Church is missionary because (according to the Father's plan) she has her origin in the mission of Son and Spirit. The Church exists to bring all men into the communion of the Father, Son and Spirit.

To Save All (851)

God "desires all men to be saved and to come to a knowledge of the truth. (1Tim.2:4) Therefore, the Church must go out to those who are seeking God, and bring them the gospel. The Church must be missionary because she believes in God's universal plan.

Led By the Spirit (852)

The Holy Spirit is the "protagonist" who guides the Church on her missionary paths leading her to follow Christ's path of service and self-sacrifice. "The blood of martyrs is the seed of the Church." (Tertullian)

Failures and Patience (853-854)

The Church recognizes the great discrepancy between her message and her human weaknesses. Only by walking the way of the cross can she extend Christ's reign.

This missionary endeavor begins by proclaiming the gospel to unbelievers and then establishing communities of believers and finally by founding a local church. This involves a process of enculturation, so the gospel takes flesh in each culture. Only by degrees can the Church penetrate the culture.

The Obstacle of Divisions (855)

The missionary endeavor stimulates efforts to Christian unity because the divisions among Christian churches is a serious obstacle to missionary activity. Because of division, the Church cannot display its full Catholic unity.

The Truths in Each Culture (856)

The missionary task must appreciate those elements of truth which God has already given to the unbelievers. Proclaiming the Good News should raise up this truth, while purifying it from error and evil.

THE CHURCH IS APOSTOLIC

Apostolic in Three Ways (857)

The Church is apostolic in three ways:
1. She is built on "the foundation of the apostles", those witnesses chosen by Christ.
2. The Church hands on the teaching of the apostles (the deposit of faith).
3. The Church is guided by the successors of the apostles, the bishops in union with the Pope. Jesus is "the eternal shepherd who never leaves his flock untended." (Preface of Apostles)

106

The Original Twelve and Their Successors (858-860)

Jesus "named twelve as his companions whom he would send to preach the good news." (Mk.3:14)

Apart from Jesus, the apostles could do nothing (Jn.5:19) for they had received from Christ their mandate and their power. They knew that they were "ambassadors of Christ" (2Cor.6:4) and "stewards of the mysteries of God." (1Cor.4:1)

The original apostles were witnesses of Christ's resurrection and the foundation stones of the Church. They took care to appoint successors, because Jesus promised to remain with them until the end of time. (Mt.28:20)

The Duty to Pass On the Office (861-862)

The apostles gave their successors the duty of completing their work and urged them to shepherd the Church of God. (Acts 20:28) They also required that, when these successors died, other proven men should take over their ministry.

The apostles' task of shepherding the Church "was destined to be exercised without interruption by the sacred order of bishops." (Second Vatican Council) The bishops, by divine institution, have taken the place of the apostles. Whoever listens to them listens to Christ. Whoever despises them, despises Christ.

Sharing in the Mission (863 - 864)

Because the Church is in communion with the apostles all Church members share in this mission. "Apostolate" means "every activity of the Mystical Body" which "aims to spread the kingdom of Christ over the whole world." (Second Vatican Council)

Because Christ is the source of the Church's apostolate, ordained ministers and lay people must be in a vital union with Christ. Guided by his Spirit, their apostolate assumes many forms.

The Kingdom Fully Revealed (865)

The Church is one, holy, catholic and apostolic because the kingdom of heaven already exists in her. This kingdom has come in Christ, grows within the hearts of believers and will be fully manifested on the last day, when all are gathered into one People of God. This kingdom is the heavenly Jerusalem which has the names of the twelve apostles of the Lamb written on its foundation. (Rev.21:14)

In Brief 866 – 870

Quotes to Remember

The Church's unity comes from the undivided Trinity.

The Church also has a rich diversity of peoples.

The Church is unfailingly holy because Christ loves the Church as his Bride.

The Church is Catholic because Christ is present in her and because her mission is to all the world.

The Church is Apostolic because she is built upon the Apostles, she hands on the Apostles' teaching, and she is guided by the successors of the Apostles (Pope and bishops).

The Church of Christ subsists in the Catholic Church.

Where there is charity, there is unity. (Origen)

15
Christ's Faithful and the Communion of Saints (871-987)

Sharing in the Threefold Office (871-872)
The Christian faithful incorporated into Christ by their Baptism and made members of God's People, share in Christ's threefold office priest, prophet and king. They are called to exercise God's mission for his Church according to their state. (Canon 204)

Because all share in the baptismal rebirth in Christ, there is a true equality in dignity and activity whereby all cooperate in building up the Body. (Canon 208)

THE CHURCH'S HIERARCHY

Diversity of Ministries (873-874)
A diversity of ministries exists which serves the Church's mission. To some (the apostles and their successors), Christ entrusted the office of teaching, sanctifying and governing. The laity have their own roles. From both hierarchy and laity, come Christian faithful who are consecrated to God and serve the Church through the profession of the evangelical councils. (Canon 207) Christ established a variety of offices for the good of all. Those who hold offices invested with sacred powers, must dedicate themselves to the salvation of all.

Receiving a Mandate – Holy Orders (875)
Faith comes from hearing. No one can "hear without a preacher" and no preacher can give himself a mandate. Only from Christ can ministers receive the mission and sacred power to "act in the person of Christ." This ministry is called "a sacrament", and is conferred by a special sacrament. (Holy Orders)

A Service (876)
Besides having a sacramental nature, Church ministry must also have the character of service. Just as Christ took "the form of a slave" (Phil.2:7) so the minister must be a "slave of Christ".

A College of Service (877)

Church ministry has a collegial character. Jesus chose the twelve apostles and sent them out together to serve the faithful and to witness to the communion of the Trinity. Therefore, every bishop has his ministry only within the episcopal college in union with the Pope, and every priest serves in the presbyterate only in union with the diocesan bishop.

A Personal Quality (878-879)

Church ministry also has a personal character, because each person is to be a personal witness with a personal responsibility. Each person acts in Christ's name, e.g. "I absolve you."

Sacramental ministry is both collegial (exercised in communion) and personal (in Christ's name). Bishops are bonded within the college and within their head, the Pope. The bishop must care for his diocese and have solicitude for the whole Church.

The Apostolic College (880-881)

Christ constituted the twelve apostles as a college, a permanent assembly with Peter as the head. Therefore, Peter's successor (the bishop of Rome) and the apostles' successors (the other bishops) are united to one another in the episcopal college. (Second Vatican Council)

Christ bestowed the power to bind and to loose upon Peter himself (Mt.16:19) and then upon all the apostles, including Peter. (Mt.18:18) This pastoral office of Peter and of the other apostles belongs to the Church's very foundation and continues with the bishops under the primacy of the Pope.

Foundation of Unity (882)

The Pope, the bishop of Rome, is Peter's successor and the visible foundation of unity (for the bishops and for all the faithful). As pastor of the entire Church, the Pope has full, supreme and universal power over the whole Church, which he can always exercise in an unhindered way. (Second Vatican Council)

The College of Bishops (883-885)

Although the college of bishops has "supreme and full authority" over the Church, this authority cannot be exercised without the agreement of the Roman Pontiff.

The college of bishops exercises this power in a solemn manner in an ecumenical council. (Canon 337) However, an ecumenical council must be confirmed or at least recognized as such by Peter's successor.

The college of bishops (comprised of many members) expresses the variety and the unity of the People of God assembled.

Unity in the Diocese and the Province (886-887)

The individual bishops are the visible foundation of unity in their dioceses. Each bishop must also have concern for the whole Church.

Neighboring dioceses form provinces or larger groupings (called patriarchates or regions). These bishops can meet in synods and provincial councils. Also, national conferences contribute to the concrete realization of the collegiate spirit.

TEACHING – SANCTIFYING -GOVERNING

Infallibility in Faith and Morals (888-890)

As teachers of the apostolic faith, bishops must "preach the gospel to all".

To preserve the purity of apostolic faith, Christ gave the Church a share in his own infallibility. By their "supernatural sense of faith", the People of God (guided by the Church's Magisterium) unfailingly adhere to this faith. (Second Vatican Council)

The Church's Magisterium keeps God's people from deviating from truth and guarantees professing the true faith without error. In this way, the faithful can abide in the truth because Christ endowed the Church's shepherds with the charism of infallibility in faith and morals.

Pope and Bishops (891)

The Pope is infallible when, as supreme pastor and teacher of the faith, he proclaims by a definitive act a doctrine pertaining to faith and morals.

This infallibility is also present in the body of bishops when, (together with the Pope) they exercise the supreme Magisterium, above all in an Ecumenical Council. When the Church proposes a doctrine as Christ's teaching "for belief as being divinely revealed", the faithful must adhere by "the obedience of faith." This infallibility extends to the entire deposit of divine revelation.

Non-Infallible Definitions (892)

Sometimes the pope and/or the bishops do not give an infallible definition or pronounce in "a definitive manner." Instead, by the ordinary Magisterium, they propose a teaching which leads to a better understanding of faith or morals. In these cases, the faithful must give "religious assent" to these teachings.

Sanctifying the Church (893)

The bishop (with his priests) sanctifies the Church especially through the Eucharist and by their ministry of word, their ministry of sacraments and by their good example.

The Bishop and His Diocese (894-896)

The bishops, as vicars of Christ, govern their dioceses by exhortations, example, and by their authority and sacred power.

In his diocese the bishop has proper, ordinary and immediate authority which he exercises as the Vicar of Christ (although its exercise is ultimately controlled by the Church's supreme authority). Although not a vicar of the pope, the bishop must be in union with the pope, (whose universal authority confirms the bishop's authority).

The bishop must have compassion on the ignorant and erring. He must listen to his people, who should be one with their bishop. "Let all follow the bishop as Jesus Christ follows his Father." (St. Ignatius of Antioch)

THE LAITY

The Mission of the Lay Faithful (897-899)

"Laity" are all the baptized (except for those in Holy Orders or in the religious state). By Baptism, they are incorporated into the People of God, share in Christ's office and have their own part to play in the Church's mission, especially by directing temporal affairs according to God's will. They must bring God's enlightenment and order to society.

Their initiative is absolutely required so that the demands of the gospel permeate temporal realities. The laity are on the front lines and must have a clear consciousness of actually being the Church. (Pope Pius XII)

Right to Preach the Gospel (900)

Because of Baptism and Confirmation, they have the right and duty (individually or grouped in associations) to preach the gospel to all. Their activity in ecclesial communities is so important that pastors cannot be fully effective without them.

Consecrating the World and the Family (901-902)

The laity are called to produce the Spirit's fruits. Their works, prayers and apostolic undertakings (even the patient bearing of hardships) must be accomplished as spiritual sacrifices. By these holy actions the laity consecrate the world to God, offering worship by their daily holiness.

In a very special way, parents, as Christian spouses and teachers of their children, share in this work. (Canon 835)

Permanent and Other Ministries (903)

Those laity with the required qualities can receive the permanent ministries of lector and acolyte. Even without these ministries, laity can fulfill certain offices (read the word, confer Baptism or distribute Holy Communion).

Witness of Life and Word (904-905)

Christ establishes both hierarchy and laity as witnesses. "To teach in order to lead others to faith is the task of every preacher and of each believer." (St. Thomas Aquinas)

The layperson must proclaim Christ by word and example. This witnessing has a special power in the ordinary circumstances of the world. Laypersons must seek opportunities to announce Christ to believers and non-believers.

Bringing Their Special Competence (906-907)

By special training, lay people can help in catechetics, in the sacred sciences and in the mass media. According to their special competence, lay people must make their opinions known to their pastors and even to other faithful (with due regard for the integrity of faith and for the common good).

Changing the World (908-909)

Christ gave his followers a "royal freedom", so they might overcome the reign of sin in themselves. "That man is rightly called a king who makes his own body an obedient subject." (St. Ambrose)

When the world's institutions and conditions are an inducement to sin, the laity should "unite their forces" to change them, and impregnate human works with a moral value.

Helping Their Pastors (910-911)

The laity must help their pastors by exercising various ministries or charisms for the good of the Church. (Pope Paul VI) Canon law provides many opportunities for the laity to cooperate in the power of Church governance such as diocesan synods, parish finance councils and parish pastoral councils.

Church and Society (912-913)

The faithful must distinguish between their rights and duties within the Church and within human society. They must unite the two, and be guided by a Christian conscience. Every person according to the gifts bestowed by Christ must be a living instrument of the Church's mission.

CONSECRATED LIFE

Evangelical Counsels (914)

The consecrated life is constituted by the profession of the evangelical counsels. Although not part of the Church's hierarchy, this life belongs to the Church's life and holiness.

Poverty, Chastity and Obedience (915-916)

In the consecrated life, the perfection of charity entails the obligations of chastity in celibacy, of poverty and of obedience in a permanent state of life recognized by the Church.

The religious state is a "more intimate consecration" of Baptism. The person serves the kingdom and proclaims the glory of the world to come.

Many Religious Families (917-919)

This seed of consecrated life has brought forth a tree with various forms, lived in both solitude or in community. There are various religious families which have spiritual resources for their members and for the Church.

From the very beginning, men and women have practiced the evangelical counsel. This has resulted in religious families accepted and approved by the Church. Bishops discern new gifts of the consecrated life but the approval of new forms is reserved to Rome.

The Hermit in Solitude (920-921)

Hermits devote their life to God "through a stricter separation from the world in the silence of solitude, assiduous prayer and penance." (Canon 603) Hermits manifest the Church's interior mystery, (a personal intimacy with Christ). The hermit finds in the desert the glory of Christ crucified.

The Consecrated Virgin (922 – 924)

Christian virgins cling to the Lord with a greater freedom and live in an approved state of virginity "for the sake of the kingdom". (Mt.19:12) Virgins are consecrated to God by the diocesan bishop ... and are dedicated to the service of the Church. (Canon 604)

The order of virgins establishes a woman living in the world (nun) in prayer, service and apostolic activity. These virgins can form themselves into associations. (Canon 604, #2)

Consecrated In Canonical Institutes (925-926)
Religious life is lived within canonical institutes which are distinguished from other consecrated forms by their liturgical character, public profession of the counsels, common life and common witness.

In religious life, the Church offers a stable way of life to the faithful who are called to profess the counsels. In this way, the Church can manifest Christ and show that she is his Bride.

United With the Bishop (927)
All religious (whether exempt or not) are collaborators with the bishop. Missionary work and Church expansion have always required the help of religious. History shows the outstanding contributions of monastic institutions, medieval orders and more recent congregations.

Consecrated Life In the World (928-929)
In a secular institute, the faithful live in the world and work for its sanctification from within. They are a "leaven in the world", trying to order temporal things according to God's plan. They commit themselves to the evangelical counsels and to a fellowship appropriate to their "particular secular way of life." (Canon 713)

Apostolic Life in Common (930)
Members of societies of apostolic life have no religious vows but they pursue their society's apostolic purpose and lead a life in common. In some societies, the members embrace the evangelical counsels "according to their constitutions." (Canon 731)

Consecrated and Serving (931 - 932)
By these states of consecrated life, the Church shows the wonderful actions of the Spirit. Therefore, the members must live out their consecration. They must also engage in the Church's missionary activity. (Canon 783)

The consecrated life imitates Christ's self-emptying and is a special sign of redemption. Following this "narrower path", the consecrated members encourage others and show that the world can be transfigured with the spirit of the beatitudes.

While Awaiting Jesus' Return (933)
Every consecrated person's life takes its origin in Christ's final return. Their example reveals to believers the heavenly good already present in this age and the future glory of the heavenly . (Second Vatican Council)

In Brief - 934 - 945

THE COMMUNION OF SAINTS

Forming One Body (946-948)
The doctrine of the "Communion of Saints" helps to explain the Church.

The baptized all form one body and the good of each is shared by all. "Because Christ (the Church's most important member) is the head, his riches are given to all the members through the sacraments." (St. Thomas Aquinas)

The Church has all her riches in a "common fund." Her two-fold communion is both "in holy things" and "among holy persons." "God's holy gifts for God's holy people." (Elevation Proclamation in Eastern liturgies)

Five Communions (949-953)
The disciples "devoted themselves to the apostles' teaching and fellowship, to the breaking of the bread and the prayers." (Acts 2:42)

There are five Communions:
1. The Communion of faith - This faith of the Church was received from the apostles.
2. The Communion of sacraments. - Sacraments, especially Baptism, link all the faithful to each other and to Christ. The word "communion" "is especially "suited for the Eucharist which brings about this communion." (Roman Catechism)

1. The Communion of charisms - These are "manifestations given by the Spirit for the common good." (1Cor.12:7)
2. The Communion of goods in common -Whatever a Christian has is really possessed in common with everyone else.
3. The Communion of Charity - "If one members suffers, all suffer together, if one member is honored, all rejoice together." (1Cor. 12:26)

Three States of the Church (954 - 956)

Right now there are three states of the Church. Some disciples are on earth, others have died and are being purified, and others are in full glory

A union exists between believers who are still on this earth and those who have died. This union is reinforced by an exchange of spiritual goods. "Yet, we all form one Church and in Christ we cleave together." (Second Vatican Council)

Saints In Heaven (957-958)

The saints in heaven establish the whole Church in holiness. Their merits are offered through Christ, the one Mediator. By their concern, our weaknesses are helped. "Do not weep, for I shall be more useful to you after my death." (St. Dominic) "I want to spend my heaven in doing good on earth." (St. Therese of Lisieux)

Our union with the saints in heaven joins us to Christ. "We love the martyrs. May we also be their companions and fellow disciples." (Martyrdom of Polycarp)

Souls in Purgatory (959)

The Church has always had great respect for the dead. "It is a holy and wholesome thought to pray for the dead that they may be loosed from their sins." (2Macc. 12:45) By our prayers, we help them and make their intercession for us effective.

In Brief - 960 - 962

Mary (963)

Because she joins with Christ in bringing about the birth of believers, Mary is both Mother of Christ and Mother of the Church.

MOTHER OF THE CHURCH

From Conception to Cross to Ascension (964-965)

Mary's role flows directly from Christ. She stood at the cross, consented to the immolation of her son and then received the beloved disciple at Jesus' words 'Woman, behold your son.' (Jn.19:26-27) After Jesus' Ascension, she aided the early Church by her prayers and implored the gift of the Spirit who had already overshadowed her in the Annunciation.

Being Assumed into Heaven (966)

Pope Pius XII declared Mary's Assumption. "When the course of her earthly life was finished, she was taken up body and soul into heavenly glory." The Assumption is Mary's unique participation in Christ's resurrection and an anticipation of our resurrection. "In your Dormition you did not leave the world, O Mother of God, but were joined to the source of Life." (Byzantine Liturgy)

A Unique Member (967-968)

Mary adhered to the Father's will, to her Son's work and to the Spirit's promptings. She is a wholly unique member of the Church. By fully cooperating in the redemption "she is mother to us in the order of grace." (Second Vatican Council)

Annunciation to Assumption (969-970)

This motherhood began by her consent at the Annunciation which she unwaveringly sustained at the cross. Her motherhood continues until the fulfillment of all the elect. She has never set aside this saving office of intercession and is invoked as Advocate, Helper and Mediatrix. (Second Vatican Council)

Mary's function does not diminish Christ's unique mediation. As the priesthood of Christ is shared in various ways, so the unique mediation of the Redeemer has many cooperators.

Devotion to Mary (971)

Mary said that, "All generations will call me blessed." (Lk.1:48) From ancient times the Church has honored her as "the Mother of God." The Church has special devotion to Mary which differs essentially from the adoration given to the Trinity. Her liturgical feasts and the rosary ("the epitome of the whole gospel") express this devotion.

Mary – What We Will Be (972)

In Mary we can see what the Church will someday be when she arrives home after a long journey. In heaven, the Church is awaited by her mother. In the meantime, Mary is the beginning of a Church to be perfected on earth and hope to God's people.

In Brief 973 – 975

FORGIVENESS OF SINS

Forgive or Retain (976)

The forgiveness of sins is associated with the Holy Spirit, the Church and the Communion of Saints. Jesus said, "Receive the Holy Spirit. If you forgive the sins of any, they are forgiven, if you retain the sins of any they are retained." (Jn.20:22-23)

(Part Two will teach of the forgiveness of sins through sacraments. Here we study briefly some basic facts.)

Through Baptism (977 – 978)

Jesus joined forgiveness of sins to faith and Baptism when he said that if anyone believed and was baptized they would be saved. (Mk. 16:15-16) Baptism is the first sacrament of forgiveness.

"While being baptized, the forgiveness we received was so full and complete that there remained in us absolutely nothing left to efface, nor any penalty to suffer for sin. Yet we are not delivered from nature's weakness. On the contrary, we still must combat the movements of concupiscence." (Roman Catechism)

Forgiveness After Baptism (979-980)

Who of us can escape every wound of sin? "If the Church has the power to forgive sins, then Baptism cannot be her only means. The Church must be able to forgive all penitents their offenses, even if they should sin until the last moment of their lives." (Roman Catechism)

By the sacrament of Penance, the baptized are reconciled with God and the Church. "This sacrament of Penance is necessary for salvation for those who have fallen after Baptism, just as Baptism is necessary for salvation for those who have not yet been reborn." (Council of Trent)

The Keys of Forgiveness (981)

The apostles and their successors communicated forgiveness in Baptism and reconciled men to God by the power of the keys. "The Church has received the keys of the kingdom so that sins may be forgiven through Christ's blood and the Holy Spirit's actions." (St. Augustine)

Power Over All Sins (982-983)

No sin is so serious that the Church cannot forgive it. "There is no one so wicked who cannot hope for forgiveness if his repentance is honest." (Roman Catechism) Christ always wants the Church's gates of forgiveness to be open for those turning from sin.

The Church wants the faithful to believe fully in the Church's power to forgive sins through the ministry of priests. "His lowly servants accomplish in his name all that he did when he was on earth." (St. Ambrose) "God above confirms what priests do here below." (St. John Chrysostom) "Were there no forgiveness of sins in the Church, there would be no hope of life to come." (St. Augustine)

In Brief - 984 – 987

Quotes to Remember

I want to spend my heaven in doing good on earth.
(St. Therese of Lisieux)

....

16
Resurrection of the Body and Life Everlasting
(988-1065)

Rising Like Christ Did (988-991)
The righteous will rise and live with the Risen Christ. Our resurrection, like his, is a work of the Trinity. "The Spirit who raised Jesus from the dead will give life to your mortal bodies through his Spirit who dwells in you." (Rom. 8:11)

"The resurrection of the flesh", (the literal wording of the Apostles' Creed) means that besides our immortal soul, our "mortal body" will also come to life.

The resurrection of the dead has always been a central Christian belief. "If there is no resurrection of the dead, then Christ has not been raised. But, in fact, Christ has been raised from the dead, the first fruits of those who have fallen asleep." (1Cor.15:12-14)

Progressively Revealed (992)
God revealed this resurrection of the dead progressively. Hope in bodily resurrection comes from faith in God as creator of man's body and soul. God both created and remained faithful to his Covenant. The martyrs in Maccabees expressed this hope. "The King of the universe will raise us up to everlasting life because we have died for his laws. (Macc.7:9 and 14)

Pharisees and Sadducees (993)
In Jesus' time, the Pharisees believed in the resurrection of the dead. At the same time, Jesus castigated the Sadducees (who did not believe in the resurrection). "You are wrong. You know neither the scriptures nor the power of God", for God is the 'God of the living.'" (Mk.12:24-27)

Promises and Signs (994-996)
Even more important, Jesus joined the resurrection of the dead to his own person. "I am the Resurrection and the life." (Jn.11:25) He promised resurrection to those who eat his flesh and drink his blood. (Jn.6:53-59) He raised people from the dead as a sign of his future resurrection (even though his was of another

order). He proclaimed the "sign of Jonah", that he would be raised after three days in the tomb. (Mt.12:39) The apostles became "witnesses to the Resurrection" because "they ate and drank with Jesus after he rose form the dead" .(Acts 10:41)

Faith in the resurrection of the body has always met opposition. "On no point does the Christian faith encounter more opposition than on the resurrection of the body." (St. Augustine)

HOW THIS HAPPENS

Reunited With The Soul (997-998)

At death, the human body decay. The soul goes to meet God (while awaiting reunion with the body). God will definitely grant incorruptible life to our bodies by reuniting them with our souls. All will rise. "Those who have done good to the resurrection of life, and those who have done evil to the resurrection of judgment." (Jn.5:29)

Those Blessed in Christ (999)

This gift comes from Christ who "will change our lowly body to be like his glorious body." (Phil.3:21) "The dead will be raised imperishable, for this mortal nature must put on immortality." (1Cor.15:35-37)

By The Eucharist (1000)

Although "how" this happens is accessible only to faith, our sharing in the Eucharist gives us a foretaste. "Just as the bread is no longer ordinary bread but Eucharist, so too our bodies which partake of the Eucharist are no longer corruptible but possess the hope of resurrection." (St. Irenaeus)

At The End of Time (1001)

This will happen at "the end of the world" (the last day) because this resurrection is associated with Christ's second coming. "The Lord himself will descend from heaven and the dead in Christ will rise first." (1Thess.4:16)

A Hidden Gift (1002-1003)

By Baptism, we have already risen with Christ. "You were buried with him in Baptism, in which you were also raised with him through faith." (Col.2:12)   This life, however, is "hidden with Christ in God." (Col.3:3)   Because the Father has already "raised us up with him". (Eph.2:6)   We belong to Christ's Body and on the last day "will appear with him in glory." (Col.3:4)

Respect For the Body (1004)
Every believer's body and soul already share in Christ's dignity. Therefore, each believer must respect his own body and the bodies of others. "The body is meant for the Lord, and the Lord for the body." (1Cor.6:13)

DYING WITH CHRIST

Physical Death (1005)
To rise with Christ, the believer must experience physical death and "be away from the body and at home with the Lord." (2Cor.5:8)   In death, the soul departs from the body. They are reunited at the resurrection of the dead.

The Mystery of Death (1006-1007)
Death is the great mystery of the human condition. Faith sees death as the "wages of sin". (Rom.6:23)   For those dying in Christ's grace death is a participation in Christ's death and resurrection.

Because of death, human life has an urgency. We have only a limited time to fulfill God's goals. "Remember your Creator in the days of your youth before the dust returns to the earth. (Eccl.12:1,7)

Jesus Transforms Death (1008-1009)
Death entered the world due to man's sins because God had not destined man to die, "Through one person, sin entered the world, and through sin, death came to all." (Rom.5:12)   Thus, "The last enemy to be destroyed is death." (1Cor.15:26)

Jesus, by accepting his death, has transformed death from a curse into a blessing. "As sin reigned in death, grace also might reign for eternal life through Jesus Christ. (Rom.5:21)

Death In Christ's Grace (1010-1011)

Because the believer has already "died with Christ", death now has a positive meaning. "If we have died with him, we shall also live with him." (2Tim.2:11) Dying physically (while in Christ's grace) completes the believers baptismal incorporation. "It is better for me to die in Christ Jesus than to reign over the ends of the earth." (St. Ignatius of Antioch)

By death, God calls man to himself. Paul wrote, "My desire is to depart and be with Christ." (Phil.1;23) "There is living water in me that says within, 'Come to the Father'." (St. Ignatius of Antioch) "In order to see God, I must die." (St. Teresa of Avila) "I am not dying, I am entering life." (St. Theresa of Lisieux)

No Reincarnation (1012-1013)

Death ends the time which God gives us to complete his plan and to decide our ultimate destiny. There is no reincarnation after death. We shall have no other earthly lives. "It is appointed for men to die once." (Heb.9:27)

Providing For Death (1014)

The Church prays that we be delivered from "a sudden and unforeseen death." We ask Mary to "pray for us now and at the hour of our death." "Death would have no great terrors for you if you had a quiet conscience. If you aren't fit to face death today, it is very unlikely you will be tomorrow." (Imitation of Christ) "Woe on those who will die in mortal sin! Blessed are they who will be found in your most holy will, for the second death will not harm them." (St. Francis of Assisi)

In Brief   1015 - 1019

PARTICULAR JUDGEMENT

Returning to the Creator (1020)

In the funeral liturgy, the Church speaks with assurance to the dying, "Go forth, Christian soul from this world. May you return to your Creator who formed you from the dust of the earth. May you see your Redeemer face to face." (Prayer of Commendation)

Judged Immediately (1021 – 1022)

Death ends the time to accept or to reject Christ's grace. The New Testament speaks of a judgment immediately after death. The parable of the rich man and Lazarus, and Jesus' words to the good thief speak of a final destiny of the soul which is different for each person.

Every man receives his eternal retribution immediately after death. He enters into Christ's blessedness (immediately or after a purification) or into everlasting damnation. "At the evening of life, we shall be judged on our love", (St. John of the Cross)

Going to Heaven (1023 – 1025)

Those who die in God's friendship and are perfectly purified will see God face to face. "The souls of the blessed have been, are, and will be in heaven before they take up their bodies again and before the general judgment. They see God face to face, without the mediation of any creature." (Pope Benedict XII)

This perfect life with the Father, Son and Holy Spirit (and with all the saints and angels) is called "heaven." It is complete happiness and the fulfillment of the deepest human longings. Although retaining their own identity, the elect live "in Christ." (Phil.1:23) "Where Christ is, there is life, there is the kingdom." (St. Ambrose)

Doors Opened by Jesus (1026)

Jesus Christ has "opened heaven to us", giving us full possession of the fruits of his redemption and making us partners in his heavenly glorification. Heaven is the community which is perfectly incorporated with him.

Images of Heaven (1027)

This communion with God is beyond all human understanding. The New Testament uses images to express heaven (wedding feast, wine of the kingdom, the Father's house, paradise). "No eye has seen, nor ear heard, nor the heart of man conceived what God has prepared for those who love him." (1Cor.2:9)

Seeing God (1028-1029)

God can be seen only because he gives man the capacity to see him. This is the "beatific vision." "How great will your happiness be, to be allowed to see God and to delight in the joy of immortality." (St. Cyprian)

The blessed in heaven continue to fulfill God's will. With Christ they "reign forever and ever." (Rev.22:5)

PURGATORY AND HELL

Those Purified (1030-1032)

Those who die in God's grace but are not yet perfectly purified are guaranteed eternal salvation. They undergo purification after death to gain the holiness needed to enter heaven.

This "Purgatory" (cf Councils of Florence and Trent), is totally different from the punishment of the damned. It is a cleansing fire. "The person will be saved, but only through fire." (1Cor.3:15) "As for certain lesser faults, there is a purifying fire." (Pope St. Gregory the Great)

The Church has always prayed for the dead and offered Mass for them. Judas Maccabees "made atonement for the dead that they might be freed from their sins." (1Macc.12:46) "Let us not hesitate to help those who have died and to offer our prayers for them." (St. John Chrysostom)

Hell - Final Separation From God (1033)

We are united to God only if we freely choose to love him. We cannot love God if we sin gravely against him, our neighbor or ourselves. "He who does not love, remains in death." (1Jn.3:14) Jesus warns us that we could be separated from him if we fail to help the poor in their serious needs. (Mt.25:31-46) To die in unrepented mortal sin separates us from God forever by our own free choice. This self-exclusion from God's presence is called "hell."

Jesus' Teaching (1034)

Jesus spoke of hell. "It is better to lose one of your members than to have your whole body thrown into Gehenna." (Mt.5:29) "Be afraid of the one who can destroy both body and soul in Gehenna." (Mt.10:28) Jesus will send his angels who "will gather all evil doers and throw them into the furnace of fire." (Mt.13:41-42) Jesus will say to some "Depart from me, you cursed, into the eternal fire." (Mt.25:41)

127

The Church Teaching (1035-1036)

The Church teaches that hell exists and that those who die in mortal sin will suffer "eternal fire." This means a definitive separation from God (who alone is man's happiness).

These teachings on hell call man to use his freedom in view of his eternity. "Enter by the narrow gate; for the gate is wide and the way is easy, that leads to destruction." This call is urgent because "those who find it are few." (Mt.7:13-14) "Since we do not know the day nor the hour we should watch constantly." (Second Vatican Council)

No One Predestined to Hell (1037)

God predestines no one to hell (Council of Trent). Damnation comes about only by a persistence in mortal sin until death. God wants "all to come to repentance." (2Pet.3:9) The Church prays "save us from final damnation and count us among those you have chosen". (Roman Canon)

FINAL JUDGMENT

For All (1038 – 1040)

The Last Judgment is "the hour when all who are in the tombs will hear the Son of Man's voice and come forth, those who have done good, to the resurrection of life, and those who have done evil, to the resurrection of judgment." (Jn.5:28-29) Matthew's gospel speaks of angels gathering all the nations, with those on Christ's right (the sheep) going into eternal life, and those on Christ's left (the goats) going into eternal punishment. (25:31,32,46)

In the presence of Christ (Truth himself), the person's relationship to God will be laid bare. Everything will be revealed, the good that the person has done or has failed to do. Augustine portrays Jesus saying to the wicked, "You have placed nothing in the hands of the poor; therefore you have found nothing in my presence."

The Father will determine the time when Christ returns in glory. Through Jesus, the Father will then pronounce the final word of history, revealing the whole purpose of creation. Then we will see that his justice has triumphed over man's injustices.

A Help to Conversion (1041)

The Last Judgment calls us to conversion. Each day is "an acceptable time of salvation." (2Cor.6:2) This truth inspires a holy fear, a commitment to justice, and also a hope, because the Lord will "be glorified in his saints." (2Thes.1:10)

The Renewal of All Creation (1042–1044)

After the final judgment, the righteous will reign with Christ and the universe will be renewed. "The universe itself, so closely related to man, will be perfectly reestablished in Christ." (Second Vatican Council)

Scripture calls this mysterious renewal "new heavens and a new earth" (2Pet.3:13), a summing up of "all things in Christ". (Eph.1:10) There will be no more death nor crying in pain, for the "former things have passed away." (Rev.21:4)

The Unity of the Human Race (1045)

There will be the final and complete unity of the human race. Those united with Christ will be his community, "the Bride, the wife of the lamb." (Rev.21:29) Sins will be no more. All will enjoy the beatific vision, by which God opens himself to the elect as man's everlasting happiness.

Unity With Creation (1046)

Man and material creation have a common destiny. "Creation itself will be set free from its bondage to decay. Not only creation, but we ourselves ... groan inwardly as we wait for adoption as sons." (Rom.8:19-23) The visible universe will be transformed, "restored to its original state, and sharing in man's glorification in the risen Jesus Christ." (St. Irenaeus)

How or When? (1047-1050)

We know neither the time nor the way of this transformation. We do know that the form of this world is passing away and that God is preparing a new earth. Although earthly progress is certainly distinct from the increase of Christ's kingdom, this progress is vital to the kingdom by contributing to the ordering of human society. (Second Vatican Council)

All the fruits of our earthly enterprise will be cleansed and transfigured when Christ presents an eternal kingdom to his Father. "Thanks to his mercy, we too, men that we are, have received the inalienable promise of eternal life." (St. Cyril of Jerusalem)

In Brief - 1051 - 1060

The Meaning of "Amen" (1061-1062)
The Creed, the Bible, New Testament prayers and Church petitions end with the Hebrew word "Amen." "Amen" and "believe" both mean trustworthiness and faithfulness. "Amen" expresses God's faithfulness to us and our trust in him.

"Amen" and "I Believe" (1063-1065)
Jesus frequently said "Amen, amen", emphasizing the trustworthiness of his words. The Creed's the final "amen" repeats its opening words "I believe." "May your Creed be as your mirror. See if you believe everything you say you believe." (St. Augustine)

Jesus Christ is the definitive "Amen". "All the promises of God find their Yes in him." (2Cor.1:20)

QUOTES TO REMEMBER

If there is no resurrection of the dead, then Christ has not been raised. (1Cor. 15:12)

....

Christ will change our lowly body to be like his glorious body. (Phil. 3:21)

....

Blessed are they who will be found in your most holy will, for the second death will not harm them. (St. Francis of Assisi)

....

PART TWO – THE CELEBRATION OF THE CHRISTIAN MYSTERY (1066-1690)

17
Liturgy and Sacraments (1066-1212)

Accomplishing the Father's Plan (1066-1067)

The Creed outlines the Trinity's work. The Father gives His Son and His Spirit to accomplish his "plan of mystery." (Eph.3:9) This is "the economy of salvation".

God's Old Testament works were a prelude to Christ's redemption of mankind, a work accomplished by his death, Resurrection and Ascension. "Dying he destroyed our death, rising he restored our life."

WHY THE LITURGY

Proclaiming These Mysteries (1068)

In her liturgy, the Church proclaims these mysteries so the faithful may live them and bear witness to them. "In the liturgy, especially the Eucharist, our redemption is accomplished and the faithful can express in their lives and manifest to others the mystery of Christ." (Second Vatican Council)

Sharing in God's Work (1069)

"Liturgy" originally meant service on behalf of the people. In Christian tradition, it means God's People participating in "the

131

work of God." Through the liturgy, Christ continues his redemptive work in the Church.

Actions of Christ (1070)

In the New Testament, liturgy refers to <u>worship</u>, proclaiming the <u>gospel</u> and acts of <u>charity</u>. The Church shares in Christ's <u>priesthood</u> (worship), which is <u>prophetic</u> (proclaiming the gospel) and <u>kingly</u> (acts of service). In liturgy, full public worship is performed by the Mystical Body. Since these are actions of Christ and His Church, they surpass all others. No other action can equal their efficacy. (Second Vatican Council)

Actions of the Church (1071-1072)

This work also manifests the Church as a visible sign of communion between God and man. It engages the faithful and involves everyone's fruitful participation. Evangelization, faith and conversion must precede liturgy, which then produces new life in the Spirit.

Summit of Prayer and Activity (1073-1074)

Because liturgy participates in Christ's prayer to the Father, all Christian prayer finds it source and goal in the liturgy. All Church activity is directed to the summit of the liturgy and all her power flows from the liturgy. (Second Vatican Council) All catechesis is linked to the liturgy, especially to the Eucharist.

From Visible to Invisible (1075)

Liturgical catechesis leads people from the visible sign (<u>sacraments</u>) to the invisible realities (the <u>mysteries</u>). This Catechism (which serves the whole Church) will present what is universally common and fundamental in the celebration of liturgy (<u>Section One</u>) and in the sacraments and sacramentals (<u>Section Two</u>).

Dispensing Christ's Gifts (1076)

By the outpouring of the Spirit at Pentecost, the new age of the Church began. In this "dispensation of the mystery" Christ lives and acts in the Church and communicates his salvation through the liturgy until he comes. Both East and West call this "the <u>sacramental economy</u>", dispensing Christ's gifts through the

Church's "sacramental" liturgy. We will explain this "sacramental dispensation" and its essential features.

THE FATHER

Blessed By the Father (1077-1079)
Paul writes that, in Christ, the Father has bestowed on us "every spiritual blessing" so "we should be holy and blameless." He destined us to be his sons by his "grace which he freely bestowed on us in the Beloved." (Eph.1:3-6)

To bless is a life-giving action which comes from the Father. For man, the word "blessing" means adoration and surrender to the Creator. The inspired authors proclaim that God's plan of salvation is one vast divine blessing from the very beginning until the end of time.

Old Testament Blessings (1080-1081)
From the beginning, God blessed all living beings, especially man and woman. In spite of man's sins which had brought a curse to the ground, he renewed this blessing with Noah. With Abraham, God's blessing entered and redirected human history, moving from death back toward life. When Abraham, "the father of all believers" embraced this blessing, salvation history was inaugurated.

The Old Testament records many blessings (the escape from Egypt, the Promised Land, the Law and the Prophets). The Psalms recall these blessings and respond with praise.

Two Dimensions of Liturgy (1082-1083)
In the Church's liturgy, the Father is adored as the source and goal of all these blessings. Through the obedient and Risen Jesus, he fills us with the Holy Spirit who contains all gifts.

The Christian liturgy has two dimensions. First, the Church by her adoration blesses the Father "for his inexpressible gift." (2Cor.9:15) Secondly, until the end of time, the Church presents to the Father His own gifts, begging him to send the Holy Spirit upon this offering, upon the Church and upon all the faithful.

Making the Events Present (1084 - 1085)

Christ, seated at the Father's right hand, pours out his Spirit through the sacraments (which he instituted) and makes present the grace they signify.

In the liturgy, Christ principally makes present his own death and resurrection. Jesus predicted these events and then lived them out. These events are unique because they do not pass away like other human events. The Paschal events cannot remain only in the past, because Christ's death destroys death. All that he did for us participates in the divine eternity. It transcends all time and is present at all times, drawing everything toward life.

Set in Motion (1086)

Just as Christ was sent by the Father, so he sent his disciples to proclaim that his death and resurrection had freed us from Satan's power and brought us into the Father's Kingdom. This work of salvation which they preached is set in motion through the sacrifice and sacraments around which the liturgy is centered.

Structured By Liturgy (1087)

When Jesus said "Receive the Holy Spirit" (Jn.20:21), he gave the apostles sanctifying power and made them his sacramental signs. They gave this same Spirit to their successors. This "apostolic succession" structures the Church's liturgical life and is handed on by the sacrament of Holy Orders.

Always Present (1088-1089)

To accomplish this great work of salvation, Christ is always present in all liturgical celebrations. He is present in the Mass in the Eucharistic species, not just in the person of the minister. Christ is the one who baptizes, who speaks in the Scriptures and is present when the Church prays. "Where two or three are gathered in my name, I am in their midst." (Mt.18:20 In these works, Christ always associates with himself the Church (his Bride) who worships the Father through Christ.

Sharing in Heaven's Liturgy (1090)

In the earthly liturgy, we have a foretaste of the heavenly Jerusalem where Christ is the Minister of the sanctuary. We sing with all the heavenly warriors, venerating the saints and eagerly awaiting Our Lord Jesus Christ so we can appear with him in glory. (Second Vatican Council)

The Spirit and the Church (1091-1092)

In the liturgy, the Spirit is both the teacher of the faith and the artisan of "God's masterpieces", the sacraments. He wants us to live in the risen Christ. In this way, the liturgy is the work of the Spirit and the Church.

In this sacramental dispensation, the Spirit prepares the Church to meet Christ, and unites the Church with Christ's life and mission.

THE SPIRIT

Retaining Old Testament Images (1093-1095)

Because the Spirit fulfills the Old Covenant, the liturgy retains certain Old Covenant elements (such as readings from the Old Testament, the praying of the Psalms and the recalling of the saving events, especially the Exodus and the Passover).

The Church's catechesis reveals the mystery of Christ which is hidden in Old Testament images. The flood, Noah's ark, the cloud and the crossing of the Red Sea symbolize Baptism. The water from the Rock prefigures the spiritual gifts of Christ, and the manna prefigures the Eucharist, "the true bread from heaven." (Jn.6:32)

The Church re-reads and relives salvation history in the "today" of her liturgy. Catechesis must lead to a spiritual understanding of this economy of salvation revealed in the liturgy.

Jewish Source But Christian Faith (1096)

Knowing the Jewish people's faith helps us to understand the Christian liturgy. The structure of the Liturgy of the Word originates in Jewish prayer. The Eucharistic Prayers draw inspiration from the Jewish tradition. However, the differences between the two are important. Christians and Jews both celebrate the Passover, but the Jews see it as history, while Christians see the Passover as being fulfilled by Jesus' death and resurrection (while still expecting its divine fulfillment).

Preconditions For the Encounter (1097-1098)
Every New Covenant liturgical action is an encounter between Christ and his Church. The Spirit gathers people of every race and social background in a unified assembly, "a communion of the Spirit."

To prepare itself, the assembly must allow the Spirit to awaken faith, conversion and adherence to the Father's will. These are the preconditions for producing fruits of a new life.

The Spirit and God's Word (1099-1102)
The Spirit (the Church's living memory) and the Church itself manifest Christ and his work in the liturgy.

The Spirit gives life to the proclaimed word of God. Scripture is extremely important in the liturgy. It provides the readings, inspires the hymns and prayers, and gives meaning to the actions.

The Spirit gives a spiritual understanding of God's word to the people and ministers, placing in them a relationship with Christ so they can live out what they celebrate.

The Spirit gives the grace of faith so that the saving word of God elicits a response of faith and the assembly "a communion in faith."

Making a Remembrance (1103)
In the Liturgy of the Word, the Spirit "recalls" all that Christ had done. The celebration "makes a remembrance of all God's works." By this remembering ("anamnesis") the Spirit awakens the memory of the Church which then gives thanks.

Making the Mystery Present (1104-1105)
Besides recalling, the Christian liturgy also actualizes the saving events. Christ's Paschal mystery is celebrated (not repeated). In these celebrations the Holy Spirit makes the mystery present.

At the invocation (epiclesis) the priest asks the Father to send the Spirit upon the bread and wine so that they become the body and blood of Christ.

Spirit's Transforming Power (1106-1107)

This remembering (anamnesis) and this begging the Father to send the Spirit (epiclesis) is at the heart of the sacramental celebration. St. John Damascene explains how the bread and wine become the body and blood of Christ, "Let it be enough for you to understand that it is by the Holy Spirit, just as it was of the Holy Virgin and by the Holy Spirit that the Lord took flesh."

The Holy Spirit's transforming power hastens the coming of the kingdom, causing us to anticipate our full communion with the Trinity.

Fruits of the Liturgy (1108-1109)

In every liturgical action, the Holy Spirit (the sap of the Father's vine) brings about fruit. He abides indefectibly in the Church and makes the Church the great sacrament of divine communion. Communion with the Trinity and other believers are the fruit of the Spirit in the liturgy.

This "fellowship of the Holy Spirit" (2Cor.13:13), transforms the faithful and helps them to participate in the Church's mission.

In Brief - 1110 - 1112

THE SACRAMENTS

The Seven Sacraments (1113)

The Church has seven sacraments: Baptism, Confirmation, Eucharist, Penance, Anointing of the Sick, Holy Orders and Matrimony. First, we will discuss what is common in their doctrinal aspects. Then, we will discuss what is common in their celebration and finally what is distinctive about each sacrament.

All Initiated By Christ (1114-1116)

The Council of Trent, "adhering to the teaching of Scripture, to the apostolic traditions and to the consensus of the Fathers", professed that "the sacraments of the new law were ... all instituted by Jesus Christ, our Lord."

Jesus' words and actions had saving power and anticipated the power of his death and resurrection. These powerful mysteries are now dispensed in the Church's sacraments. "What was visible in our Savior has passed over into his mysteries." (Pope Leo the Great)

The Church's Treasures (1117-1118)

Through the Spirit (who guides "to all truth" Jn.16:14), the Church has gradually recognized Christ's treasures and has seen that, among her liturgical celebrations, there are seven (in the strict sense) that are sacraments instituted by Christ.

These sacraments are "by the Church", because she is the sacrament of Christ's actions. They are "for the Church" because they manifest and communicate to men the mystery of God's communion.

The Baptized and the Ordained (1119-1120)

In the sacraments, the Church acts with Christ as "an organically structured priestly community." Through Baptism and Confirmation, people are enabled to celebrate the liturgy. Those who have received Holy Orders are appointed to "nourish the Church ... in the name of Christ.

The ministerial priesthood serves the baptismal priesthood by guaranteeing that it is really Christ who acts in the sacraments. The ministerial priesthood is the sacramental bond which links the liturgical action to the apostles' actions and, through them, to Christ's words and actions.

The Seal of Three Sacraments (1121)

These three sacraments (Baptism, Confirmation and Holy Orders) bestow a "character" or seal which is indelible (remaining forever). By this seal the person is configured with Christ according to the different states in the Church. This seal disposes for grace, guarantees divine protection, and calls the person to worship and service in the Church. These three sacraments can never be repeated.

SACRAMENTS OF FAITH AND SALVATION

Evangelizing Implies Sacraments (1122)

Christ sent his apostles to all nations to preach "repentance and forgiveness of sins." (Lk.24:47) They were to baptize everyone who believed. (Mt.28:19 Therefore, this mission to baptize (sacramental ministry) is implied in the mission to evangelize. "The preaching of the word is required for sacramental ministry because the sacraments are sacraments of faith, drawing their origin and nourishment from the Word." (Second Vatican Council)

Instructed In Faith (1123-1124)
Besides sanctifying the faithful and giving praise to God, the sacraments instruct. They are "sacraments of faith" because they presuppose faith and nourish it.

The person's faith is preceded by the Church's faith (received from the apostles). Because the Church "prays according to its beliefs" the Liturgy is a constitutive element of the Church's living tradition.

Not To Be Changed (1125-1126)
No minister or community can modify a sacramental rite. Even the Church's supreme authority cannot act arbitrarily and can change the liturgy only in the obedience of faith. Because the sacraments express the faith of the Church, they are an essential criteria of ecumenical dialogue.

Sending the Spirit "Ex Opere Operato" (1127-1129)
If celebrated worthily in faith, the sacraments bestow the grace signified because Christ himself is at work. In each sacrament, the Father sends the Spirit, who (like a fire) transforms whatever comes under his power.

The Church calls this power of the sacrament "ex opere operato" (just by the action being accomplished). This power comes from God, "not from the minister nor the recipient." (St. Thomas Aquinas) Christ and his Spirit act independently of the personal holiness of the minister (although the results do depend on the recipient's dispositions).

The sacraments are necessary for salvation. (Council of Trent) Each bestows by a special "sacramental grace", by which the Spirit transforms the recipients.

Prefiguring Eternal Glory (1130)
The Church will celebrate these sacraments until the Lord comes, because the Spirit groans for Christ's return. (1Cor 16;22) In the sacraments, the Church has already received a guarantee of

heaven even while "awaiting the appearing of our Savior Christ Jesus." (Titus 1:13) "A sacrament commemorates what precedes it (Christ's passion), demonstrates what the passion accomplished (grace) and prefigures what is pledged (future glory)." (St. Thomas Aquinas)

In Brief - 1131 - 1134

Four Questions (1135)

This chapter explains what is common to the celebration of these seven sacraments, by answering four questions:
1. Who celebrates the liturgy?
2. How is the liturgy celebrated?
3. When is the liturgy celebrated?
4. Where is the liturgy celebrated?

CELEBRATING LITURGY

The Whole Christ (1136)

The liturgy is celebrated by the "whole Christ", including those who celebrate in heaven.

Celebrants in Heaven (1137-1139)

The Book of Revelation reveals that in heaven there is "one seated on the throne." (4:2) The Lamb is "standing, as though it had been slain" (5:6). "The river of the water of life" flows from the throne of the Lamb .(22:1)

This book reveals the participants who are "recapitulated in Christ." These include the heavenly powers, all creation (the four living creatures), the servants of the Old and New Covenant (the twenty four elders), the new people of God, and the 144,000. There are also the martyrs and the woman and finally, "a multitude which no one could number." We participate in this heavenly liturgy whenever we celebrate the sacraments.

Celebrants on Earth (1140)

Because liturgical services are celebrations of the Church (holy people united with their bishops) the whole community celebrates. The sacrament's effects touch individual members differently, according to their role and actual participation. The rites, therefore, "should be celebrated with the faithful present and actively participating." (Second Vatican Council)

The celebrating assembly is the community of the baptized who are consecrated by the holy priesthood of Christ, the sole priest. Mother Church wants the faithful to have active participation because they are a "royal priesthood" and have a right and obligation coming from their Baptism. (Second Vatican Council)

Various Functions (1143-1144)

Not all members "have the same function." (Rom.12:4) Ordained ministers are called by God and consecrated by Holy Orders. They are an "icon" of Christ and act in the person of Christ. This ministry of the bishop (as well as priests and deacons) is most evident in the Eucharist.

Other particular ministries (servers, readers, commentators, choir), although not consecrated by Holy Orders, exercise true liturgical functions. Therefore, the whole assembly acts in the liturgy. Each should carry out "all and only those parts which pertain to his office." (Second Vatican Council)

HOW CELEBRATED?

Meanings of the Signs (1145)

The celebration uses signs and symbols whose meaning comes from creation, human culture, the events in the Old Testament and the revelation given in the life of Christ

Signs from the Human World (1146-1149)

In human life, man expresses and perceives spiritual realities through physical signs and symbols. As social beings, we communicate by language, gestures and actions. By means of the material cosmos, God speaks to man. Light, word, water, fire and the earth itself speak of God's greatness and nearness.

These same realities can express actions by which God sanctifies man and man worships God. Social realities (washing, breaking bread, drinking from a cup) can express God's presence and man's thankfulness.

Mankind's great religions witness to the cosmic meaning of religious rites. The Church's liturgy sanctifies these elements and confers on them the dignity of signs of Christ's grace.

Signs of the Covenant (1150)
God gave the Chosen People distinctive signs and symbols (circumcision, anointings of kings and priests, sacrifices and, above all, the Passover). These went beyond cosmic signs and social gestures, and prefigured New Covenant sacraments.

Signs Taken Up by Christ (1151-1152)
Jesus used signs to make known the kingdom's mysteries. He gave new meaning to Old Covenant deeds and signs (especially the Exodus and Passover).

Since Pentecost, the Spirit does his work through sacramental signs which fulfill the figures of the Old Covenant. They make present Christ's saving power and anticipate heaven's glory.

A Dialogue With The Father (1153)
In the sacraments, God's children meet their Father in a dialogue of actions and words. These symbolic actions (which are already a language) are accompanied by the Word of God and a response of faith. Liturgical actions signify what God's Word expresses.

Liturgy's Word and Action (1154-1155)
In the liturgy of the Word, the signs (the veneration of the book, a prominent place for the lectern, the intelligible reading, the proclamation of the homily and the assembly's response) nourish faith.

The liturgical word and action are inseparable. The Holy Spirit awakens faith by the Word of God and then makes present the "wonders" of God by the sacraments.

Pre-eminence of Music (1156)
The Church's musical tradition has a pre-eminence, because the sacred music and words form a necessary part of the liturgy. (Second Vatican Council) The Old Covenant had the singing of inspired psalms. The Church continues this tradition "making

melody to the Lord with all your heart." (Eph.5:19)   "He who sings prays twice." (St. Augustine)

Three Criteria (1157 - 1158)

These signs should fulfill three criteria:
1. a beauty expressive of prayer
2. the unanimous participation of the assembly
3. the solemn character of the celebration

"How I wept, deeply moved by your hymns, songs and the voices that echoed through your Church.   Tears streamed down my face – tears that did me good." (St. Augustine)

This harmony of songs, music, words and actions must be expressed in the cultural richness of God's people.   The Church wants "the voices of the faithful to be heard" and "texts which conform to Catholic doctrine and are taken chiefly from the Scripture and liturgical texts." (Second Vatican Council)

Icons of Christ (1159 - 1160)

The liturgical icon represents principally Christ.   Before his birth, the invisible God could not be represented.   "Now that God has made himself visible in the flesh I can make an image of what I have seen of God and contemplate the glory of the Lord, his face unveiled." (St. John Damascene)

Christian icons express the gospel message in images.   "The production of representational artwork accords with the history of preaching the gospel" because "the incarnation of the Word of God was real and not imaginary." (Council of Nicaea II)

Icon of Mary (1161-1162)

Even images of the Mother of God and of the saints truly signify Christ, for they manifest the "cloud of witnesses". (Heb.12:1)   The Council of Nicaea II (787) defined that "the figures of Christ, Our Lady, angels and saints can be exhibited in the holy churches of God, in houses and on streets."   "The beauty of the images moves me to contemplation." (St. John Damascene)

WHEN CELEBRATED?

Feasts Throughout the Year (1163-1164)

The Church believes that she should celebrate Christ's words throughout the year. Every Sunday, the Church recalls the memory of Christ's resurrection. Once a year, she recalls his passion and resurrection. Throughout the year, the Church makes present to the faithful the riches of Christ's power and merits so they "are filled with saving grace." (Second Vatican Council)

After the Mosaic Law, the Israelites observed fixed feasts to commemorate God's actions, to give thanks and to teach new generations. In this age of the Church the liturgy shows forth the newness of Christ's mystery.

Today (1165)

The Church's prayer is marked by the word "today." Man is called to enter into this "today", "the hour" of Jesus' Passover which underlies all history. "Therefore, a day of long eternal light is ushered in for us who believe in him. This is the mystical Passover, a day which is never blotted out." (St. Hippolytus)

Sunday – The First and Eighth Day (1166-1167)

Because of apostolic tradition, the Church celebrates Christ's death and rising on Sunday, (which is both the first day of creation and the eighth day of creation). After the seventh day of rest, Christ inaugurates the "day that knows no evening." "If pagans call Sunday, 'the day of the sun', we willingly agree, for today the light of the world is raised." (St. Jerome)

On Sunday (the pre-eminent liturgical day) the faithful gather to thank God who "has begotten them again by the resurrection of Jesus Christ." (Second Vatican Council) "Blessed is Sunday for on it began creation, the world's salvation and the renewal of the human race. Blessed is Sunday, for on it were opened the gates of paradise." (the Syriac Office of Antioch)

Easter – "The Feast of Feasts" (1168-1169)

The brilliance of the Resurrection fills the whole liturgical year. The year is transfigured by the liturgy because God is at work.

144

Easter is the "feast of feasts" (just as the Eucharist is the "sacrament of sacraments"). Easter is "the Great Sunday" (St. Athanasius) and Holy Week is "the Great Week." The Resurrection permeates our history until all is subject to him.

When Celebrated (1170)
Easter is celebrated on the Sunday after the first full moon after the vernal equinox. (Nicaia- 325) However, when Pope Gregory XIII reformed the calendar (1582) a discrepancy of several days resulted between calendars of the East and the West. An agreement on a common date for Easter is being sought by both Churches.

The Beginning of Salvation (1171)
Another cycle of feasts (Annunciation, Christmas and Epiphany) surround Christ's birth, which commemorates the beginning of our salvation.

Honoring the Saints (1172-1173)
The annual liturgical year also honors the Blessed Mary, Mother of God, because she is inseparably linked with her Son's redeeming work. "In Mary, the Church contemplates the faultless image which she desires to be." (Second Vatican Council)

Liturgical feasts of martyrs and saints proclaim Christ's death and rising in those faithful servants.

Sanctifying the Whole Day (1174)
In the "divine office", the mystery of Christ celebrated in the Eucharist permeates the whole day. This divine office "makes the whole course of the day and night holy by praise of God. In this public prayer all exercise the priesthood of the baptized." (Second Vatican Council)

All Should Participate (1175-1176)
Because the Liturgy of the Hours is the prayer of the whole People of God (priests, religious and laity), all should participate. Pastors should see that vespers be said in Church on Sundays and on more solemn feasts. The laity are encouraged to say the divine office, even individually. (Second Vatican Council)

Meditating on the Word (1177-1178)

The Liturgy also uses hymns and litanies according to the liturgical season. Readings from the Word and the writings from spiritual masters reveal the mystery being celebrated. In this way, meditating upon God's word (Lectio Divina) is rooted in the liturgy.

Celebrated Anywhere (1179)

Because the whole earth is sacred, Christians can worship "in Spirit and in truth" everywhere. However, they must truly be the "living stones" (2Cor.6:16) in the spiritual temple of Christ's Body from which flows the living waters.

Constructing Churches (1180)

When there is religious liberty, Christians construct churches which make visible the dwelling of God with men. The Church building must be constructed in good taste, manifesting that Christ is present and active.

Church Furnishings (1181-1184)

The altar is the Lord's Cross, the table of Our Lord, and a symbol of Christ's tomb.

The tabernacle should be in the most worthy place, thus fostering adoration. The sacred chrism (together with the oil of catechumens and of the sick) should be reserved and venerated in the sanctuary.

The chair of the priest should express his role of presiding over the assembly. The lectern (ambo) should provide a suitable place for proclaiming God's Word.

Places For Sacraments (1185)

A Church must have a place for the celebration of Baptism and for fostering a remembrance of Baptism (holy water fonts). There must be a place for the sacrament of Penance and a place for silent prayer.

Crossing the Threshold (1186)

By entering the Church, the person crosses the threshold from a world wounded by sin into the world of Christ's new life. The Church is a symbol of the Father's house, open and welcoming to all God's children.

In Brief - 1187 - 1199

Diverse Traditions (1200-1201)

Until Christ's Second Coming the one mystery of Christ's death and rising is celebrated in many liturgical forms.

These various traditions show the unfathomable richness of the mystery of Christ. They complement each other and enrich one another.

Diverse Geographical Areas (1202-1203

Diverse traditions arise from the Church's mission. Churches give liturgical expression to the mystery of Christ according to their culture. They have their own theological understandings and forms of holiness. The Church is catholic, able to integrate and purify all authentic cultural riches.

Liturgical rites (currently in use) are the Latin, Byzantine, Alexandrian and Coptic, Syriac, Armenian, Maronite and Chaldean. All these recognized rites are of equal dignity and should be preserved.

Redeeming the Culture (1204)

Liturgy must correspond to the culture and redeem the culture, so that the mystery of Christ be "made known to all the nations." (Rom.16:26) In this way, God's children have access to the Father through their own culture and are transfigured by Christ.

Diversity Not To Damage Unity (1205-1206)

All liturgy has an immutable part which is divinely instituted (such as the sacraments) and a changeable part which the Church can adapt to various cultures.

Liturgical diversity can be a source of enrichment or of tensions (or even a cause of schism). Diversity should not damage unity but must express fidelity to the common faith, and to hierarchical communion. Sometimes, a true conversion demands a breaking away from ancestral customs which are incompatible with Catholic faith. (Pope John Paul II)

In Brief - 1207 - 1209

GROUPING THE SACRAMENTS

Seven Sacraments (1210)
The seven sacraments instituted by Christ are Baptism, Confirmation (chrismation), Eucharist, Penance, Anointing of the Sick, Holy Orders and Matrimony. These seven touch all the important stages and important moments of life.

Three Groups (1211)
The Seven Sacraments are divided into three groupings:
1. the sacraments of initiation (Baptism, Confirmation and Eucharist)
2. the sacraments of healing (Reconciliation and Anointing of the Sick)
3. the sacraments serving the Church and the mission of the faithful (Holy Orders and Matrimony)

This order (not the only possible one) shows that the sacraments form an organic whole. Each sacrament has its vital place. All the sacraments are ordered to the Eucharist (the "Sacrament of sacraments")

Three Initiation Sacraments (1212)
Baptism, Confirmation and Eucharist lay the foundations of the Christian life. Just as every natural life has an origin, development and nourishing, so the faithful are born anew (Baptism), are strengthened (Confirmation), and receive the food of eternal life (Eucharist).

18
Baptism (1213 – 1284)

Baptism – Door to the Spirit (1213)
Baptism is the door to the Holy Spirit and to the other sacraments. (Council of Florence) By Baptism, the believer is freed from sin, reborn as God's child, made a member of Christ and of the Church, and given a share in the Church's mission.

Various Names (1214-1216)
1. <u>Baptism</u> means to <u>plunge</u> or <u>immerse.</u> This plunging into water symbolizes the believer's burial with Christ, followed by his rising up as a "new creature." (2Cor.5:17)
2. "<u>The</u> <u>washing</u> of <u>regeneration</u> <u>and</u> <u>renewal</u> <u>by</u> <u>the</u> <u>Holy</u> <u>Spirit</u>" (another name for Baptism) refers to the birth by water and the Spirit which is needed to "enter the kingdom of God." (Jn.3:5)
3. Enlightenment "This bath is called <u>enlightenment</u> because those instructed 'are enlightened in their understanding'." (St. Justin)

St. Gregory of Nazeanzus wrote that "Baptism has many names: <u>gift</u> (because conferred freely), <u>grace</u> (because given to the guilty), <u>enlightenment</u> (because it radiates light), <u>clothing</u> (because it veils our shame), <u>bath</u> (because it washes), and <u>seal</u> (as a sign of God's Lordship)."

HISTORY OF SALVATION

Events Prefiguring Baptism (1217-1222)
The Easter Vigil liturgy commemorates the saving events which prefigured Baptism:
1. In the beginning, the Spirit <u>breathed</u> <u>on</u> <u>the</u> <u>water</u> "making them a wellspring of all holiness."
2. <u>Noah's</u> <u>ark</u> prefigured salvation through Baptism. The flood waters are "a sign of the waters of Baptism."
3. The <u>Red</u> <u>Sea</u> symbolized death. Baptism signifies communion with Christ's death.

149

4. The Israelites crossing the Red Sea prefigured liberation. This freeing action is "an image of the people set free in Baptism."
5. The Israelites' crossing the Jordan and receiving the Promised Land also prefigured Baptism.

Fulfilled in Jesus (1223)
These prefigurations are fulfilled in Jesus. Jesus was baptized by John and, after his resurrection, he commanded the apostles to "make disciples of all nations" and to baptize "in the name of the Father, and of the Son and of the Holy Spirit." (Mt.28:19-20)

John's Baptism (1224)
Jesus submitted to John's Baptism to "fulfill all righteousness" (Mt.3:15). At this moment, the Spirit (present over the waters at the first creation) came upon Christ (the new creation), and the Father revealed that he was His "beloved Son." (Mt.3:16-17)

The Cross (1225)
Jesus spoke of his passion as a "baptism" which he had to receive. (Mk. 10:38) The water and blood flowing from his side symbolized Baptism and Eucharist. After Jesus' death, men could "be born of water and the Spirit." (Jn.3:5) "See where Baptism comes from ... from the cross of Christ, from his death." (St. Ambrose)

Baptizing After Pentecost (1226)
On Pentecost day, Peter told the crowd "Repent, and be baptized every one of you in the name of Jesus Christ for the forgiveness of your sins; and you shall receive the gift of the Holy Spirit." (Acts 2:38) After Pentecost, the Apostles provided Baptism for anyone who believed in Jesus (Jews, God-fearers and pagans). Paul told the jailer in Philippi that he and his household would be saved if he believed in the Lord Jesus. At once the jailer "with all his family" was baptized. (16:31-33)

Entering Christ's Death (1227 - 1228)
Paul teaches that the believer, through Baptism, enters into Christ's death, burial and resurrection, "so that as Christ was raised from the dead ... we too might walk in newness of life." (Rom.6:3-4)

In Baptism, the imperishable seed of God's Word produces life-giving effects. "The word is brought to the material element and it becomes a sacrament." (St. Augustine)

HOW CELEBRATED?

Six Essential Elements of Conversion (1229)
Although becoming a Christian is a journey (rapid or slow) with several stages, there are always six essential elements:
1. The word is proclaimed.
2. The Gospel (together with the needed conversion) is accepted.
3. The faith is professed.
4. The person is baptized.
5. The Spirit is given.
6. The believer is admitted to Eucharistic communion.

The Rite Has Varied (1230-1231)
Over the centuries, this initiation rite has varied greatly. Originally, a lengthy catechumenate (including liturgical rites) culminated in the three sacraments of initiation.

When infant Baptism became common, the preparatory rites were very much abridged. Therefore, infant Baptism demands post-baptismal teaching and formation.

Restored Catechumenate (1232-1233)
The Second Vatican Council restored the catechumenate for adults with several stages (found in the Rite of Christian Initiation of Adults). In mission countries, initiation rites already in use were allowed, if adopted to the ritual.

Today, adults enter a catechumenate and then receive the three initiation sacraments at once. In the East, infants also receive Confirmation and Eucharist with their Baptism. In the Roman rite, infants receive Confirmation and Eucharist many years later.

Ten Parts of the Rite (1234-1245)
The rite of Baptism shows clearly the sacrament's meaning and graces:

1. The sign of the cross (the imprint of Christ), signifies the redemption won for us by Christ.
2. The Word of God enlightens the person and calls forth a response of faith.
3. The exorcism shows freedom from sin and from the devil's power. This is completed by the laying on of hands and the anointing with the oil of catechumens. The person can then profess the faith of the Church.
4. The consecration of the Baptismal water asks that the Father send the Spirit upon the water (epiclesis), so the person will be "born of water and the Spirit."
5. The Baptism itself is the essential rite and brings about death to sin and entry into new life. This is conferred by a triple immersion into the water or by pouring the water three times over the candidate's head.
   The words used (in the Latin Church) are "I baptize you in the name of the Father, and of the Son and of the Holy Spirit." The last uses similar words "The Servant of God is baptized in the name of the Father and of the Son and of the Holy Spirit."
6. The anointing with sacred chrism signifies that the newly baptized has received the Holy Spirit and is anointed priest, prophet and king. In the East, this anointing is Chrismation (Confirmation). In the Roman liturgy, this anointing announces that Confirmation will be received years later.
7. The white garment symbolizes the person's sharing in Christ's new life.
8. The candle symbolizes the inner enlightenment by Christ, "the light of the world." The newly baptized (now a child of God) can say "Our Father."
9. First Holy Communion. The neophyte can now be admitted to "the marriage supper of the Lamb." (Rev.19:9) The Latin Church (reserving Eucharist to those who have attained the age of reason) express this Eucharistic orientation by having the baptized child brought to the altar for the "Our Father."
10. Three final blessings (of which the blessing of the mother has a special place) complete the rite.

WHO CAN RECEIVE?

Not Yet Baptized? (1246)
"Every person not yet baptized" and only such a person is "able to be baptized" (In the West, Canon 864; in the East, Canon 679).

The Catechumenate (1247-1249)
Where the gospel is newly preached the catechumenate has an important role in disposing the adult for the full initiation gift.

The catechumenate must bring the person to conversion and to mature faith. The person is led (by successive rites) into the Church's faith, liturgy and charity.

Because the catechumens (even before Baptism) are joined to the Church and are leading a life of faith, "the Church embraces them as her own." (Second Vatican Council)

Infant Baptism (1250-1252)
Children need the new birth of Baptism to be freed from darkness and brought into God's family. Because infant Baptism shows God's total gratuitousness, the Church (and parents) would deny the children a priceless gift if they were not baptized shortly after birth. Infant Baptism has certainly been practiced since the second century and quite possibly from the very beginning of the Church since scripture speaks of "households" being baptized. (See Acts 16:15, 33; 18:8; 1Cor.1:16)

Need For Beginning Faith (1253 - 1255)
To be baptized, the person needs only a "beginning faith" (not a perfect and mature faith). This beginning faith requires a community of believers within which the believer's faith can develop. Because this Baptismal faith must grow, every year at Easter time the Church celebrates the renewal of baptismal promises.

Especially important is the role of the parents. Also, godparents must be firm believers and ready to help the person's faith. Actually, the whole Church bears responsibility for developing the grace of Baptism.

Who Can Baptize? (1256)

The ordinary ministers are the bishop, the priest and (in the Latin Church, the deacon). In necessity, anyone (even someone not baptized) can baptize. They must have the intention to will what the Church does when she baptizes and use the Trinitarian baptismal formula. The Church sees this possibility for other to baptize because Baptism is necessary for salvation.

NECESSITY OF BAPTISM

The Only Door We Know (1257)

Jesus clearly told the apostles to baptize their disciples. (Mt.28:19) "Whoever believes and is baptized, will be saved; whoever does not believe will be condemned." (Mk.16:16) Because Baptism is the only door to eternal happiness which the Church knows, she makes sure that all are baptized. Although God has bound salvation to Baptism, he himself is not bound by his sacraments. (He can save by other means.)

Death Before Baptism (1258)

Some, (although not baptized) have suffered death because of faith in Christ. This Baptism of blood (like the desire for Baptism) brings about the fruits of the sacrament.

Catechumens who die before Baptism are assured of eternal salvation by their desire for Baptism and their repentance for sins.

Salvation of Those Not Baptized (1259-1261)

Because God wants everyone to be saved, the Spirit gives everyone a chance to share in Christ's death and rising. Those who are ignorant of the Gospel and the Church, yet seek the truth and do God's will (according to their understanding) can be saved. It is supposed that such persons would desire Baptism explicitly if they knew its necessity. Concerning children who have died without Baptism, the mercy of God (who wills all to be saved) and Jesus' tenderness toward the children, allow the Church to hope that these children are saved. The Church calls parents not to prevent their children from receiving Baptism.

THE GRACES OF BAPTISM

Two Main Effects (1262)
The immersion in water signifies Baptism's two main effects – purification from sins and new birth in the Holy Spirit. Peter promised his hearers (on Pentecost) that by Baptism they would receive "forgiveness for your sins" and "the gift of the Holy Spirit." (Acts 2:38)

Forgiving Sin/Removing Punishment (1263)
Baptism forgives all sins (original and personal) and all punishment for sin. (Council of Florence – 1439) Nothing remains to impede entrance into heaven.

Consequences Remain (1264)
Some consequences of sin (sickness, death, weakness of character) remain. There is also an inclination to sin called concupiscence with which we must struggle. However, this inclination does no harm if resisted by Christ's grace. (Council of Trent – 1546)

Effects of Baptism (1265-1266)
Baptism makes the believer an adopted child of God, a sharer in God's nature, a co-heir with Christ and a temple of the Holy Spirit.

By sanctifying grace (the grace of justification), the baptized:
1. are enabled to believe in God, hope in him, and love him (theological virtues)
2. can live according to the power of the Holy Spirit (the sanctifying gifts)
3. can grow in goodness (the moral virtues)

Baptism bestows the whole organism of the supernatural life.

Joined With Others (1267-1268)
By Baptism "we are members one of another." (Eph.4:25) This Body of Christ transcends all cultures, because "by one Spirit we were all baptized into one body." (1Cor.12:13)

The baptized have become "living stones." They are a royal nation, a holy priesthood, God's own people (1Pet.2:9) sharing in the common priesthood of all believers.

Duties of Baptized (1269-1270)

The baptized belong to Christ and have the duty to serve others in the Church and to obey Church leaders. They have a right to the sacraments, to the nourishment of God's Word and to all the Church's spiritual helps. They must participate in the Church's missionary activity.

One With All the Baptized (1271)

Baptism is the sacramental bond of unity (even for those not in full communion with the Catholic Church). By faith and Baptism, all "are incorporated into Christ, have a right to be called Christians and to be accepted as brothers." (Second Vatican Council)

Effects of Baptismal Seal (1272-1273)

Baptism seals the Christian with an indelible spiritual mark (the "character of Baptism") which sin cannot erase. Therefore, Baptism cannot be repeated.

This sacramental seal consecrates the person for Christian religious worship and requires them to participate in the Church's liturgy and to bear witness by their holy lives.

Sealed Forever (1274)

This "seal of the Lord" is for "the day of redemption." The Christian who is faithful to this seal will die "marked for eternal life" with hope in seeing God. "Baptism is the seal of eternal life." (St. Irenaeus)

In Brief - 1275 – 1284

Quotes to Remember

Because Baptism is the only door to eternal happiness which the Church knows, she makes sure all are baptized. However, God himself is not bound by his sacraments. (He can save by other means.)

19
Confirmation (1285-1321)

Completes Baptism (1285)

Confirmation is necessary to complete the baptismal grace. "By Confirmation, the baptized are more bound to the Church, enriched by a special strength of the Spirit, and more strictly obliged to spread and defend the faith." (Second Vatican Council)

IN THE HISTORY OF SALVATION

The Spirit and the Messiah (1286)

The prophets announced that the Spirit would rest upon the Messiah. The Spirit's visible descent upon Jesus (at Baptism) was the sign that he was the Messiah. Jesus was conceived by the Spirit and his whole mission was fulfilled in the Spirit who was given "without measure." (Jn.3:34)

Given Now To All (1287)

Jesus often said that this Spirit would be given to the whole Messianic people. "You will receive power when the Holy Spirit comes down upon you." (Acts 1:8) This promise was fulfilled at Pentecost. Peter proclaimed this outpouring as a sign of the messianic age. All who believed and were baptized received the Spirit.

Laying On Of Hands (1288)

The apostles, at Samaria, laid hands so that the newly baptized would receive the Holy Spirit as a completion of the Baptismal gift. "Peter and John ... prayed for them, that they might receive the Holy Spirit, for it had not yet fallen upon any of them; they had only been baptized in the name of the Lord Jesus." (Acts 8:15) "Baptism and the laying on of hands" are the first elements of Christian instruction. (Heb.6:2) "This imposition of hands (which perpetuates the grace of Pentecost) is rightly recognized as the origin of the sacrament of Confirmation." (Pope Paul VI)

Chrism (1289)

Later, perfumed oil (chrism) was added to signify the Spirit's anointing. The word "Christian" means "anointed" (deriving from the title "Christ" meaning "the anointed one"). The word "Confirmation" suggests a ratification of Baptism. In Eastern Churches, the sacrament is called "Chrismation."

Joined Or Separated? (1290)

Originally, Baptism and Confirmation were given together, (called the "double sacrament" by St. Cyprian). However, due to increased infant baptisms and the growth of dioceses, the West deferred Confirmation so the bishop could be present. The East has kept the sacraments united. When the priest confirms, he must use the "myron" (chrism) consecrated by a bishop.

Double Anointing (1291)

In the West, St. Hippolytus (Apostolic Traditions) recorded a "double anointing" immediately after Baptism – the first by a priest and the second by the bishop. This facilitated the present practice of a double anointing (in which the priest anoints the believer after Baptism and the bishop anoints again at Confirmation). In adult Baptism, there is only one anointing, the sacrament of Confirmation.

Different Stress (1292)

The Eastern practice stresses the unity of Christian initiation. The Western practice expresses the communion of the believer with the bishop (the guarantor of apostolic unity).

THE SIGNS AND RITE

What Anointing Expresses (1293-1294)

Anointing (in biblical symbolism) is a sign of abundance, joy, cleansing and healing. The Good Samaritan "poured oil and wine over his wounds." (Lk.10:34)

The pre-baptismal anointing with the oil of catechumens signifies cleansing and strengthening. The anointing of the sick expresses healing and comfort. The anointing in Confirmation and Holy Orders is a sign of consecration. By Confirmation, Christians share more fully in Christ's mission and in his Spirit.

Seal of Christ's Ownership (1295-1296)

This anointing bestows a "mark" (a <u>seal</u> of the Spirit), which symbolizes Christ's ownership (as a slave is sealed by his master).

Jesus claimed that the "Father had set his seal" on him. (Jn.6:27) This same gift belongs to every Christian. "He has put his seal on us and given us the Spirit." (2Cor.1:21-22) By this seal, the Christian is promised his protection in the trials of the last day. (cf.Rev.7:2-3)

Consecration of Oil (1297)

The bishop consecrating the chrism on Holy Thursday is, in a sense, part of the sacrament. In some Eastern Churches, only the Patriarch can consecrate the chrism.

The Syriac liturgy (Antioch) says "Father send your Holy Spirit on this oil so that all who are anointed are marked with an anointing of gladness, an imperishable happiness, the indelible seal and a buckler of faith."

Need For Renewing Baptismal Vows (1298)

When Confirmation is separated from Baptism, the liturgy always begins with a renewal of baptismal promises and the profession of faith, to show that Confirmation follows Baptism.

Involving the Spirit (1299)

In the Roman Rite, the bishop extends his hands over all to be confirmed. From the apostolic age this gesture has signified the gift of the Spirit. He then invokes the Holy Spirit "Send your Holy Spirit upon them to be their helper and guide."

Essential Rite (1300)

The essential rite follows, that is the anointing with chrism on the forehead and the words, "Be sealed with the Gift of the Holy Spirit." The Eastern Churches anoint many more parts of the body (forehead, eyes, nose, ear, lips, breast, back, hands and feet) accompanying each anointing with the words, "The seal of the gift that is the Holy Spirit."

Communion With Bishop (1301)

The sign of peace demonstrates the communion between the bishop and the faithful.

Six Effects (1302-1303)

Confirmation's effect is the full outpouring of the Holy Spirit. Therefore, Confirmation:

1. increases and deepens baptismal grace
2. causes us to cry out "Abba, Father"
3. unites us more firmly to Christ
4. increases the Spirit's gifts
5. bonds us more to the Church
6. strengthens us to proclaim our faith boldly.

"Recall then that you have received the spiritual seal. God the Father has marked you. Christ the Lord has confirmed you and placed the Spirit in your hearts." (St. Ambrose)

Indelible Mark (1304-1305)

Confirmation also gives an "indelible spiritual mark" (character), showing that the confirmand has been clothed with power from on high to be Christ's witness. (Council of Trent)

This "character" perfects the common priesthood of the faithful. "The person has the power to profess Christ publicly and officially." (St. Thomas Aquinas)

WHO CAN RECEIVE

The Baptized (1306)

Every baptized person is obliged to receive Confirmation "at the appropriate time" (Canon 890). Although Baptism is valid and efficacious without Confirmation and Eucharist, Christian initiation remains incomplete.

When Received (1307-1308)

In the Latin Church, the person receives Confirmation at "the age of discretion." However any child in danger of death should be confirmed, even before the age of discretion." (Canon 891; 883)

Although Confirmation is the "sacrament of Christian maturity", we must not confuse adult faith with the natural growth of age. "Age of body does not determine age of soul. Even in childhood man can attain spiritual maturity. Many children, through the strength of the Holy Spirit have even shed their blood for Christ." (St. Thomas Aquinas)

Preparing (1309)

Preparation for Confirmation should aim at a personal union with Christ and a familiarity with the Spirit's actions. Also, the person should receive a sense of belonging to the Church (both universal and local).

State of Grace (1310 - 1311)

To receive Confirmation, the person must be in the state of grace (hopefully purified by the sacrament of Penance). Preparation should include intense prayer to receive the graces of the Spirit. Candidates must seek the spiritual help of a sponsor. Having the same sponsor as at Baptism stresses the unity of these sacraments.

Who Can Confirm? (1312-1314)

The original minister of Confirmation is the bishop. In the East, ordinarily the priest baptizes and confirms at the same time (using the sacred chrism consecrated by the bishop). This same practice is followed in the West for adult Baptism and for reception into full communion of adults who were never confirmed.

In the Latin Rite, the bishop is the ordinary minister. Even though for grave reasons, he can give priests the faculty to confirm (Canon 884), the bishop should confer the sacrament himself because this sacrament is meant to unite the faithful more firmly to the Church.

Danger of Death (1315)

In danger of death, any priest can confirm. The Church wants none of her children, even the youngest, to die without this sacrament.

In Brief - 1316 - 1321

20
The Eucharist (1322-1419)

Full Initiation (1322-1323)
Those baptized and confirmed are fully initiated into the Church by receiving first Eucharist.

At the Last Supper, Our Lord instituted the Eucharistic sacrifice to perpetuate the sacrifice of the cross throughout the ages. In this memorial of his death and resurrection "Christ is consumed, the mind is filled with grace and a pledge of future glory is given." (Second Vatican Council)

SOURCE AND SUMMIT OF CHURCH LIFE

All Oriented to the Eucharist (1324)
All the Church's sacraments and ministries are oriented to the Eucharist, "the source and summit of Christian life". In the Eucharist, the whole spiritual good of the Church (Christ himself) is contained.

Culmination of God's Saving Acts (1325-1327)
The Church is kept in being by the Eucharist (the sign and cause of the unity of God's People). In the Eucharist we are united with the heavenly liturgy and anticipate eternal life with God. "Our thinking is attuned to the Eucharist and the Eucharist in turn confirms our way of thinking." (St. Irenaeus)

Ten Names (1328-1332)
This inexhaustible richness has many names. It is called:
1. Eucharist – as an action of thanksgiving which recalls the Jewish blessings that proclaim God's mighty works
2. Lord's Supper – as a memorial of the Last Supper which anticipates the heavenly wedding feast of the Lamb
3. Breaking of the Bread – in recollection of the Jewish practice of blessing and distributing bread which Jesus used at the Last Supper. After the resurrection, the two disciples recognized Jesus in the breaking of the bread. (Lk.24:31) After Pentecost, the disciples "devoted themselves ... to the breaking of the bread" (Acts 2:42) (the earliest Christian term for Eucharist).

4. Eucharistic assembly as the sacrament should be celebrated communally
5. Memorial –as a recollection of the Lord's Passion and Resurrection
6. Holy Sacrifice – in making present the sacrifice of the cross
7. Holy and Divine Liturgy, in Eucharist, the Church's liturgy finds its most intense expression.
8. The Most Blessed Sacrament –This name is also given to the reserved Eucharistic species because the Eucharist is the sacrament of sacraments.
9. Holy Communion –highlights our union with Christ. (Also used are – holy things, bread of angels, bread from heaven, medicine of immortality.)
10. Holy Mass - the liturgy concludes with a sending forth (Missio)

THE HISTORY OF SALVATION

Becoming Christ's Body and Blood (1333)

The bread and wine become Christ's Body and Blood by the words of Christ and the invocation of the Holy Spirit. On the eve of his passion "He took bread" and "He took the cup filled with wine." The signs of bread and wine become the Body and Blood of Christ, while continuing to signify the goodness of creation. Melchizedek prefigured the Eucharist when he "brought out bread and wine." (Gen.14:18)

Jewish Bread and Wine (1334)

In the Old Covenant, bread and wine received a new meaning as the Israelites left Egypt. The annual Jewish Passover was unleavened bread, a memorial of their hasty departure. During their travel across the desert, God fed them with manna. "The cup of blessing" at the end of the Jewish Passover recalls the joy of messianic expectation. In the Eucharist, Jesus gives a new and definitive meaning to the blessing of bread and wine.

163

Gospel Miracles (1335-1336)

Jesus' miracle of the multiplication of loaves and fishes prefigures the superabundance of the Eucharist. The miracle of Cana makes manifest the kingdom's wedding feast.

When Jesus first announced the Eucharist (Jn. C6), the disciples were divided, (just as they were when he announced his passion and death). Although the Eucharist and the cross are stumbling blocks, Christ invites all ages to learn that he has "the words of eternal life." (Jn.6:68)

Instituting the Eucharist (1337)

At the Last Supper, knowing that his hour had come to leave this world, Jesus washed the apostles' feet, gave them the command of love and then instituted the Eucharist. When he commanded the apostles to "do this in memory of me" (Lk.22:19), "he constituted them priests of the New Testament." (Council of Trent)

Four Accounts (1338)

Paul, Matthew, Mark and Luke give an account of the institution of the Eucharist. John (C. 6) prepares for this institution by recording Christ's words at Capernaum, "I am the bread that came down from heaven." (C.6)

Luke's Account (1339)

At Passover, Jesus gave the apostles his Body and Blood. Luke writes that on "the day of Unleavened Bread", Jesus sat at table with his apostles. "He took bread and when he had given thanks he broke it and gave it to them saying, 'This is my body which is given for you. Do this in remembrance of me'. And, likewise the cup after supper saying, 'This cup which is poured out for you in the New Covenant is my blood'." (22:7-20). Other accounts of the institution of Eucharist are found in Matthew (26:17-29), in Mark (14:12-25) and in Paul. (1Cor.11:23-26)

The New Passover (1340)

At this Last Supper (deliberately celebrated at Passover) Jesus gave definitive meaning to the Jewish Passover. The Supper anticipated Jesus' passing over to his Father (by his death and rising). Now, the Eucharist celebrates this new Passover and anticipates the Church's final Passover into the kingdom.

LITURGICAL CELEBRATION

Until He Comes (1341)

We certainly must remember all that Jesus did for us. However, his command to repeat his words and actions "until he comes" is directed also to the liturgical celebration of this memorial of his life, death, resurrection and intercession before the Father.

Celebrated From Beginning (1342-1344)

The Church has always been faithful to this command. Immediately after Pentecost, the earliest believers "devoted themselves ... to the breaking of the bread and the prayers." (Acts 2:42)

On Sunday (the day of the Lord's resurrection) Christians met for Eucharist. When Paul was at Troas, "On the first day of the week, we gathered to break bread." (Acts 20:7) Since then, the Eucharist has been the center of Church life.

By celebrating Eucharist, the Church proclaims these mysteries of Jesus "until he comes", and leads the elect to the table of the kingdom.

St. Justin's Outline (1345)

Around 155, St. Justin outlined the structure of Mass for the pagan emperor Antonius Pius. This order has remained until now. He wrote:

1. Christians gather on Sunday
2. The writings of apostles and prophets are read.
3. The presider challenges the hearers to imitate these things.
4. All then offer prayers of intercession.
5. They exchange a kiss of peace.
6. The gifts of bread and wine (mixed with water) are brought forth.
7. The presider prays for a "considerable time" as "he gives thanks" (Eucharist).
8. At the end, all say "Amen."
9. The deacons give the "Eucharistized" bread, wine and water to all present and take some to those absent.

Two Parts (1346-1347)

This liturgical structure (preserved for centuries) has two great parts – the liturgy of the Word (readings, homily and intercessions) and the liturgy of the Eucharist (presentation of the gifts, consecration and communion). Together they form "one single act of worship".

This structure is similar to the Risen Jesus' encounter with the two disciples. After explaining the Scripture, he sat at table, "took bread, blessed and broke it, and gave it to them." (Lk.24:13-35)

Christ Presides Invisibly (1348)

Christ himself is the principal agent of the Eucharist, presiding invisibly over every Eucharistic celebration. The bishop (or priest) acts in the person of Christ the head, giving the homily, receiving the gifts and saying the Eucharistic prayer. Others exercise various ministries. All the people participate by their "Amen."

Reading, Homily and Intercessions (1349)

The Liturgy of the Word includes both the Old and New Testament, followed by the homily which exhorts all to put the Word into practice. Finally, all intercede. "I urge that supplications, prayers, intercessions and thanksgiving be made for all men." (1Tim.2:1-2)

Presentation of the Gifts (1350-1351)

The bread and wine are brought to the priest who (like Christ) took "the bread and a cup." The Church uses these created elements, and "alone offers this pure oblation to the Creator." (St. Irenaeus) This presentation puts the Creator's gifts into Christ's hands who perfects all human attempts to offer sacrifices.

Besides bread and wine, Christians took up a collection for the poor. "What is gathered is given to him who presides to assist all who are in need." (St. Justin)

Six Parts of Eucharistic Prayer (1352-1355)

The Eucharistic Prayer (Anaphora) is the heart and summit of the celebration and contains the following:

1. Preface – The whole community joins in unending praise, giving thanks for God's creation, redemption and sanctification.
2. Epiclesis – The Church asks the Father to send the Spirit on the bread and wine so they might become the body and blood of Christ and that all those participating would be one.
3. Institution Narrative – The power of the words, the action of Christ and the power of the Spirit make Christ's body and blood sacramentally present under the species of bread and wine.
4. Anamnesis - After recalling Christ's Passion, resurrection and glorious return, the Church presents this reconciling offering to the Father.
5. The intercessions – This shows that the Eucharist is celebrated in communion with the whole Church in Heaven and on earth.
6. Communion - The faithful receive "the bread of heaven" and "the cup of salvation." "Because this bread and wine have been made Eucharist", the recipients must believe in the Church's teaching, be baptized, and live by what Christ taught.
   (St. Justin)

THANKSGIVING-MEMORIAL-PRESENCE

Celebrating For Centuries (1356-1357)

Throughout the centuries, Christians have celebrated the Eucharist in this form for centuries because Jesus commanded "Do this in remembrance of me." (1Cor.11:24-25)

We offer to the Father his creation of bread and wine which (by the Spirit's power and Christ's words) have become Christ's body and blood. Christ is really and mysteriously made present.

167

Three Aspects (1358)

The Eucharist, therefore, is:
1. thanksgiving and praise to the Father, a sacramental memorial of Christ and his Body,
2. the presence of Christ by the power of his word and of his Spirit

Thanksgiving and praise to the Father (1359 – 1361)

In the Eucharist, we thank the Father for creation. Through Christ's death and resurrection, the whole of creation is offered to the Father.

The Church thanks God for all his benefits- creation, redemption and sanctification.

In the Eucharist, the Church offers acceptable praise to the Father.

A Living Memorial (1362-1364)

The Eucharist is a memorial, making present and sacramentally offering Christ's sacrifice. Therefore, every liturgy contains a memorial prayer (anamnesis) after the words of institution.

This "memorial" is not just a recollection of past events. In the liturgy, these events become present and real. Similarly, the Jews believe that the events of liberation from Egypt are made present to them each time they celebrate the Passover.

The sacrifice of Christ is made present and remains ever present. Whenever Eucharist is celebrated, "The work of our redemption is carried out."

Also a Sacrifice (1365-1366)

As a memorial of Christ's Passover, the Eucharist is a sacrifice. The words of institution manifest this clearly. "This is my body which is given for you" and "This cup which is poured out for you is the New Covenant in my blood." (Lk.2:19-20) This body and blood is "poured out for many for the forgiveness of sins." (Mt.26:28)

The Eucharist re-presents the sacrifice of the cross and applies its fruits. Christ left the Church "a visible sacrifice" by which "the cross would be re-presented, its memory perpetuated and its salutary power be applied to the forgiveness of sins." (Council of Trent – 1562)

The Cross And the Eucharist (1367-1368)

The sacrifice of the cross and the sacrifice of the Eucharist are one single sacrifice. "The victim is one and the same ... the same Christ who offered himself once in a bloody manner on the altar of the cross is offered in an unbloody manner." (Council of Trent 1562)

The Eucharist is also the Church's sacrifice because she herself is offered whole and entire. In this way the prayers and sufferings of all the faithful are united with Christ and all generations can be united with his offering.

In the catacombs the Church is often portrayed as a woman, her arms outstretched like Christ, offering herself for all.

The Whole Church On Earth (1369)

In every Mass, the Pope (the sign of the universal Church's unity) and the local bishop (the sign of the local Church's unity) are always mentioned. "Let only that Eucharist be regarded as legitimate which is celebrated under the bishop or his representative." (St. Ignatius of Antioch) "The Eucharist is offered through the priests' hands in the name of the whole Church." (Second Vatican Council)

The Church In Heaven and Purgatory (1370-1372)

Those in heaven are united to this offering because the Eucharist is celebrated at the foot of the cross with Mary.

The Eucharist also includes those who "have died in Christ but are not wholly purified." On her deathbed, St. Monica said to her sons, "Don't trouble yourselves about my body. I simply ask you to remember me at the Lord's altar wherever you may be."

"We pray for all who have fallen asleep, in the belief that it is of great benefit to the soul to offer supplication while the holy and tremendous Victim is present." (St. Cyril of Jerusalem)

The "society of the saints is offered to God as a universal sacrifice by the high priest so as to make us the Body of so great a head." (St. Augustine)

THE PRESENCE OF CHRIST

The Risen Christ – Especially Present (1373)
Although the risen Christ is present in many ways to his Church (in his word, in the prayers, in the poor, in the sacraments), "he is present ... most especially in the Eucharistic species." (Second Vatican Council)

The Real Presence (1374)
The Eucharist is raised above all the other sacraments because the mode of Christ's presence is unique. In the Eucharist, "the body and blood, together with the soul and divinity of Our Lord Jesus Christ, and therefore, the whole Christ is truly, really and substantially contained." (Council of Trent – 1551) "This presence is called real because it is presence in the fullest sense. It is a substantial presence by which Christ, God and man, makes himself wholly and entirely present." (Council of Trent – 1551)

Power of Priest's Words (1375)
"The priest in the role of Christ, pronounces these words but their power and grace are God's. 'This is my body' he says. This word transforms the things offered." (St. John Chrysostom) Speaking of this conversion into Christ's body and blood, St. Ambrose wrote, "This is not what nature formed but what the blessing has consecrated. By the blessing, nature itself is changed. Could not Christ's words which can make from nothing what did not exist change existing things into what they were not before?"

Declaration of Trent (1376)
The Council of Trent declared "by the consecration of the bread and wine there takes place a change of the whole substance of the bread into the substance of the body of Christ our Lord and of the whole substance of the wine into the substance of his blood." The holy Catholic Church has fittingly and properly called this change "transubstantiation." (Council of Trent – 1561)

Continuing Presence (1377)
This Eucharistic presence begins at the moment of consecration and continues as long as the species of bread and wine subsist. Christ is present whole and entire in each of the

species and in each of their parts in such a way that breaking the bread does not divide Christ. (Council of Trent)

Signs of Adoration (1378)
We express our faith in Christ's real presence by genuflecting or bowing. This cult of adoration is offered to the Eucharist both during Mass and outside of Mass (as when the reserved host is exposed for solemn veneration). (Pope Paul VI)

Importance of Tabernacle (1379)
The tabernacle (originally intended for reserving communion for the sick) became more important as the Eucharistic faith deepened. Therefore, the tabernacle must be located in an especially worthy place.

Love Until the End (1380 1381)
When departing from his disciples in his visible form, Christ wanted to stay with his Church. Therefore, he gave us his sacramental presence. "By his death he loved us to the end." (Jn.13:1) "Let us not refuse the time to go to meet him in adoration. Let our adoration never cease." (Pope John Paul II)

The truth of the Real Presence "cannot be apprehended by the senses but only by faith which relies on divine authority." (St. Thomas Aquinas) "Receive the words of the Savior in faith. He cannot lie." (St. Cyril of Alexandria)

THE PASCHAL BANQUET

Sacrifice and Sacrament (1382-1383)
The Mass is both the sacrificial memorial of the cross and a sacred banquet. The Eucharistic celebration is totally directed to the union of the faithful with Christ in Communion.

The altar is both the altar of sacrifice and the table of the Lord. It is the symbol of Christ himself present as both victim and food. "The altar represents the body of Christ and the Body of Christ is on the altar." (St. Ambrose)

The Roman Canon speaks of the offering "borne to your altar in heaven" ... "so that we may receive in communion at this altar the most holy Body and Blood of your Son."

171

Preparing For Communion (1384-1385)

Jesus said that "unless you eat the flesh of the Son of man and drink his blood, you have no life in you." (Jn.6:53)

St. Paul teaches that we must be prepared for Communion. Those who receive Communion "in an unworthy manner will be guilty of profaning the body and blood of the Lord." Before Communion, "Let a man examine himself." (1Cor.11:27-29) Anyone conscious of a grave sin must receive the sacrament of Reconciliation before receiving Communion.

A Worthy Reception (1386-1387)

Before Communion, the faithful borrow the Centurion's words, "Lord I am not worthy that you should enter under my roof." "Like the good thief I cry 'Jesus remember me when you come into your kingdom'." (St. John Chrysostom)

A worthy reception demands observance of the required fast. Bodily demeanor and proper clothing show respect.

Need To Receive (1388-1389)

The faithful, if properly disposed, should receive Communion every time they participate in Mass. "This more perfect form of participation in the Mass is warmly recommended." (Second Vatican Council)

The faithful must take part in Mass on Sundays and holydays of obligation. They are required by Church law (C. 920) to receive Communion once a year. They are encouraged to weekly and even daily Communion.

Under One Species (1390)

Since Christ is sacramentally present under each species, receiving under the species of bread has become the more common form. However, Communion under both forms is a more complete sign of the Eucharistic meal. This is the usual form in Eastern Rites.

THE FRUITS

The Seven Effects of Holy Communion (1391-1398)

Holy Communion has the following seven effects:

1. <u>Increases our union with Christ.</u> "He who eats my flesh and drinks my blood, abides in me and I in him." (Jn.6:56) "He who eats me, will live because of me." (Jn.6:57) "Life and resurrection are conferred on whoever receives Christ." (Syriac Office of Antioch) The flesh of the risen Christ increases our Baptismal life of grace.

2. <u>Separates us from sin -</u> Since Christ's body was "given for us" and his blood was shed "for the forgiveness of sins", the Eucharist cleanses past sins and preserves from future sins. Because the blood is "poured out for the forgiveness of sins, I should always receive it, so it may always forgive my sins. Because I always sin, I should always have a remedy." (St. Ambrose)

3. <u>Wipes away venial</u> sins - The Eucharist gives us a living charity which wipes away venial sins. Also, Christ helps us to break our disordered attachments. "Having received this gift of love, let us die to sin and live for God." (St. Fulgentius of Ruspe)

4. <u>Preserves us from future mortal sin -</u> The Eucharist is not directly ordered to the forgiveness of mortal sins. This is proper to the sacrament of Reconciliation.

5. <u>Brings about the Unity of the Mystical Body</u> – By Communion, the person's Baptismal incorporation into the Church is deepened. "Because there is one bread, we who are many are one body, for we all partake of the one bread." (1Cor.10:16-17) "You hear the words 'the Body of Christ' and respond 'Amen'. Be then a member of the Body of Christ that your Amen may be true." (St. Ambrose)

6. <u>Commits us to the poor</u> - Receiving Communion demands that we recognize Christ in the poor. "You have tasted the Blood of the Lord, yet you do not recognize your brother." (St. John Chrysostom)

7. <u>The unity of Christians -</u> "O sign of unity! O bond of charity." The painful experience of Church division

which breaks common Eucharistic participation makes our prayers for unity even more urgent.

CHRISTIAN UNITY

Intercommunion With Orthodox (1399)
Members of Eastern Churches which are separated from Rome but possess true sacraments and apostolic succession are encouraged to receive Eucharist and other sacraments "given suitable circumstances and the approval of Church authority." (cf C.844,#3)

With Other Churches (1400)
Unfortunately, Eucharistic intercommunion is not possible with Ecclesial communities which have not preserved the proper reality of the Eucharist, especially because of the absence of Holy Orders. However, their commemoration of Christ's death and resurrection in the Holy Supper does signify life in communion with Christ and their awaiting for his coming.

In Grave Necessity (1401)
Catholic ministers can give the sacraments of Eucharist, Penance and Anointing of the Sick in a grave necessity (determined by the Ordinary) to other Christians not in full communion with the Catholic Church who ask for them, are properly disposed, and have Catholic faith regarding these sacraments. (Canon 844, #4)

Anticipating Heavenly Glory (1402-1403)
In the Eucharist "the soul is filled with grace and a pledge of life to come is given to us. (Ancient prayer) The Eucharist anticipates heavenly glory.

At the Last Supper, Jesus said that he would not drink this cup "until that day when I drink it new with you in my Father's kingdom." (Mt.26:29) At every Eucharist, the Church looks to him who is to come. "May your grace come and the world pass away." (Didache)

Our Sign of Hope (1404-1405)

We await "the coming of our Savior, Jesus Christ" and look forward to "that day when we shall see you, our God, as you are."

The Eucharist is our surest sign of hope in the new heavens and the new earth. "The Eucharist is the medicine of immortality, the antidote for death, the food that makes us live forever in Jesus Christ." (St. Ignatius of Antioch)

In Brief - 1406 – 1419

Quotes to Remember

The Church is kept in being by the Eucharist.

This is my Body. This cup which is poured out for you in the New Covenant is my blood. Do this in remembrance of me. (Lk.22:7-20)

Don't trouble yourselves about my body. I only ask you to remember me at the Lord's altar. (St. Monica)

Let us not refuse the time to meet Christ in adoration. (Pope John Paul II)

Anyone conscious of a grave sin must receive the Sacrament of Reconciliation before receiving Communion.

The bread and wine become Christ's Body and Blood by the words of Christ and the invocation of the Holy Spirit.

21
Penance and Reconciliation (1420-1498)

Two Sacraments Confronting Sin and Death (1420-1421)
We carry this new life "in earthen vessels." (2Cor.4:7) We are in "an earthly tent" subject to suffering, illness and death, this new life can be weakened and even lost by sin.

Christ, who forgave the sins of the paralytic (and then healed him) wants his work of healing and salvation to continue. Therefore, he gave us the sacraments of Penance and Anointing of the Sick.

Two Effects of Penance (1422)
Those who approach the Sacrament of Penance receive God's mercy for their sins and are reconciled to the Church. (Second Vatican Council)

The Five Names (1423-1424)
The sacrament has the following names:
1. Sacrament of conversion – making Jesus' call to conversion sacramentally present.
2. Sacrament of Penance – consecrating the person's conversion, penance and satisfaction.
3. Sacrament of confession – because disclosing sins to a priest is an essential element. It is also a confession of God's holiness and mercy.
4. Sacrament of forgiveness – By the priest's sacramental absolution God gives pardon and peace.
5. Sacrament of Reconciliation – The person is "reconciled to God" (2Cor.5:20), and "reconciled to his brother." (Mt.5:24)

Need For Post-Baptismal Forgiveness (1425-1426)
"If we say we have no sin, we deceive ourselves and the truth is not in us." (1Jn.1:8) Jesus taught us to pray "Forgive us our trespasses." (Lk.11:4)

Although the initiation sacraments make us "holy and without blemish" (as Christ's Bride the Church), these sacraments do not abolish the weakness of human nature nor the inclination to sin (concupiscence). The Christian life is a struggle for holiness and eternal life.

CONVERSION AND PENANCE

First and Second Conversion (1427-1429)

"Repent and believe in the gospel." (Mk.1:15) This first conversion is for those who do not know Christ. By faith and Baptism, a person first gains forgiveness of sins and new life.

The "second conversion" (of Christians) is the uninterrupted task of the Church (who "clasps sinners to her bosom"). This conversion is beyond merely human endeavor and must come from a contrite heart which responds to God's mercy.

St. Peter himself wept at Jesus' look of mercy (Lk.22:61) and made a three-fold profession of love. (Jn.21:15-17) There is a communitarian dimension to this second conversion because Christ says "repent" to the whole Church. "There are water and tears: the water of Baptism and the tears of repentance." (St. Ambrose)

A Radical Reorientation (1430-1431)

Jesus' primary call is to an interior conversion which gives fruitfulness to the exterior works of penance.

Interior repentance is a radical reorientation of life, a total turning to God and away from sin, which includes a resolution to change one's life. This conversion entails a certain pain, called "affliction of spirit" and "repentance of heart."

A Gift From God (1432-1433)

Only God can give us "a new heart" (Ezek.36:26-27) Man is converted by gazing on Jesus Crucified. "Let us fix our eyes on Christ's blood and understand how precious it is to his Father." (St. Clement of Rome)

The Holy Spirit, who proves "the world wrong about sin" (Jn.16:8-9), is also the Consoler who gives grace for repentance and conversion.

Forms of Penance (1434)

Interior penance is best expressed externally in three forms:
1. toward oneself by fasting
2. toward God by prayer

3. toward our neighbor by almsgiving

There also should be tears, reconciliation with others, concern for other's salvation, intercession of the saints and charity "which covers a multitude of sins." (1Pet.4:8)

Many Means (1435)

Conversion comes about by an examination of conscience, admission of faults, spiritual direction, acceptance of suffering and of persecution and concern for the poor.

Source and Times of Conversion (1436-1438)

The Eucharist nourishes this daily conversion. "It is a remedy to free us from our daily faults and to preserve us from mortal sins." (Council of Trent – 1551)

Every sincere act of worship or devotion (Bible reading, personal prayer) revives the spirit of conversion and contributes to forgiveness of sins.

The Church has established Lent and Fridays as intense moments of conversion. At these times, spiritual exercises and voluntary self-denial are important.

Process of Conversion (1439)

The parable of the Prodigal Son is the best example of the process of conversion and repentance. The son seeks freedom but ends up feeding on pig's husks. This leads to reflection and a decision to return home. His journey back and his father's joy are characteristics of conversion. The robe, the ring and the banquet are symbols of new life. Only Christ could so simply reveal his Father's love.

THE SACRAMENT

Reconciliation With God and the Church (1440)

Sin is primarily an offense against God, but it also damages communion with the Church. Conversion, then, entails God's forgiveness and reconciliation with the Church. These are liturgically accomplished by the Sacrament of Penance.

Only God forgives sins (1441 – 1442)

Jesus has said, "The Son of man has authority on earth to forgive sins" (Mk.2:10) and "Your sins are forgiven." (Mk.2:5, 10 and Lk.7:48) Jesus also gave this authority to his apostles. (Jn.20:21-23)

Christ wanted his whole Church to be a sign and instrument of the forgiveness which he gained by shedding his blood. He entrusted this power of absolution to the apostles who received the "ministry of reconciliation." (2Cor.5:15) Paul makes the appeal "Be reconciled to God." (2Cor.5:20)

Power Given To Apostles (1443-1445)

During his public life, Jesus forgave sinners and reintegrated them into the People of God. His eating with sinners was an astonishing gesture of God's forgiveness.

Jesus gave the apostles the power to forgive sins and to reconcile sinners with the Church. This is best seen from Christ's promise to Peter. "I will give you the keys of the kingdom of heaven, and whatever you bind on earth shall be bound in heaven, and whatever you loose on earth shall be loosed in heaven." (Mt.16:19) Later, Jesus gave these powers to all the apostles united with Peter. (Mt.18:18)

"Bind and loose" mean that whoever is excluded from your communion will be excluded from God's communion. Whoever is welcome back into your communion is welcomed back into God's communion.

Recovering Baptismal Grace (1446)

Christ instituted the Sacrament of Penance for all sinful members of the Church, especially for those who have fallen into grave sins after Baptism. This sacrament gives Christians the possibility to recover Baptismal grace. Penance is "the second plank (of salvation) after the shipwreck which is the loss of grace." (Tertullian)

Two Different Forms (1447)

Over the centuries, the Church has had two forms of this sacrament. In the early Church, there was an "order of penitents" for those who committed grave sins (as idolatry, murder or adultery). This involved a rigorous discipline, (often for years).

179

People were admitted rarely to this order and sometimes, only once.

In the seventh century, Irish missionaries to Europe (inspired by the Eastern monastic practice) began "private penance", the form we have today. The sins were told secretly to a priest and the penance was not prolonged. This allowed for frequent receiving of the sacrament and the forgiving of both grave sins and venial sins at the same time.

Two Unchanging Elements (1448)

Although the forms have changed, two equally essential elements remain. First, the person undergoing conversion makes acts of contrition, confession and satisfaction. Secondly, the Church (through the priest) forgives the sins in the name of Jesus Christ so that the sinner is healed and returned to Church communion.

The Absolution (1449)

The Church's absolution formula expresses the three essential elements:
1. The Father is the source of the forgiveness.
2. He reconciles by Christ's death and resurrection and by the Spirit's gift.
3. The action happens through the ministry of the Church.

ACTS OF THE PENITENT

Three Acts (1450)

The sinner must be contrite of heart, confess with their lips and make fruitful satisfaction. (Roman Catechism)

Two Types of Contrition (1451-1454)

The penitent's contrition (sorrow for sin and a resolution to sin no more) is the penitent's primary act.

Perfect contrition (when the penitent loves God above all else) forgives venial sins and mortal sins (when there is a firm resolve to use the sacrament of Penance as soon as possible).

Imperfect contrition (when a hatred for the sin or a fear of damnation or other penalties causes sorrow) by itself does not obtain forgiveness of sins. However, it does begin an inner process which leads the person to sacramental absolution (which completes the forgiveness).

Before confession, the penitents must examine their conscience in light of Jesus' gospel teachings.

Telling All Mortal Sins (1455-1456)

The confession of sins facilitates reconciliation. An admission of guilt opens the door of reconciliation (to God and to others).

"All mortal sins must be told in confession, even the most secret, for these can wound the soul even more grievously than those committed openly." (Council of Trent 1551) "By confessing their sins, they place all before divine mercy for pardon. Those who knowingly withhold some, place nothing before the divine goodness for remission by the priest. Medicine cannot heal a person who is too ashamed to tell the doctor." (Council of Trent 1551)

Necessary Confession (1457)

Catholics have an obligation to confess serious sins at least once a year. (Canon 989) Anyone aware of mortal sin must not receive Communion unless he has a grave reason for receiving and no possibility of going to confession. All must receive first confession before first Communion.

Devotional Confession (1458)

The regular confession of venial sins helps to form conscience and to fight against evil tendencies. Frequent confession helps us to be merciful as the heavenly Father is merciful. (Lk.6:36) "Man is what God has made. Sinner is what man himself has made. Destroy what you have made, so God can save what he has made. The beginning of good works is the confession of evil works." (St. Augustine)

Need To Repair (1459)

Simple justice requires that the penitent repair any harm he has caused (return stolen goods, restore another's reputation etc.). The person, to recover full spiritual health must "make satisfaction", that is, do penance.

Imposing A Penance (1460)

The confessor, therefore, must impose a penance according to the gravity of the sins and the person's situation. Through these penances (prayer, works of mercy, etc.) we become co-heirs with Christ. However, this satisfaction is not ours. Only in Christ can we "bring forth fruits that befit repentance. These fruits have their efficacy from him." (Council of Trent 1551)

Who Has the Power? (1461-1462)

The bishops (as successors of the apostles) and priests (as collaborators of the bishop), by the sacrament of Holy Orders, have the power to forgive all sins, "in the name of the Father, and of the Son, and of the Holy Spirit."

Because forgiveness also brings reconciliation with the Church, the bishop (the visible head of the local church) has the ministry of reconciliation. Priests also exercise this ministry to the extent that they have received a commission.

Forgiving Excommunication (1463)

Excommunication, the most severe Church penalty, can only be forgiven by the Pope, the local bishop or by priests authorized by him. Any priest (even if deprived of faculties) can absolve from all sins and excommunications when the penitent is in danger of death. (Latin Canon 976; Easter Canon 725)

Encouraging Frequent Confession (1464-1466)

Priests must encourage frequent confession and be available for the sacrament whenever reasonably requested. As confessor, the priest has the ministry of the Good Shepherd. While being a just judge, the priest must also be a sign of God's mercy. The priest must know Christian behavior, be sensitive to human failures, be faithful to Church teaching, lead the person to healing, and do penance for the penitent.

Seal of Confession (1467)

Out of respect for the sacrament and the person, the Church binds every priest (under severe penalties) to maintain absolute secrecy concerning sins confessed by his penitents, making no use of this knowledge. This secret (called the seal of confession) admits no exceptions because the sins are "sealed" by the sacrament.

EFFECTS

Restores To God's Friendship (1468)

This sacrament restores the person to God's friendship. This reconciliation with God "brings a serenity of conscience with strong spiritual consolation" (Council of Trent – 1551) and restores all the blessings of being God's child.

Reconciles To the Church (1469)

The person is also reconciled to the Church. The sinner shares again in the holy exchange of spiritual goods with other members. Reconciliation with God leads to the person's reconciliation "within himself, with his brethren, with the Church and with all creation." (Pope John Paul II)

Anticipates Particular Judgment (1470)

The sacrament anticipates the person's particular judgment after death. In this life the person can choose the road of conversion away from those sins which exclude from the kingdom. By repentance, the sinner "does not come into judgment." (Jn.5:24)

INDULGENCES

Plenary and Partial (1471)

Indulgences are closely linked to the sacrament. An indulgence is the remission of the temporal punishment due to already forgiven sin. This remission comes from the action of the Church which dispenses from its spiritual treasury. A plenary indulgence removes all temporal punishment due to sin. A partial indulgence removes part of the temporal punishment.

Hell and Purgatory (1472-1473)

Sin has "a double consequence. Grave sin brings "eternal punishment" (depriving the person of heaven). All sins, even venial, must be purified (either on earth or in purgatory). These

183

two punishments come not from God's vengeance but from the very nature of sin. A conversion made because of fervent charity can remove all punishment due to sin.

Often, even after eternal punishment is removed by God's forgiveness, a temporal punishment remains. By patient acceptance of trials and by facing death serenely the Christian accepts temporal punishment as a grace. By acts of penance, the person strives to put off "the old man" and put on the "new man." (Eph.4:22-24)

The Church's Treasury (1474-1477)

The Christian is not alone in trying to purify himself. He is one with all other Christians in the single mystical person of Christ.

A perennial link exists between the saints in heaven, the saints in purgatory, and the saints on earth. There is a "wonderful exchange" whereby the holiness of one member profits everyone.

This is called the "Church's treasury", which has infinite value through Christ's merits gained by His redemption.

The treasury also includes the immense and unfathomable merits of the Blessed Virgin Mary and all the good works of those saints who have attained their own salvation and now cooperate in saving their brothers/sisters in Christ. (The Doctrine of Indulgences - #5)

Opening The Church Treasury (1478-1479)

By the power of binding and loosing, the Church intervenes for individual Christians and opens her treasury so they can obtain the remission of temporal punishment due for sins. This should spur them to works of devotion.

We can obtain this remission of punishment also for the souls in purgatory.

CELEBRATION OF THE SACRAMENT

Aspects of the Sacrament of Penance (1480)

The sacrament of Penance is a liturgical action which includes an examination of conscience, a greeting and blessing from the priest, reading of God's word and exhortation, confession (acknowledgement to a priest of sins committed) the imposition and acceptance of a penance, the priest's absolution and blessing.

The Byzantine Absolution (1481)

The Byzantine liturgy has several forms of absolution which acknowledge the sorrow of King David, the tears of Peter, the sorrow of the prostitute and of the prodigal son. The Byzantine form asks forgiveness so the person can "appear before his awe-inspiring tribunal without condemnation."

Communal Celebration (1482)

The sacrament can take place in a communal celebration in which the personal confession of sins and individual absolution are inserted into a liturgy. This expresses more clearly the ecclesial character of penance. This sacrament , in whatever form, is always a liturgical, public action.

General Confession in Grave Necessity (1483)

In case of grave necessity, a communal celebration can include general confession and general absolution. This certainly happens when a large number of people are in danger of death with insufficient time for individual confessions. It also occurs when an insufficient number of confessors and lack of time would cause penitents to be deprived of sacramental grace and Holy Communion for a long time. For the absolution to be valid, the penitent must intend to use individual confession later. The diocesan bishop is the judge of these conditions. A large gathering on a given occasion is not a case of grave necessity.

Personal Confession (1484)

Individual, integral confession and absolution remain the only ordinary way for receiving forgiveness unless physical or moral impossibility excuses. Jesus wants each person to hear his words "My son, your sins are forgiven." (Mk.2:5) Personal confession best expresses the person's reconciliation with God and the Church.

In Brief - 1485 - 1498

Quotes to Remember

Admission of guilt opens the door to reconciliation.

....

22

Anointing of the Sick (1499-1532)

To Raise Up the Sick (1499)

By this sacred anointing, the Church asks the glorified Lord to raise up and save the sick person. The person is asked to help the Church by their union with Christ's sufferings and death. (Second Vatican Council)

BASIS FOR THE SACRAMENT

Man's Gravest Problem (1500-1501)

Illness presents the gravest of problems to a person who sees his powerlessness and even a glimpse of his death.

Illness can lead to self-absorption, despair and even revolt against God. It can also lead to maturity and provoke a search for God.

Sin and Redemption (1502)

The man of the Old Testament lives his sickness before God, laments his illness and implores healing. For Israel, illness is mysteriously linked to sin, while faithfulness to God restores life. "For I am the Lord, your healer." (Ex.15:26)

Sickness can have a redemptive power. (Is.53:11) Isaiah prophesies a time when "No one who dwells there will say 'I am sick'; the people who live there will be forgiven their guilt." (Is.33:24)

Jesus' Love For the Sick (1503-1505)

Christ has the power to forgive and to heal, as when he forgave the paralytic his sins and healed him. (Mk.2:5-12) Jesus identified with the sick. "I was sick and you visited me." (Mt.25:36) Following Jesus, Christians make tireless efforts in their preferential care of the poor.

Jesus asked the sick to believe. In fact, many tried to touch him "for power came forth from him and healed all." (Lk.6:19) In the sacraments, Christ continues to touch and to heal us.

Jesus' healings were signs of the coming of the kingdom of God and announced his victory over sin and death. Jesus took away the "sin of the world" (of which illness is a consequence). On the cross Christ gave a new meaning to suffering, making it the door to union with him.

The Power To Heal (1506-1508)

Jesus shared his ministry of healing with others. "They cast out many demons and anointed with oil many who were sick and healed them." (Mk.6:12-13) The risen Jesus made healing a sign of the Church's mission "They will lay their hands on the sick and they will recover." (Mk.16:17-18)

Although the Spirit gives a special charism of healings to some, even intense prayer does not always gain the healing of illnesses. Paul learned to endure suffering, completing "what is lacking in Christ's afflictions for the sake of his Body, the Church." (2Cor.12:9)

Sacraments of Healing (1509-1510)

Through Christ's life-giving presence in the sacraments, especially in the Eucharist, the Church strives to carry out the Lord's command "Heal the sick." (Mt.10:8)

St. James attests to the early Church's own rite for the sick. The elders (presbyters) should pray over the sick person, anoint him with oil in the Lord's name. The Lord will raise him up and forgive his sins. (Jas.5:14-15) Tradition has recognized this rite as one of the seven sacraments.

Healing As A Sacrament (1511-1513)

The Church believes that Christ made the anointing of the sick (alluded to by Mark and promulgated by James) a sacrament of the New Testament. (Council of Trent 1551)

Traditions (from East and West) show the practice of anointing the sick with blessed oil. In time, the anointing of the sick was limited to those at the point of death. Still, the prayer was for the person to be restored to health if this helped his eternal salvation.

The Roman Rite requires that this sacrament be given to the seriously ill by anointing the forehead and hands with blessed oil while saying, "Through this holy anointing may the Lord in his love and mercy help you with the grace of the Holy Spirit. May the Lord who frees you from sin save you and raise you up."

WHO RECEIVES AND WHO ADMINISTERS

In Danger of Death (1514-1515)
The sacrament is for those in danger of death (not just at the point of death) from sickness or old age.

If the person recovers, he can be anointed again in case of another grave illness. If the person becomes more serious, in the same illness, the sacrament can be received again. Also, someone about to undergo an operation or the elderly whose frailty becomes more pronounced can receive.

Ministers of the Sacrament (1516)
Only bishops and priests can administer the sacrament. Pastors should instruct the faithful of the sacraments' importance. These should encourage the sick to call the priest. The whole parish should surround the sick with prayer and attention.

CELEBRATION AND EFFECTS

Three Sacraments (1517-1519)
Whether for an individual or a group, whether in the home, or in the Church, this anointing is always a liturgical action which should be preceded by <u>Penance</u> and followed by <u>Eucharist</u> as the last sacrament of the earthly journey (Viaticum).

The principal elements of the celebration are the priest laying hands in silence, the prayer of faith, and the anointing with oil blessed by the bishop (if possible). These prayers and actions show the sacrament's grace.

Three Effects – Peace, Healing and Forgiveness (1520)
The person receives peace and strength against temptations and discouragement in their illness. The sacrament's power should lead the person to a healing of soul and the body (if God wills). Also, "If he has committed sins, he will be forgiven." (Jas.5:15 and Council of Trent)

Consecrated To Christ's Sufferings (1521-1523)
The person is consecrated into a likeness of Christ's sufferings and can see suffering as a participation in Jesus' passion.

By uniting himself to Christ's passion, the sick person contributes to the Church's sanctification. The Church, through the communion of saints, intercedes for the sick person.

For those dying, the sacramental anointing (sometimes called "the sacrament of the departing") completes the earlier anointings of Baptism and Confirmation and fortifies the person for their final struggles.

Sacraments For The Journey (1524-1525)

Besides anointing the sick, the Church offers the Eucharist as viaticum for this special moment of "passing over" from this world to the Father. At this point, Jesus' words mean so much "He who eats my flesh and drinks my blood has eternal life and I will raise him up on the last day." (Jn.6:54)

Therefore, Penance, Anointing of the Sick, and Eucharist are the sacraments that prepare for our heavenly homeland and complete our earthly pilgrimage.

In Brief - 1526 – 1532

Quotes to Remember

Illness presents the gravest of problems because the person sees his powerlessness, and perhaps, even a glimpse of death.

St. James attests to the early Church's rite for the sick.

For those dying, the anointing of the sick completes the earlier anointings of Baptism and Confirmation.

On the cross, Christ made suffering the door to union with him.

23
Holy Orders (1533-1600)

Two Sacraments of Service To Others (1533-1535)
The initiation sacraments (Baptism, Confirmation and Eucharist) call the believer to holiness and confer the graces needed for our pilgrimage.

Holy Orders and Matrimony (although contributing to the person's salvation) are directed primarily to the salvation of others.

Believers (already consecrated by Baptism and Confirmation) receive a particular consecration through Holy Orders "to feed the Church by the word and grace of God". Christian spouses, through Matrimony, are consecrated to the duties of married life.

Bishop – Priest – Deacon (1536)
(The teaching on the institution and ministry of Holy Orders is given in numbers 874 – 896. This section teaches the sacramental means by which the ministry is handed on.) Through Holy Orders, the mission given by Christ to his apostles is continued until the end of time in three degrees, bishop, priest and deacon.

HOLY ORDERS IN ECONOMY OF SALVATION

Placing In An Order (1537 – 1538)
In Roman times, ordination incorporated a person into an order, an established governing body. Catholic Tradition (with a basis in Scripture) has three orders, bishops, priests and deacons. Order is also used of groups of catechumens, virgins, widows, etc.

In the Church, people entered these orders by a liturgical ordination rite. Today ordination is used only of the order of bishops, priests and deacons and goes beyond mere election or delegation by the community. By ordination, the Spirit bestows a sacred power which comes from Christ through his Church. Ordination (also called consecration – a "setting apart") is conferred by the bishop's laying on of hands and the consecratory prayer.

The Old Testament Priesthood (1539-1540)

Although Israel was "a kingdom of priests", God set aside the tribe of Levi for liturgical service. By a special rite of consecration, they were "appointed to offer gifts and sacrifices for sin." (Heb.5:1)

This priesthood remains powerless to achieve definitive salvation which is accomplished only by Christ's sacrifice.

Prefiguring Christ's Priesthood (1541-1543)

Catholic liturgy sees the priesthood of Aaron, the service of the Levites and the anointing of the seventy elders (Num.11:24-25) as prefiguring the ordained ministry of the New Covenant. The Church recalls these Old Testament figures:

1) In the consecratory paragraph for bishops, "You established rulers and priests and did not leave your sanctuary without ministers to serve."
2) At the ordination of priests, "You extended the spirit of Moses to seventy wise men. You shared among the sons of Aaron the fullness of their father's power."
3) At the ordination of deacons, "As ministers of your tabernacle you chose the sons of Levi."

Christ's Single Offering (1544 - 1545)

The fulfillment of the Old Covenant priesthood came about in Christ, the "one mediator between God and man." (Tim.2:5) Christian tradition sees Melchizedek ("priest of God Most High") as a prefiguration of the priesthood of Christ who "by a single offering has perfected for all time those who are sanctified." (Heb.10:14)

Christ's sacrifice (although unique and accomplished once for all) is made present in the Eucharistic sacrifice. The one priesthood of Christ is made present through the ministerial priesthood. "Only Christ is the true priest, the others being only his ministers." (St. Thomas Aquinas)

Two Priesthoods – Hierarchical and Common (1546-1547)

Christ has made his Church "a kingdom of priests for his God and Father." (Rev. 1:6) Through Baptism and Confirmation the faithful are "consecrated to be a holy priesthood." (Second Vatican Council)

The ministerial, hierarchical priesthood (bishop, priest and deacon) and the common priesthood (all the faithful) are ordered to one another but differ essentially. The common priesthood is the unfolding of baptismal grace so the person lives in the Spirit. The ministerial priesthood is directed to the unfolding of the baptismal grace in all Christians. This priesthood is given by another sacrament, namely, Holy Orders.

Acting In the Person of Christ (1548-1549)

Through the ordained minister, Christ himself is present to the Church as Head of his Body. The priest, therefore, acts "in the person of Christ the Head."

By ordination the minister is made like Christ and has "authority to act in the power and place of the person of Christ himself." (Pope Pius XII) "The priest of the new law acts in the person of Christ." (St. Thomas Aquinas)

The bishop is "the living image of God the Father." (St. Ignatius of Antioch)

The Sins Of the Minister (1550-1551)

In spite of this, the minister is not preserved from all human weakness or even from sin. The guarantee of the Spirit extends to the sacraments so that the minister's own sins cannot impede their grace. In other acts, however, the minister can harm the fruitfulness of the Church.

This priesthood is ministerial (ordained to service). It is entirely dependent on Christ and ordered for the good of others. Because the sacrament gives him the sacred power of Christ, the minister must follow the model of Christ.

Representing Christ and the Church (1552-1553)

Besides representing Christ to the faithful, the ministerial priesthood offers prayers to God in the "name of the whole Church."

The priests are not delegates of the community. Because the whole Church (head and members) prays and offers itself, the ministers are ministers of Christ and of the Church. Because the ministerial priesthood represents Christ, it can represent the Church.

THREE DEGREES OF ORDER

Bishop – Priest – Deacon (1554)

From the very beginning, the three degrees of Church ministry have been called bishop, priest and deacon. Catholic doctrine recognizes two degrees of ministerial participation in Christ's priesthood – the episcopacy and the presbyterate. The deaconate is meant to serve these two orders. Therefore, the word sacerdos (priest) denotes bishops and priests. However, all three orders (the two degrees of priesthood and the degree of service) are conferred by sacramental "ordination" (Holy Orders).

"Let everyone revere the deacons as Jesus Christ, the bishop as the image of the Father and the priests as the senate of God for without them one cannot speak of the Church." (St. Ignatius of Antioch)

Bishop – The Fullness of Sacred Orders (1555-1557)

In the chief place are the bishops who (because of the unbroken succession going back to the beginning) are transmitters of the apostolic line. (Second Vatican Council)

The apostles received a special outpouring of the Spirit and they passed this gift on by the laying on of hands. Paul told Timothy, "Keep alive the gift that God gave you when I laid my hands on you." (2Tim.1:6)

The fullness of the sacrament of Holy Orders is conferred by episcopal consecration.

Three Powers (1558)

This Episcopal consecration confers the offices of sanctifying, teaching and ruling. By the laying on of hands and the words of consecration, the Holy Spirit is given and a sacred character is impressed. The bishop takes the place of Christ himself and acts as his representative. "By the Holy Spirit, the bishops have been constituted true and authentic teachers, pontiffs and pastors." (Second Vatican Council)

The Episcopal Body (1559)

By this consecration and by hierarchical communion with the Pope and other bishops, the bishop becomes a member of the episcopal body. The Church's ancient practice of several bishops consecrating every new bishop witnesses to the bishop's collegial

193

nature. Today, a lawful episcopal ordination also requires the intervention of the Pope.

The Local Church (1560-1561)

As Christ's vicar, the bishop has two duties – the pastoral care of his particular Church and a solicitude for all the Churches. By divine institution, all bishops have a responsibility for the Church's apostolic mission. Therefore, Eucharist celebrated by the bishop has special significance.

Ordaining Priests As Co-Workers (1562-1564)

Bishops entrust various Church members with offices of ministry. The function of the bishop's ministry is handed over in a subordinate degree to priests as co-workers of the episcopal order to fulfill the Church's apostolic mission.

Joined to the episcopal order, priests share in Christ's authority. Therefore, the priesthood of priests is given by its own particular sacrament. Through the sacrament and the Spirit's anointing, priests receive a special character, are configured to Christ and are able to act in the person of Christ.

Although dependent on the bishop, priests are associated with him by their sacerdotal (priestly) dignity. By Holy Orders they are consecrated to preach the Gospel, to pastor the faithful and to celebrate divine worship.

For The Whole World (1565-1566)

The priest's spiritual gift is not for a limited or restricted mission but for a universal mission. They are prepared to preach the Gospel to the end of the world.

They exercise the supreme degree of their office in the Eucharistic assembly. In the sacrifice of the Mass they make present again Christ's spotless offering to the Father. From this unique sacrifice, their priestly ministry draws its strength.

The Brotherhood Of the Priests (1567-1568)

With their bishop, priests constitute a unique sacerdotal college (presbyterium). In each local assembly, they represent the bishop, assume his duties and exercise their ministry in communion with him. The bishop sees them as co-workers and sons. To the bishop, the priests owe love and obedience.

All priests are bound together in an intimate sacerdotal brotherhood. Especially in a diocese, they form (with the bishop) a priestly body. Their unity is expressed liturgically by their imposition of hands (after the bishop) upon the newly ordained.

Deacons, A Ministry For the Bishop (1569-1571)

Deacons, at a lower level of hierarchy, receive the imposition of hands "not for the priesthood but for the ministry." The bishop alone lays hands, signifying the deacon's special attachment to him.

Deacons receive a permanent imprint (character) which configure them to Christ. Among other tasks, the deacon assists at the Eucharist, distributes Communion, preaches, baptizes, blesses marriages and does works of charity.

The Latin Church restored the deaconate as a permanent rank of hierarchy which can be conferred on married men. It is important that men who carry out Church ministry are "strengthened by the imposition of hands, bonding their tasks more closely to the altar and made more fruitful by sacramental grace." (Second Vatican Council)

CELEBRATING THE SACRAMENT

Essential Rite (1572-1573)

These three ordinations are so important that they should take place preferably on a Sunday at the cathedral within the Eucharistic liturgy. All three ordinations follow the same pattern.

The essential rite for all three is the bishop's imposition of hands and the specific consecratory prayer asking for an outpouring of the Holy Spirit and the specific gifts of the ministry.

Rites - Signs of the Effects (1574)

Additional rites surround the celebration. The early parts (such as the presentation of the candidate) show that the choice is according to Church order. After the act of consecration, several rites show what has been accomplished. Bishops and priests receive an anointing with oil symbolizing the giving of the Spirit. The bishop receives the Gospel book, ring, miter and crozier (signs of his ministry). The priest receives the paten and chalice (signs of the people's offering). The deacon receives the book of gospels (a sign of his preaching task).

195

Who Confers? (1575-1576)

Now at the Father's right hand, Christ continues to protect his Church through the apostles and to guide it through those pastors (bishops) who continue his work. Christ's gifts "make apostles and pastors." (Eph.4:11)

Since Holy Orders is the sacrament of apostolic ministry, only validly ordained bishops (those in the line of apostolic succession) validly confer these three degrees of order.

Who Receives? (1577-1578)

Because Jesus chose men as his apostles and the apostles also chose men as their successors, only baptized men can validly receive ordination. (Canon 1024) Because the college of bishops (with whom priests are united) makes the college of the apostles ever-present, the Church is bound by Christ's own choice. Therefore, the ordination of women is not possible. (Pope John Paul II – 1977)

No one can claim a right to receive Holy Orders. Anyone who recognizes God's call must submit his desire to the Church who has the right to call men to sacred orders (always an unmerited gift).

Celibacy (1579-1580)

All ordained ministers (excepting deacons) are usually chosen from men of faith who are celibate and intend to remain celibate. They have undivided hearts given totally to "the affairs of the Lord." (1Cor.7:32) Celibacy, practiced with a joyful heart, proclaims the reign of God.

The Eastern Churches have a legitimate tradition that bishops are chosen from celibates, while married men can be ordained deacons and priests. The Eastern Churches hold celibacy in great honor and a man who is already ordained cannot marry.

THE EFFECTS

The Seal of An Indelible Character (1581-1584)

Holy Orders configures the recipient to Christ and enables him to act as a representative of Christ.

As in Baptism and Confirmation, this share in Christ's office is given once for all. This sacrament also confers an <u>indelible</u>

spiritual character and cannot be repeated or conferred temporarily.

A validly ordained man (even if discharged from his obligations) cannot become a layman again in the strict sense because the spiritual character marks him permanently.

The unworthiness of the minister does not prevent Christ from acting. "Christ's gift is not profaned: what flows through him keeps its purity and what passes through him remains clean." (St. Augustine)

Each Configured To Christ (1585-1589)
The Spirit configures the ordained to Christ.

The bishop receives primarily the gift of strength, the "governing spirit" to guide and defend the Church. This grace impels him to proclaim the gospel and be a model of holiness to his flock. "May he be a shepherd to your holy flock and a high priest blameless in your sight" (Consecratory Prayer).

The priest receives the gift to proclaim the gospel, fulfill the ministry of the word and to offer spiritual gifts and sacrifices (Byzantine liturgy).

The deacon receives the gift of service to the liturgy, to the Gospel and to the poor.

"Who is the priest? He stands with angels, gives glory with archangels, shares Christ's priesthood, refashions creation and, even greater, is divinized and divinizes." (St. Gregory of Nazianzus) "If we really understood the priest on earth, we would die not out of fright but out of love." (Cure' of Ars)

In Brief - 1590 – 1600

Quotes to Remember

No one can claim a right to receive Holy Orders.
A person's desire must be submitted to the Church.

·····································

Catholic tradition has three orders –
bishops, priests and deacons.

·····························

24
Matrimony (1601 – 1666)

Definition of Matrimony (1601)
By their matrimonial covenant, a man and a woman establish a partnership of the whole of life. This covenant is by nature ordered to the good of the spouses and the procreation and education of offspring. Between the baptized, Christ has raised this covenant to the dignity of a sacrament. (Canon 1055, #1)

GOD'S PLAN

Marriage – At the Beginning and the End (1602)
Scripture begins with the creation of man and woman and concludes with the "wedding feast of the Lamb." (Rev.19:7,9) Scripture speaks extensively of marriage, its mystery, its origin and its purpose. It describes the difficulties caused by sin and the renewal of marriage by Christ.

God's Laws For Marriage (1603)
In creating man and woman, God himself established marriage with its own proper laws. Although customs and laws vary, marriage is not a purely human institution but has some common permanent characteristics. Every culture has some sense of the greatness of the matrimonial union "because the well-being of the person and the society depends on a healthy conjugal life." (Second Vatican Council)

All Called To Love (1604)
The mutual love of man and woman is an image of God's unfailing love. God intends man and woman to "Be fruitful and multiply", because mankind has the task to "fill the earth and subdue it." (Gen.1:27)

Leaving All (1605)
From the beginning, God said that "It is not good that the man should be alone", God gave him woman, "flesh of his flesh." She is clearly his equal and helpmate. So, man "leaves his father and his mother and cleaves to his wife." (Gen.2:18-25)   Jesus

approves this plan of an unbreakable union." "They are no longer two, but one flesh." (Mt.19:6)

Disorder Within Marriage (1606)
Evil (experienced everywhere by man) is also felt in the man/woman relationships. Evil threatens their union with conflicts, hatred and even separation. This disorder (although having different manifestations according to cultures and individuals) seems to happen everywhere.

Source Of the Disorder (1607 - 1608)
This disorder does not come from the nature of man/woman or from their relationship. It comes from sin. Original sin (a breaking from God) ruptured the original communion of man and woman. They experienced recriminations in their relationship and lust in their mutual attraction. Their vocations to have offspring and to till the soil were burdened by the pain of childbirth and the toil of work.

Nevertheless, God's order of creation endured. God, by making "garments of skin for the first couple" (Gen.3:21), showed that he still provided the grace needed to achieve marital union.

Dual Punishment (1609)
The dual punishments (pain in childbearing and toil by "the sweat of your brow") actually embody remedies to sin. Marriage helps to overcome self-absorption and leads to mutual self-giving.

MARRIAGE IN THE SCRIPTURES

Old Testament Divorce (1610-1611)
Although the polygamy of Abraham, Isaac and Jacob and of the Israelite kings was not explicitly rejected, the Old Testament (through Moses' law) aimed to protect wives. However, in allowing divorce, this law showed "hardness of heart."

The prophets (using the image of faithful married love to exemplify God's covenant) prepared Israel to understand marriage's unity and indissolubility. The books of Ruth and Tobit are excellent examples of married love. The Song of Songs sees love "as strong as death." (9:6-7)

199

Jesus Reviews the Marriage Covenant (1612-1615)

The nuptial covenant between God and Israel prepared the way for the Son of God to unite himself to all mankind and prepare for "the wedding feast of the Lamb." (Rev.19:7,9)

By performing his first miracle at a wedding feast, Jesus confirmed the goodness of marriage and proclaimed marriage as an efficacious sign of his presence.

Jesus swept aside Moses' permission to divorce one's wife. He taught that marriage was indissoluble "as at the beginning." "What God has joined together, let no man put asunder." (Mt.19:6)

Jesus did not come to place impossible burdens. He restored the Reign of God (including the graces gained by his cross) so couples can regain the original meaning and joy of marriage.

Christ's Love For His Church (1616-1617)

Paul, therefore, writes, "husbands love your wives, as Christ loved the Church." In light of Christ's love for his Church, a man "is joined to his wife, and the two shall become one." (Eph.5:25-26)

This spousal love (Christ for his Church) marks the whole Christian life. Baptism is the nuptial bath (Eph.5:26-27) and the Eucharist is the wedding feast. Christian marriage signifies the covenant between Christ and his Church.

Virgins – Bonded to Christ (1618-1620)

Union with Christ takes precedence over every human bond. From the Church's beginning, some have even renounced the goods of marriage to "follow the Lamb wherever he goes." (Rev.14:4)

Virginity is a sign that our bonds with Christ come first and that marriage belongs only to this age (which is passing away).

Matrimony and virginity both come from the Lord. "Whoever denigrates marriage also diminishes the glory of virginity." (St. John Chrysostom)

Eucharist and Penance (1621-1622)

In the Latin Rite, marriage between two Catholics usually takes place during Mass. The spouses should seal their consent to each other in Christ's offering and should receive the Body and Blood of Christ so they might be "one body" in Christ.

Because marriage is a sacramental action which should be both valid and fruitful, the spouses should receive the sacrament of penance.

Rule of the Spouses (1623-1624)

In the Latin Church, the spouses are the ministers. They confer the sacrament on each other by their mutual consent. In Eastern liturgies, the priest is the minister of the sacrament (called "crowning"). After receiving their consent, the priest places crowns on each of the spouses as a sign of the covenant.

The spouses receive the Holy Spirit as their covenant seal and the ever-available source of strength.

A Free, Human Consent (1625-1628)

The parties are a baptized man and woman, who are free to marry, and who freely give their consent. They must not be under constraint nor be impeded by any law.

Their exchanging of consent is the indispensable element in making the marriage. Without consent, there is no marriage.(Canon 1057, #1)

The consent ("I take you to be my husband" and "I take you to be my wife") must be a human act of mutual self-giving which binds the spouses and finds its fulfillment when the two "become one flesh." (Gen.2:24)

This consent must come from each person freely and not be coerced by grave fear. (Canon 1103) Because no human power can substitute for this consent, a marriage is invalid where freedom is lacking. (Canon 1057, #1)

Church Tribunal (1629)

For this reason (and others) a Church tribunal can declare as null a marriage entered into without the necessary freedom. Then, the spouses (having fulfilled any natural obligations) are free to marry.

Before A Priest And Two Witnesses (1630-1631)

The priest receives their consent and gives the Church's blessing. His presence (and that of the witnesses) shows that marriage is a Church reality.

The Church obliges people to be married before a priest and two witnesses because:

1) Marriage should be celebrated in the Church's public liturgy.
2) Marriage bestows a Church order with rights and responsibilities.
3) There must be certainty about the state of life in the Church (the need for witnesses).
4) The public character strengthens the consent and the spouses' fidelity.

Marriage Preparation (1632)

Because consent must be freely given, marriage preparation has great importance. Although parents and families are the first teachers, the parish is God's family which transmits human and Christian values (so needed because of family breakdown). Young people need suitable instruction about the dignity of married love so they can have an honorable courtship and enter marriage freely.

Problems In A Mixed Marriage (1633-1634)

Frequently a Catholic wishes to marry a baptized non-Catholic or a non-baptized person.

Although spouses can overcome the problems arising from religious differences, the difficulties of mixed marriage should not be underestimated. The spouses will experience the historical separation of the Christian Churches in their own home.

When the spouse is not baptized, even greater problems can exist. There can be religious indifference or differences over the correct idea of marriages, and of the children's Christian education.

Duty Of the Catholic (1635-1637)

A Catholic marrying a baptized non-Catholic needs Church permission. (Canon 1124) A Catholic marrying a non-baptized person needs a dispensation for the marriage to be valid (Canon 1086). This permission and dispensation are granted only when both parties accept the essential goals of marriage and when the Catholic party assumes the obligation of baptizing and educating the children in the Catholic faith. (Canon 1125)

In some regions, churches have cooperated in preparing for a mixed marriage. This encourages respect for what separates them and helps couples to overcome religious differences.

Concerning a non-baptized spouse, Paul writes "The unbelieving husband is consecrated through his wife and the unbelieving wife is consecrated by her husband." (1Cor.7:14) Hopefully, the Catholic will have the joy of seeing his/her spouse freely convert to the Catholic Church.

EFFECTS OF MARRIAGE BOND

A Perpetual And Exclusive Bond (1638)
A valid marriage brings about a perpetual and exclusive bond between the spouses. In Christian marriage, the spouses are strengthened and consecrated by a special sacrament. (Canon 1134)

Never To Be Broken (1639-1640)
Their mutual consent is sealed by God himself and results in a institution which is confirmed by divine law and accepted in the eyes of society.

A marriage bond which is concluded and consummated by baptized spouses can never be dissolved. The spouses' consent and consummation forge an irrevocable covenant which even the Church cannot break.

Christ's Graces (1641-1642)
Because of their Christian state, spouses receive graces to perfect their love, to help them obtain holiness and to welcome and educate their children.

Christ encounters the spouses through the sacrament of Matrimony. He gives them the strength to begin again when they fail, to forgive each other, to be subject to one another and to enjoy a taste of the heavenly wedding feast. "How can I even express the happiness of a marriage joined by the Church. How wonderful the bond between two believers. Where the flesh is one, one also is the spirit." (Tertullian)

CONJUGAL LOVE

Three Requirements (1643)
Conjugal love involves the appeal of body and instinct, the power of feeling and affectivity, the aspirations of spirit and will. All of these aim at a union beyond the flesh, a union of heart and soul. This definitive mutual self-giving demands indissolubility, faithfulness and openness to children. In this way, natural conjugal love expresses Christian values.

No Longer Two (1644-1645)
This community of spouses embraces their entire lives for "they are no longer two, but one flesh" (Mt.19:6 and Gen.2:24). They must continually grow in self-giving. Christ confirms this human communion by the sacrament of Matrimony and deepens it by the Eucharist.

Polygamy (1645)
The unity of marriage is made clear when spouses have an equal personal dignity. Therefore, polygamy is contrary to exclusive and undivided conjugal love.

Fidelity and Indissolubility (1646-1648)
Conjugal love requires inviolable fidelity. Love is not an arrangement "until further notice." Marriage itself and the good of the children demand total fidelity.

This teaching is based upon God's fidelity to the Old Covenant and Christ's fidelity to his Church. This indissolubility receives a deeper meaning from the sacrament.

Because this seems so difficult, the spouses must hear the Good News of God's irrevocable love for them. They share in this love and witness to God's love by their own fidelity.

Separated But Still Married (1649)
Sometimes, for a variety of reasons, common life between the spouses is impossible. The Church permits the spouses to live apart (a physical separation). They are still husband and wife and are not free to remarry. If possible, they should reconcile. In either case, the Christian community must help them to live out their original indissoluble commitment.

New Civil Marriage (1650-1651)
Sometimes, spouses divorce and contract a new civil marriage. This violates Christ's clear words, "Whoever divorces his wife and marries another, commits adultery against her, and if she divorces her husband and marries another, she commits adultery." (Mk.10: 11-12) Since this situation objectively contradicts God's law, they cannot receive Eucharist. Reconciliation through Penance can be granted only if they live in complete continence (as brother and sister).

Many in this situation remain in the Church, practice their faith and bring up their children religiously. They must be encouraged by the parish not to see themselves as separated from the Church. They must persevere in prayer and bring up their children in the Catholic faith, each day imploring God's grace.

Open To Children (1652-1654)
Marriage, by its nature, has the goals of the procreation and education of children (the crowning glory of marriage). "Be fruitful and multiply." (Gen.1:28) Although having other goals, married love disposes the spouses in a special way to cooperate with the Creator to increase his family.

Parents are the first educators of their children, and must give them the fruits of a moral and supernatural life. Marriage and family are at the service of life.

Even spouses who cannot conceive can have a conjugal life filled with the fruitfulness of charity and sacrifice.

THE DOMESTIC CHURCH

The Home As The First Church (1655-1657)
From the beginning, the Church was formed from believers "and their whole household." New believers wanted their family to be saved. (Acts 18:8)

In our modern world (often hostile to religion), religious families are extremely important centers of living faith. They are "domestic churches" in which the parents are the first heralds of faith. (Second Vatican Council)

In the home, father, mother and children exercise their baptismal priesthood in a privileged way. The home is the first school of the Christian life where all learn love, repeated forgiveness and prayerful worship.

205

Single Persons (1658)

Single persons (often not married by force of circumstances) are close to Jesus' heart. Some, are without a human family. Christian families and the Church must open their doors to them. "The Church is a home and family for everyone." (Second Vatican Council)

In Brief – 1659 – 1666

Quotes to Remember

In creating man and woman, God himself established marriage with its own proper laws.

A marriage bond which is concluded and consummated by baptized spouses can never be dissolved.

Their mutual consent is sealed by God himself.

The Church permits the spouses to live apart (a physical separation) but they are not free to remarry.

The disorder in the relationship does not come from the nature of man and woman but from sin.

Virginity is the sign that our union with Christ takes precedence over any human bond.

25
Sacramentals and Christian Funerals (1667-1690)

Signs Resembling Sacraments (1667)
The Church herself has instituted <u>sacramentals</u>, (sacred signs resembling the sacraments) which signify spiritual effects obtained by the Church's intercession.

Sanctifying Persons, Places and Things 1668-1669)
The sacramentals sanctify certain ministries, certain circumstances and certain things used in daily life. They always include a prayer and a specific sign (such as the sign of the cross or sprinkling of holy water).

Because sacramentals come from the priesthood of the baptized (who are meant to be a blessing to all) lay people can preside at blessings unless they are reserved to the priest or bishop.

Preparing For Grace (1670)
Sacramentals do not confer grace (as sacraments do) but, they prepare for grace and dispose us to cooperate. Sacraments and sacramentals draw their power from Christ's resurrection.

Blessings (1671-1672)
The most important sacramentals are the blessings of persons, objects and places. These usually invoke Jesus' name with the sign of the cross.

Certain blessings have a lasting importance because they consecrate persons to God (abbots, virgins, religious profession, various ministries) or they reserve objects and places for liturgical use (dedication of Church or altar, blessing of holy oils and vessels).

Exorcism (1693)
Exorcism (of persons or objects) is the expulsion of demons or liberation from their possession by the spiritual authority given by

Jesus to his Church. The Baptismal ceremony contains a simple exorcism. A solemn (or major) exorcism must be done by a priest who has the bishop's permission. Before an exorcism takes place, it must be clear that the problems do not come from a psychological illness.

Popular Forms of Piety (1674-1675)

Catechesis must teach popular devotions and forms of piety by which Christians express their religious sense. These include the rosary, medals, stations of the cross, processions, pilgrimages, etc.

These expressions of piety should harmonize with the Church's liturgical life (which is far superior to these devotions).

An Answer To Problems (1676)

"This piety offers Christian wisdom as an answer to modern problems, creatively combining divine and human, Christ and Mary, body and spirit. This wisdom radically affirms the dignity of every person and can provide joy even in very difficult circumstances. This religious wisdom spontaneously senses when the gospel is served and when it is stifled by other interests." (Puebla 1979)

In Brief (1677 – 1679)

CHRISTIAN FUNERALS

The Life to Come (1680)

All the sacraments seek to lead the child of God into the kingdom. "I look for the resurrection of the dead, and the life of the world to come." (Nicene Creed)

From Sacraments to Eternal Life (1681-1683)

Christ's death and resurrection reveals the Christian meaning of death, namely, to be "away from the body and at home with the Lord." (1Cor.5:81)

A Christian's death inaugurates the end of his sacramental life and the beginning of the kingdom (even if final purification is needed before the nuptial banquet).

During life, Holy Mother Church carried the person sacramentally within her womb. At a funeral, the Church surrenders the baptized "into the Father's hands", with the hope of his rising to glory.

Celebration of Funerals (1684 –1685)

The funeral is neither a sacrament nor a sacramental for the person has already passed beyond all sacraments. The funeral expresses a communion with the deceased and a proclaiming of eternal life to those gathered.

The funeral rites express Christ's death and rising according to the traditions of each region (as with the color of the vestments).

Three Places of Celebration (1686-1690)

The Order of Christian Funerals envisions three different places of celebration (the home, the Church and the cemetery) and has four elements:

1. The community receives a word of greeting in faith which offers the Spirit's consolation and points beyond this world's prospective.
2. The liturgy of the word and homily need careful preparation because many might be present who rarely come to church. The homily should not be a eulogy but should illumine this mystery of death by Christ's light.
3. The Eucharistic Sacrifice expresses the Church's communion with the deceased, asks Christ to purify the person and helps the family to be one with the person who "has fallen asleep in the Lord."
4. In the final commendation, the Church gives her "last farewell to one of her members." "For even dead, we are not at all separated from one another, because we all run the same course and we will find one another again in the same place" (St. Simeon of Thessalonica).

Quotes to Remember

A Christian's death inaugurates the end of his sacramental life and the beginning of the kingdom.

PART THREE –
LIFE IN CHRIST
(1691 – 2550)

26
Dignity In Christ (1691-1748)

God's Greatest Work (1691-1692)

"Christian, recognize your dignity. Remember who is your head and of whose body you are a member. Never forget that you have been rescued from the power of darkness." (Pope St. Leo the Great)

The creeds confess God's great works (man's creation, redemption and sanctification). The sacraments communicate these gifts to man. Christians through Christ and the Spirit must live a life "worthy of the gospel of Christ." (Phil.1:27)

Called To Be Perfect (1693-1695)

Christians are invited to become "perfect as your heavenly Father is perfect." (Mt.5:48)

Because they are to be "dead to sin and alive to God in Christ Jesus" (Rom.6:11) they must become "imitators of God as beloved children." (Eph.5:1-2)

The Spirit teaches believers to "pray to the Father" (Eph.4:23) and to bring forth "the fruit of the Spirit" (Gal.5:22).

Church catechesis stresses the "two ways" (to life or to death) and the importance of moral decisions for our salvation. "There are two ways, the one of life, the other of death, but between the two, there is a great difference." (Didache)

The Seven Catechetical Needs (1696-1698)

There must be a catechesis:

1. of the Spirit – Who inspires, corrects and strengthens
2. of grace – which alone saves and bears fruit
3. of the beatitudes – which sum up Christ's way
4. of sin and forgiveness by which man acknowledges his sinfulness and learns of the possibility of forgiveness
5. of human virtues –which grasp the beauty of goodness
6. of Christian virtues – which follow the example of the saints
7. of the Ten Commandments – which give clear teaching
8. of the Church - in which the believer "shares spiritual goods"

All Catechesis must lead to Christ. Only in Christ, can the believer gain the promises. "I ask you to consider that our Lord Jesus Christ is your true Lord. All that is his is yours. You belong to him." (St. John Eudes) "For to me, to live is Christ." (Phil. 1:21)

Aspects of Man's Call (1699)

This section has three parts:

1. The vocation of man in the Spirit
2. A life of charity toward God and solidarity with man
3. Salvation

Man's Vocation (1700)

This first part has eight articles:

1. Man, the Image of God
2. Man's Call to Happiness
3. Man's Freedom
4. The Morality of Human Acts
5. The Morality of the Passions
6. Moral Conscience
7. The Virtues
8. Sin

MAN: THE IMAGE OF GOD

Nine Truths About Christ and Man (1701-1709

1. Only in Christ ("the image of the invisible God") can man understand himself and his exalted call. God's image in man has been restored by Christ.
2. When man is in communion with others, he is a likeness of the communion of the three divine persons.
3. Because man has an immortal soul, God has willed his existence for his own sake. From his conception, man is destined for eternal life.
4. By reason, man can understand that God created this world. By his free will, he can direct himself to his true good.
5. Because his soul has the power of intellect and free will, man has freedom, "an outstanding manifestation of God's image." (Second Vatican Council)
6. By his reason man can know that God wills him "to do what is good and to avoid what is evil." He must follow this law of his conscience.
7. Enticed by the Evil One, man misused this freedom. His nature is wounded by sin, inclined to evil and subject to error. "Man is divided in himself. As a result, his whole life shows itself to be a struggle between good and evil." (Second Vatican Council)
8. By his Passion, Christ delivered man from Satan and merited grace which restores what sin damaged.
9. By believing in Christ, a person becomes a son of God, capable of following Christ and gaining a perfection which blossoms into eternal glory.

In Brief 1710 – 1715

THE BEATITUDES

Blessed (1716)
Jesus calls us <u>blessed</u> if we:
1. are pure in spirit
2. mourn
3. are meek

4. hunger and thirst for righteousness
5. are merciful
6. are pure in heart
7. are peacemakers
8. are persecuted for righteousness
9. are reviled and persecuted for his sake

Paradoxical Blessings (1717)

In these blessings, Jesus goes beyond the promises made to Abraham (which were focused on territory) and bring us to the kingdom of heaven.

These sayings are paradoxes, promising hope amidst tribulations and proclaiming rewards already secured. These blessings have already begun for Mary and all the saints.

Goal of Man's Existence (1718-1719)

These blessings correspond to man's desire for perfect happiness. St. Augustine said "We all want to live happily." He also prayed "O God, my body draws life from my soul and my soul draws life from you." St. Thomas Aquinas wrote "God alone satisfies."

The goal of man's existence is nothing less than experiencing God's own happiness, a gift to every person and to the whole Church.

Entering the Kingdom (1720-1722)

The New Testament calls this happiness "the Kingdom of God", "the vision of God", "the joy of the Lord" and "God's rest." "For what other end do we have, if not to reach the kingdom which does not end?" (St. Augustine)

We are in this world to know, love and serve God so we can enter into Christ's glory with the Father and the Spirit.

This gift is "supernatural", going far beyond our intellect and being freely given by God. "He goes so far as to grant those who love him the privilege of seeing him. For what is impossible for man is possible for God." (St. Irenaeus)

Confronted With Moral Choices (1723-1724)

These promised blessings confront us with decisive moral choices and invite us to purify ourselves. They teach us that true riches cannot be found in any human achievement. "All bow down before wealth and measure happiness by wealth. Wealth is one idol of the day and notoriety is a second. Notoriety may be called newspaper fame." (John Cardinal Newman)

The Ten Commandments, the Sermon on the Mount and Church teaching describe the path to the kingdom which we must walk each day.

In Brief - 1725 - 1729

MAN'S FREEDOM

Free To Choose (1730)

Man is created by God as a human person who can begin and control his own actions. He is meant to seek God and gain perfection by cleaving to him.

Good or Evil (1731-1733)

By freedom (rooted in his intellect and will) man has the power to act or not to act. He can shape his own life, mature in goodness and gain a perfection which is rooted in God.

Until man attains God, he can choose to do good or evil, to grow in perfection or to sin. Because human acts are free, they are worthy of praise or blame.

By constantly doing good man grows in freedom. Doing evil leads man into a "slavery of sin." (Rom.6:17)

Responsible For Acts (1734-1735)

A person is responsible for his voluntary acts. By progress in virtue, in knowledge of good and in self-discipline, he gains greater mastery. Man's responsibility and imputability can be lessened or nullified by ignorance, fear, habits or inordinate attachments or other factors.

God's Confrontations (1736-1737)

God confronted Eve, "What is this that you have done?" (Gen.3:13) He also confronted Cain, "What have you done?" (Gen.4:10) A person is responsible for any directly willed act. Also, an action can be indirectly voluntary (from negligence or ignorance).

214

A person is not responsible for an evil act if he did not will it and did not intend it as a means to an end, for example, a person might incur death while trying to help another. A person is responsible if they could have avoided the evil (as a drunk driver killing someone).

Respecting Freedom (1738)
Every human person must recognize the right of freedom in others. Exercising freedom (especially in moral or religious matters) is an inalienable right of the human person. This must be protected by civil authorities within the limits of public order.

Abuse of Freedom (1739-1740)
Human freedom refused God's love and became a slave to sin. The first sin has led to so many others. Human history attests that the problems of man come from man's abuse of freedom.

Freedom does not give man the right to say and do everything, because man's purpose is not his own earthly satisfaction. Man's blindness and injustice destroy the cultural conditions needed for freedom. Deviating from the moral law violates man's own freedom and imprisons him within himself.

Grace and Freedom (1741-1742)
"For freedom, Christ has set us free" (Gal.5:1) and saved us from sin's power. "Where the Spirit of the Lord is, there is freedom." (1Cor.17)

Christ's grace is not a rival to man's freedom. The person grows in inner freedom by being docile to God's Spirit. "Take away from us all that is harmful so we may freely accomplish your will." (Prayer – 32nd Sunday)

In Brief - 1743 - 1748

Quotes to Remember

The goal of man's existence is to experience God's own happiness.

215

27
Morality (1749-1876)

"Father of His Acts" (1749 - 1750)

Whenever man deliberately chooses, he is the "father of his acts." These freely chosen acts can be morally evaluated as good or evil.

Three Sources (1750

The three sources of morality:
1. the object chosen
2. the person's purpose
3. the circumstances of the act

The Object Chosen (1751)

The object directly chosen by the will determines the basic morality (good or bad). The person's intellect sees this as according to moral standards (good) or not according to moral standards (evil).

The Intention (1752-1753)

The person also has an intention which determines the act's morality. An intention can guide many acts or even a whole lifetime (as loving God). One act can have a multiplicity of intentions. (Doing a favor to help someone and also to receive a favor in return).

However, a good intention can never turn an evil act into a good one. A good purpose cannot justify evil means. However, an evil intention can make a good act into an evil one (such as giving alms to gain praise).

The Circumstances (1754)

Only the act and the intention make an act good or bad. The circumstances can increase or diminish the goodness or evil. For example, stealing a large amount of money increases the evil, while fear of harm can lessen a person's responsibility. Circumstances can never make an evil act into a good one.

216

Determining Good and Evil Acts (1755-1756)

An act is good when the object, the intention and the circumstances are all good. A good act is vitiated by an evil intention (praying in order to be seen as good). Some acts are evil in themselves (as fornication) and are always wrong to choose.

Therefore, the person's intention and the circumstances (such as pressure or duress) cannot change a morally evil act (such as murder, blasphemy, adultery) into a morally good act. We cannot do evil so good will come from it.

In Brief 1757 - 1761

MORALITY OF THE PASSIONS

Their Help (1762)

The passions or feelings can help the person in his duty to choose.

Passageway From Senses to Mind (1763-1764)

Feelings (passions) are movements of the sensitive appetite. These lead us to act or not to act when experiencing a perceived good or evil.

Emotions are a passageway connecting man's life of the senses with his life of the mind. Jesus called this source of human emotions "the heart." (Mk.7:21)

Loving Good or Evil (1765-1766)

Love (the most fundamental emotion) is attracted by the good causes hope and finds pleasure in possessing its object. In contrast, seeing evil causes hatred, aversion and fear. This leads to sadness or to anger (to remove the evil).

Passions (feelings) are evil if they love what is evil and they are good if they love what is good.

Passions To Good and Evil (1767-1768)

Passions in themselves are neither good or evil. They become good or evil as they lead the reason and the will to make a choice. Passions become voluntary when the will commands them or places no obstacle to them. "Moral goodness exists when passions are governed by reason." (St. Thomas Aquinas)

Strong feelings do not decide morality. They are only the inexhaustible reservoir of images and affections. Feelings are good when contributing to good acts. They are evil when leading to evil acts. These feelings can be lifted up by virtues or perverted by vices.

The Holy Spirit And Feeling (1769-1770)
The Holy Spirit mobilizes the whole human person with his sorrows and fears. In the garden, Christ made his human feelings lead to the highest charity (his own death).

Man must choose the good with his will and with his sensitive desires. "My heart and flesh sing for joy to the living God." (Ps.84:2)

In Brief - 1771 - 1775

MORAL CONSCIENCE

An Inner Law (1776)
Deep within his conscience, man discovers a law which he must obey, namely to do good and to avoid evil. In his conscience (man's most secret core) he is alone with God whose voice echoes within man.

Conscience – Judge of Individual Acts (1777-1779)
Moral conscience urges a person to do good and avoid evil. It even judges his particular choices (past, present and future) and shows God's authority. The prudent man hears God speaking in his commandments.

By conscience, the person's reason judges the morality of his actions (past, present or future). In this judgment, man sees God's law. "Conscience is a messenger of him who speaks to us behind a veil and teaches us by his representatives. Conscience is the aboriginal Vicar of Christ." (John Cardinal Newman)

Every person must have sufficient interior awareness so he can hear and follow his conscience. "Turn inward, brethren, and in everything you do, see God as your witness." (St. Augustine)

An Upright Conscience Assumes Responsibility (1780-1782)

Human dignity requires an upright conscience which knows moral principles and applies them in each circumstance. Truth is recognized by prudent judgments. Whoever follows his conscience is indeed prudent.

By conscience, a person assumes responsibility. Even in evil deeds, conscience remains an inner witness to truth that the choice was evil. This true judgment makes clear that the person must seek forgiveness and choose good in the future. "Whenever our hearts condemn us, we reassure ourselves that God is greater than our hearts and he knows everything." (1Jn.3:19-20)

Man has a right to make his own moral decisions. He cannot be forced to act contrary to his conscience, nor be prevented from acting according to his conscience, (especially in religious matters).

Man's Duty – To Have A Right Conscience (1783-1785)

The person has a duty to have a true conscience which is formed by reason and seeks to know God's will. Only the educating of conscience can overcome negative influences and temptations.

This lifelong task begins with awakening the child to know and practice God's law. A prudent education teaches virtues, cures selfishness and guarantees peace of heart.

The Word of God guides this education. Man must examine his conscience before the cross, seek the advice of others and learn the Church's authoritative teaching.

Difficulties in Judging (1786-1789)

Conscience can make a right judgment (in accord with God's law and reason) or an erroneous judgment, (not in accord).

In some situations, moral judgments are difficult. However, in every case, the person must seek God's will in accord with his law.

The person must interpret the data, assisted by his own prudence, competent advice, and the help of the Holy Spirit.

In all cases, evil can never be done so good can result. "Whatever you wish that men would do to you, do so to them." (Mt.7:12) "Do nothing that makes your brother stumble." (Rom.14:21)

Sources of Errors in Judgment (1790-1792)

Although a person must always obey the certain judgments of his conscience, he might be in ignorance and make erroneous judgments.

Sometimes, the person is to blame for having an erroneous conscience because he took no effort to discover the truth. In this case, he is responsible for the evil he commits.

There are several sources of these errors in judgment – ignorance of Christ and of his Gospel, bad example from others, enslavement to passions, lack of conversion of heart, and rejection of the Church's teaching.

Unable to Overcome (1793-1794)

Sometimes, the person is not responsible for his erroneous judgment because he cannot overcome the obstacles to truth. This is called "invincible ignorance." Although evil is present, the person is not blameworthy. He should work to correct his errors.

Conscience must be enlightened by faith so that persons and groups will turn aside from blind choices.

In Brief 1795 – 1802

THE VIRTUES

Always Strong To the Good (1803)

Paul asks the Philippians to see "all that is true, honorable, just, pure, lovely and gracious. (Phil.4:8)

Virtue is a firm and habitual disposition, by which a person strives firmly and regularly toward the good with all of his powers. "The goal of a virtuous life is to become like God." (St. Gregory of Nyssa)

The Human Moral Virtues (1804)

Human virtues are firm, stable attitudes and dispositions which order the passions and guide conduct. They bring about self-mastery and joy. The moral virtues are acquired by human effort and dispose the person to God's love.

The Four Cardinal Virtues (1805 – 1809)

Scripture says that wisdom "teaches temperance and prudence, justice and fortitude." (Wis.8:7) These are the four cardinal virtues (meaning "hinge") around which the other virtues are grouped.

Prudence disposes man's practical reason to see what is good and to choose the right means. Prudence is "right reason in action" (St. Thomas Aquinas) guiding the person's judgment. By prudence, the person correctly applies moral teachings to individual cases without error and removes all doubts about good and evil.

Justice leads the person to give all that is due to God (the virtue of religion) and to others. Justice respects people's rights and establishes harmony. Scripture praises the conduct of the "Just Man". "You shall not be partial to the poor, nor defer to the rich." (Lev.19:15)

Fortitude makes the person firm in face of difficulties and constant in pursuing good. It helps man to resist temptations, to overcome obstacles, to face fear and even to suffer persecution. "In the world you have tribulation; but be of good cheer, I have overcome the world." (Jn.16:33)

Temperance moderates the powerful attraction of pleasures, guarantees the will's control over instincts, keeps desires honorable and directs the passions to good. "Do not follow your base desires but restrain your appetites." (Sir.18:30) Believers should "live sober, upright and godly lives." (Titus 2:12)

"Love is kept uncorrupted by temperance, undisturbed by fortitude, obedient to God by justice and discerning by prudence. (St. Augustine)

The Virtues Need Grace (1810-1811)

Divine grace elevates those human virtues which have been formed by repeated deliberate acts.

Because man is wounded by sin, he cannot easily maintain a moral balance. Through the sacraments and the help of the Holy Spirit, Christ offers the grace needed to persevere.

The Three Theological Virtues (1812-1813)

The three theological virtues (faith, hope and charity) allow man to share in God's nature. These virtues relate directly to God who directly infuses these three virtues into the soul where they make the believers capable of living as God's children and meriting eternal life.

Believing What God Revealed (1814-1816)

By faith, we believe in God, in all that he has revealed, and in all that the Church proposes for our belief. Faith leads to a total committal. "The righteous shall live by faith" (Rom.1:17).

When faith is deprived of hope and love, it does not unite the believer to Christ nor make him a living member of the body. "Faith apart from works is dead." (Jas.2:26)

Christ's disciple must spread the faith to others, even if this brings about persecution. Jesus said, "Whoever acknowledge me before men, I also will acknowledge before my Father" and "Whoever denies me before men, I will deny before my Father." (Mt.10:43-33)

Hoping and Searching For the Kingdom (1817-1818)

By hope, we seek heaven, place our trust in Christ's promises, and rely on the Holy Spirit. We must "hold fast to our confession of hope." (Heb.10:23) Through the Spirit, we have "become heirs in hope of eternal life." (Titus 3:6-7)

Into everyone's heart, God has placed a search for happiness. Hope responds to this desire. It sustains man, frees him from discouragement, preserves him from selfishness and leads to happiness on earth and in heaven.

Abraham's Hope (1819)

Israel's hope was modeled upon Abraham who trusted in God's promise even when asked to sacrifice Isaac. "Hoping against hope, he believed, and thus became the father of many nations." (Rom.4:18)

Our Hope Of Heaven Through Jesus (1820-1821)

Jesus unfolded Christian hope in the beatitudes, proclaiming that those who suffer trials on earth are blessed in heaven. This hope "does not disappoint" (Rom.5:5) because Jesus has gone ahead "as a forerunner on our behalf." (Heb.6:19-20)

Therefore, we can hope to gain heaven and to persevere "to the end." (Mt.10:22) The Church prays for "all men to be saved" (1Tim. 2:4) and she awaits union with Christ, the Bridegroom. "Hope, O my soul, hope. Watch carefully. Dream that the more you struggle, the more you will rejoice one day with your Beloved." (St. Teresa of Avila)

Loving God and Neighbor (1822-1824)

By charity, we love God for his own sake and our neighbor as ourselves for the love of God.

Jesus loved us "to the end.". (Jn.13:1) He told his disciples to "love one another as I have loved you." (Jn.15:9,12)

Charity keeps the commandments of God and of Christ, "If you keep my commandments, you will abide in my love." (Jn.15:9-10)

Paul's Description (1825-1826)

Christ demands that we love everyone, especially our enemies, our neighbors and the poor. St. Paul says that love is patient and kind, believing, helping and enduring all things. Love is not jealous, boastful, arrogant, rude, irritable or resentful.

Without charity, "I am nothing" and "I gain nothing." "So faith hope and charity abide, these three. But the greatest of these is charity." (1Cor.13:1-13)

Love Animates the Moral Life (1827-1829)

Charity binds all virtues "together in perfect harmony (Col.3:14) and gives them order. Charity purifies and raises human love to the perfection of God's love.

When charity animates his moral life, the Christian is free from servile fear and lives as a son responding to God who "first loved us." (1Jn.4:19) "If we obey out of love for him who commands, we are in the position of his children." (St. Augustine)

Charity is benevolent, disinterested and generous, bringing forth friendship and communion. "Love is the goal. Once we reach it, we shall find rest."(St. Augustine)

GIFTS AND FRUITS OF THE SPIRIT

Gifts Which Complete the Virtues (1830-1832)

The seven gifts of the Spirit (wisdom, understanding, counsel, fortitude, knowledge, piety, and fear of the Lord) belong to Christ's fullness. They complete the virtues and make us ready to obey divine inspirations. "For all who are led by the Spirit of God are sons of God." (Rom.8:14)

By the twelve fruits of the Spirit, (charity, joy, peace, patience, kindness, goodness, generosity, gentleness,, faithfulness, modesty, self-control and chastity) the Spirit forms us for eternal glory.

In Brief 1833 – 1845

SIN AND MERCY

Revealing His Mercy (1846)

The gospel reveals God's mercy to us in Christ. Jesus' name means that "he will save his people from their sins." (Mt.1:21)

Receiving His Mercy (1847-1848)

"God created us without us, but he will not save us without us" (St. Augustine) To receive God's mercy, we must admit our sinfulness. "If we say we have no sin, we deceive ourselves. If we confess our sins, he ... will forgive our sins." (1Jn.1:8-9)

God's grace is like a physician probing our wounds. Sin must be uncovered before it is forgiven. "Conversion includes an interior judgment of conscience which contains a double gift. First, the truth of conscience and secondly a gift of the certainty of redemption." (Pope John Paul II)

Defining Sin (1849-1850)

Sin offends reason, fails in love for God and neighbor, wounds man's nature and injures human solidarity. Sin is "an utterance, a deed, or a desire contrary to the eternal law." (St. Augustine)

Sin is disobedience and revolt, "love of oneself even to contempt of God." (St. Augustine) This proud self-exaltation is totally opposed to Jesus' obedience which gains our salvation.

Sin Manifested in Christ's Passion (1851)

Sin manifested itself clearly in Pilate's cowardice, the soldiers' cruelty, the people's hatred, Judas' betrayal, Peter's denial and the disciples' flight. However in that hour of darkness, Christ's sacrifice secretly became the source of the forgiveness of sins.

Works of the Flesh (1852)

Paul calls sin "works of the flesh" (fornication, impurity, licentiousness, idolatry, sorcery, enmity, strife, jealousy, factions, envy, drunkenness, carousing) and says that they exclude from the kingdom of God. (Gal.5:19-21)

Sin of Various Kinds (1853)

Sins are defined according to the virtues they oppose or the commandments which they violate. Sins are committed against God, neighbor or oneself. They are spiritual or carnal; in thought, word, deed or omission. All sin comes "out of the heart and defiles a man." (Mt. 15: 19-20)

MORTAL AND VENIAL

Distinguishing Mortal and Venial Sins (1854-1855)

The distinction between mortal and venial sins is evident from Scripture, is part of the Church's tradition and is corroborated by experience.

By mortal sin (a grave violation of God's law) man destroys charity, turns away from God, and chooses an inferior good. Venial sin offends charity but allows it to continue in the soul.

Explaining Mortal Sin (1856)

Mortal sin, because it attacks charity, requires God's mercy and a conversion of heart. This is normally accomplished in the sacrament of reconciliation. When the will chooses something which is incompatible with love for God (such as blasphemy) or against love for neighbor (homicide or adultery) the sin is mortal.

"When the will is set upon a disorder not totally opposed to charity (as thoughtlessness) such sins are venial." (St. Thomas Aquinas)

Three Conditions (1857)
A mortal sin requires three conditions:
1. the object is grave matter
2. it is committed with full knowledge
3. it is done with deliberate consent

Grave Matter (1858)
Grave matter is specified by the Ten Commandments. Jesus said, "Do not kill. Do not commit adultery. Do not steal. Do not bear false witness. Do not defraud. Honor your father and your mother." (Mk.10:19) Some sins are more grave than others. Murder is greater than thefts. Violence against parents is greater than against a stranger.

Knowledge and Consent (1859 1860)
Mortal sin requires full knowledge and complete consent. It presupposes that the person knows that the act is sinful and is opposed to God's law. It also requires a deliberate consent which is a personal choice. Feigned ignorance or hardness of heart increase the voluntariness.

Unintentional ignorance can diminish or remove grave imputability. However, no one is ignorant of the moral law written on the heart. Many factors (feelings, passions, external pressure, emotional disorders) can also diminish personal freedom. Sins of malice (a deliberate choice of evil) are the greatest.

Need For Repentance (1861)
Being free, man is capable of committing mortal sin which deprives him of sanctifying grace. This can exclude him from God's kingdom forever if he does not repent and seek God's forgiveness. When a person chooses mortal sin and refuses to turn back, he will suffer eternal death in hell.

Venial Sins (1862-1863)

A person commits a venial sin in two cases:
1. when he does not observe God's law in a less serious matter
2. when he did not have full knowledge or give full consent in a grave matter

Venial sins show disordered affections and impede the person's progress in virtue. If deliberate and unrepented, they dispose the person to mortal sins. However "Venial sin does not deprive the sinner of sanctifying grace or friendship with God" (Pope John Paul II). "When he is in the flesh, man cannot help but have at least some light sins. However, a number of light objects makes a great mass. What then is our hope? Above all, confession." (St. Augustine)

Blasphemy Against the Holy Spirit (1864)

Jesus said that "Whoever blasphemes against the Holy Spirit never has forgiveness." (Mk.3:29) This deliberate refusal to repent and receive God's mercy, rejects the Spirit's forgiveness. Such hardness can lead to final impenitence and to eternal loss.

PROLIFERATION OF SINS

Effects Of Repeated Sins (1865)

Within the person, repetition of sin brings about a proclivity to sin, resulting in perverse inclinations and erroneous judgments. Sin reinforces itself and destroys any moral roots.

The Seven Capital Sins (1866)

Some sins are called "capital" (according to St. John Cassian and St. Gregory) because they engender other sins. The seven capital sins are pride, avarice, envy, wrath, lust, gluttony and sloth.

Sins That Cry To Heaven (1867)

These sins include the blood of Abel (murder), the sin of the Sodomites (sodomy), the cry of the oppressed, the widow or the orphan, and the injustice to a wage earner.

Accomplices in Sin (1868-1869)

We have a duty not cooperate in the sins of others. Therefore, we must avoid any direct participating in, or ordering sinful acts. Also, we cannot approve sinful acts by allowing them or by protecting evildoers.

Men can become accomplices in sin and cause injustice to reign by bringing about "social sins." These sins establish sinful structures and institutions which are against God's goodness and cause people to sin.

In Brief - 1870 – 1876

Quotes to Remember

Man is "the father of his own acts".

....

Conscience is man's most secret core,
where he is alone with God.

....

God created us without us, but he will not save
us without us. (St. Augustine)

....

Sin is disobedience and revolt.

....

We must not cooperate in the sins of others.

....

Every person must have an interior awareness
to hear and follow his conscience.

....

The goal of a virtuous life is to become like God.
(St. Gregory of Nyssa)

....

28
The Human Community (1877-1948))

Individual Persons and Human Community (1877)
God's call to the human race to show forth his image is both personal (to the individual) and global (to the human community).

THE PERSON AND SOCIETY

Life In Society (1878-1881)
The communion of the three Divine Persons and the fraternity among men bear a definite resemblance.   Love of neighbor is inseparable from love of God.

Living in society is a requirement for the human person.   In society, he develops his potential in mutual exchange and service of others.

Society groups persons together organically.   It is an assembly (visible and spiritual).   Within society, man can use his talents and develop their fruits.   Man is an "heir" of society and he must be loyal to his community and to authority.

Although each community has its own goal, man must be the "subject and the goal of all social institutions." (Pope John XXIII)

Family and State Communities (1882)
The family and the state are unique communities.   The state must encourage <u>voluntary associations</u> which relate to social and economic goals.   Human beings naturally experience "socialization", the associating with one another to gain goals beyond the individual's capacity.

The State and Subsidiarity (1883-1885)
Socialization presents the danger of excessive intervention by the state. States must practice <u>subsidiarity</u>, not interfering in a community's inner life, but supporting its activities.

God entrusts certain functions to his creatures and governs the world with great regard for human freedom.   Government, therefore, should imitate God and behave as ministers of divine providence.

This principle of subsidiarity opposes all forms of collectivism, limits state interventions, aims at harmonious relationships between persons and societies, and establishes international order.

Hierarchy of Value (1886-1887)

Society must have a just hierarchy of values, subordinating the physical dimensions to the spiritual aspects. "Human society must primarily be considered something spiritual, in which men eagerly strive to make their own the spiritual achievements of others." (Pope John XXIII)

A false inversion takes place when society "sees a person only as a 'means' and creates unjust structures which make Christian living almost impossible." (Pope Pius XII)

Man – Called to Conversion (1888-1889)

Society must appeal to man's inner conversion to obtain needed social changes. This call for conversion imposes the obligation to bring needed remedies to those living conditions which are inducements to sin.

Man, by God's grace, can learn to avoid both the cowardice which gives in to evil and the violence which would make the evil even worse.

In Brief - 1890 - 1896

Need For Authority (1897-1898)

"A well-ordered society needs people who have legitimate authority to preserve society's institutions and to care for the good of all." (Pope John XXIII)

Authority means the power to make laws, give order and expect obedience. Foundations for authority lie in human nature itself because the state is necessary for unity and for the common good.

Subject To Authority (1899-1900)

"Let every person be subject to the governing authorities for there is no authority except from God. Those that exist have been instituted by God and those who resist authority will incur judgment." (Rom 13:1-2)

Obedience requires that respect and due honor be given to those in authority. Pope St. Clement asked God's favor upon authority so "they may exercise without offense the sovereignty that you have given them."

Diverse Political Structures (1901)

Authority comes from God but the choice of political structures and leaders come from the "free decision of the citizens." (Second Vatican Council) A diversity of governmental regimes is morally acceptable. However, governments which act contrary to the natural law, the public order or the fundamental rights of persons cannot achieve the common good.

Legitimate Authority (1902-1904)

Because authority does not contain its own moral legitimacy, governments must not be despotic. "Every human law has the character of law if it accords with right reason . If it falls short of right reason, it is an unjust law and thus a "kind of violence." (St. Thomas Aquinas)

Authority acts legitimately when it seeks the common good and uses moral means. Unjust laws and immoral means do not bind in conscience. In these cases "authority breaks down and results in shameful abuse." (Pope John XXIII)

Each power should be balanced by other powers. By this "rule of law", the will of any man will not be sovereign.

Good of Person and Society (1905)

The good of the person and the good of the society (always defined in reference to the human person) are necessarily related. "Do not live entirely isolated but gather together to seek the common good." (Letter of Barnabas)

Three Elements of Common Good (1906-1910)

The common good is the sum total of those social conditions which allow groups and persons to gain their goals more easily. The common good requires three elements:

1. Respect for the person - Public authorities must respect the fundamental and inalienable rights of the human person. Government must guarantee the right of persons to act in accordance with their conscience.

231

2. Social well-being - Authority must promote the development of the person and of the group. Authority must arbitrate between various particular interests and make the necessities for human life (food, clothing, establishing a family, etc.) accessible to all.
3. Peace - Authority must establish the peace of a just order by morally acceptable means. This is the basis for legitimate personal and collective defense.

In the political community the common good is best realized. The state must promote the good of its citizens and of intermediate bodies.

Community of Nations (1911-1912)

Increasing human interdependence is bringing about a unity of the human family. This implies a universal common good. Therefore, the community of nations must organize so that the basic needs of all (food, education, etc.) can be met and special situations (such as refugees and immigrants) can be alleviated.

The common good must always focus on persons. "The order of things must be subordinate to the order of persons." (Second Vatican Council)

PERSONAL RESPONSIBILITY

Duty To Participate (1913-1915)

The dignity of the human person requires that everyone can participate in society according to their role. This demands:
1. that the individual assume personal responsibility for his family, his work and the good of others
2. that citizens participate in public life.

We praise those nations which permit the largest possible participation of their citizens in genuine political freedom.

Conversion (1916)

This full participation demands renewed conversion of social partners. Fraud and other subterfuges which evade the law are incompatible with justice. Also needed are institutions to improve human life.

Inspiration (1917)

Those in authority must inspire confidence in the people so they are willing to serve others. "Humanity is in the hands of those who are capable of providing people with reason for life and optimism." (Second Vatican Council)

In Brief - 1918 - 1927

SOCIAL JUSTICE

Ensuring Human Rights (1928-1930)

Society must ensure social justice, the conditions that allow individuals and associations to gain what is their due.

Social justice demands respect for the dignity of the person. "What is at stake is the dignity of the human person." (Pope John Paul II)

Society must respect the person's inalienable rights (which existed before society and are the moral basis for society's authority). "By unjust laws, the state undermines its own legitimacy." (Pope John XXIII) The Church reminds men of their rights but distinguishes these rights from unwarranted claims.

Respecting Other's Rights (1931-1933)

Everyone should look upon his neighbor as "another self". Laws cannot do away with all the fears, prejudices and selfishness which destroy society. Such behavior will end only through charity which sees others as neighbors.

Being a "neighbor" is especially urgent toward the disadvantaged. "As you did it to one of the least of these my brethren, you did it to me." (Mt. 25:40)

This commandment of love extends to those who think differently from us and even to our enemies. The liberation of the Gospel is incompatible with hatred for an enemy (even though we truly hate the evil he does).

Removing Discrimination (1934-1935)

All men have the same nature, the same origin and an equal dignity. All are redeemed by Christ's sacrifice and are called to heavenly glory.

Equality among men rests upon the person's dignity and rights. "Every form of discrimination must be eradicated as incompatible with God's design." (Second Vatican Council)

Unequal Distribution (1936-1937)

At birth man does not have all he needs for full development. Therefore, he needs others. However, differences appear in physical and mental abilities, wealth, etc. These are not equally distributed.

This unequal distribution is part of God's plan, so that man can share his blessings with those in need. These differences actually oblige persons to practice generosity. Jesus said to St. Catherine of Siena, "I have not given everything to one single person, so that you are constrained to practice charity towards one another. I have willed that one should need another."

Sinful Inequalities (1938)

Unfortunately, there are also "sinful inequalities" which affect millions and are open contradictions to Jesus' Gospel. "We must strive for fairer conditions because the social disparity is a human scandal which militates against justice, equity and peace. (Second Vatican Council)

Need For Solidarity (1939)

Human solidarity (friendship) is demanded by human and Christian brotherhood. "Disregard for human solidarity is widespread . Yet, this law of solidarity was sealed by the sacrifice of redemption offered by Christ." (Pope Pius XII)

Requirements of Solidarity (1940-1942)

Solidarity requires a just distribution of goods, remuneration for work, a just social order, and tensions resolved by negotiations.

There must be solidarity among the poor themselves, between rich and poor, among workers, between workers and employers, and between people and nations. World peace depends on this.

Solidarity also extends to spiritual goods (which always leads to temporal development). "Seek first his kingdom and his righteousness, and all these things shall be yours as well." (Mt.6:33) "For two thousand years in the Church, this sentiment has led to the heroic charity which has created social conditions worthy of man." (Pope Pius XII)

In Brief - 1943 – 1948

Quotes to Remember

All men have the same origin, the same nature and an equal dignity. All are redeemed and called to heavenly glory.

....

Man must be the "subject and goal of all social institutions". (Pope John XXIII)

....

An inversion takes place when society only sees man as a "means" (Pope Pius XII)

....

Authority comes from God but the choice of political structures comes from a "free decision of the citizens". (Second Vatican Council)

....

There are "sinful inequalities" which affect millions and are contradictions to the Gospel.

....

Authority acts legitimately when it seeks the common good and uses moral means.

....

The community of nations must organize so the basic needs of all can be met.

....

29
Law, Grace and the Church (1949-2051)

Saved By God's Law (1949)
Although called to heaven, man is wounded and needs to be saved by God's law that guides him and by God's grace that sustains him.

THE MORAL LAW

Law – God's Instructions (1950-1951)
The moral law is God's fatherly instruction, showing the rules that lead to heaven and the evils which lead away from God.

Laws are rules of conduct given by competent authority for the common good. God's moral law presupposes a rational order of nature by which creatures can gain their final goal. All law finds its truth in God's eternal law and is established by reason participating in God's loving care.

"Among all the animals, only man was worthy to receive a law from God to govern his conduct by using his freedom and will." (Tertullian)

Expressions Of God's Law (1952-1953)
There are various expressions of moral law (God's eternal law, natural law, law revealed in the Old Testament, the law of the Gospel, Church law and civil law).

The moral law finds its fullness in Christ. "For Christ is the end of the law, that everyone who has faith may be justified." (Rom. 10:4)

A Law Engraved On Man's Heart (1954)
Man participates in the wisdom of God and in the goodness of God. By the natural law, man has the moral sense to discern good and evil.

"The natural law is engraved in the soul of every man, because human reason tells him to do good and avoid evil. It has force because it is the voice of a higher reason to which our spirit must submit." (Pope Leo XIII)

Expressed In The Ten Commandments (1955)

This "divine and natural" law and is expressed in the Ten Commandments. The law is "natural" because reason (which decrees it) belongs to human nature. "These rules are written in the book of that light which we call truth and are imprinted on the heart of man as a seal upon wax." (St. Augustine) "Natural law is the light of understanding placed in us by God through which we know what we must do and what we must avoid." (St. Augustine)

Over All Men (1956)

This natural law is universal, and its authority extends to every man, determining the basis for his rights and duties. "This true law is diffused among all men, is immutable and eternal. To replace it with a contrary law is a sacrilege." (Cicero)

Immutable (1957-1958)

The application of this law varies greatly (because it considers many different conditions). Yet, even amid diversity of cultures, the natural law bonds men together and imposes common principles.

Even amid the flux of ideas, this law is immutable and permanent throughout history, with rules which remain substantially valid. Even when rejected, the law is not destroyed but rises again in individuals and societies. "This is the law that iniquity itself does not efface." (St. Augustine)

Basis Of Society (1959)

Upon this natural law, man can build moral rules and the human community can establish a moral foundation. Natural law is the basis for that civil law which draws conclusions from its principles and creates legal structures.

THE OLD AND NEW LAW

A Need For Revelation (1960)

The natural law precepts are not easily perceived by everyone. Therefore, man needs God's revelation to know these truths "firmly and with no mixture of error." (Pius XII) Natural law is God's preparation for revealed law.

Law Revealed To Israel (1961-1962)

In preparing for Christ, God chose Israel and revealed his law. This Law of Moses authenticates many truths which can also be known by reason.

The Old Law (summed up in the Ten Commandments) is the first stage of revealed law and is the foundation for man's vocation. This light is offered to everyone's conscience to make God's ways known and to protect men from evil. "God wrote on the tables of the Law what men did not read in their hearts." (St. Augustine)

Imperfect – Yet Preparing For the Gospel (1963-1964)

This Law is holy but imperfect and does not provide the strength to keep it. It is, therefore, a "law of bondage." This Law "discloses sin" (concupiscence in the human heart). It is the first stage, disposing all (Jews and Christians) for conversion.

The Old Law prepares for the Gospel. It is a "prophecy of things to come" (St. Irenaeus), prophesying the full liberation from sin in Christ. The Law is completed by the Wisdom books and the prophets. Although the Old Law prescribed charity, it did not give the Holy Spirit. "Some under the Old Covenant possessed the grace of the Holy Spirit and longed for the promises of the New Law. Conversely, there exist carnal men under the New Covenant for whom only fear incites them to virtue." (St. Thomas Aquinas)

A New Law Given By the Spirit (1965-1966)

The Law of the Gospel (expressed by Christ in the Sermon on the Mount) perfects divine law (natural and revealed). Christ's Law is a work of the Spirit. "I will put my laws into their minds and write them on their hearts. (Jer.31: 31-34)

The New Law teaches us through the Sermon on the Mount and uses sacraments to give us the needed grace. "If anyone should meditate on the sermon on the mount, he will doubtless find there the perfect way of the Christian life." (St. Augustine)

Surpassing But Not Abolishing (1967-1968)

The New Law surpasses the Old Law. Being addressed to the poor and the afflicted, the New Law marks out the kingdom's surprising ways.

The New Law does not abolish or devalue the Old Law. It releases its hidden potential and reveals its divine and human truths. It reforms the heart of man (where he chooses good or evil) and imitates the heavenly Father by forgiveness and prayer for enemies.

Practices Of the New Law (1969-1971)

The New Law wants almsgiving, prayer and fasting directed to the "Father who sees in secret."

The Gospel Law (summed up in the new commandment to love one another as Jesus has loved us) demands a decision to put Christ's words into practice.

The New Testament also contains moral teachings which have apostolic authority. (Romans C. 12-15; 1Cor.C12-13, Colossians C3-4; Ephesians C4-5, etc.) This catechism uses the light of Christ and of the Church to guide all men in questions of conscience.

Many New Names (1972)

The New Law has many names:
1. Law of love – We act from the Spirit of love not of fear.
2. Law of grace – We act from the strength of grace.
3. Law of freedom – We act in freedom. We are friends of Christ, children of God and heirs of the kingdom.

Precepts And Counsels (1973-1974)

The New Law contains both precepts and evangelical counsels (distinguished by their relation to charity). Precepts remove what is incompatible with charity. Counsels remove what hinders the development of charity.

Living by the evangelical counsels means that the person's charity is never satisfied. These counsels point out more direct ways to love God and neighbor. "God does not want each person to keep all the counsels but only those appropriate to their diverse state as charity requires. (St. Francis de Sales)

In Brief - 1975 – 1986

Explaining Justification (1987-1988)

Justification cleanses from sin and communicates God's righteousness through faith in Christ. Paul writes, "But if we have died with Christ, we believe that we will live with him" and "You must consider yourselves as dead to sin and alive to God in Christ Jesus." (Rom. 6: 8-11)

By the Spirit's justification we die to sin and are born to new life. We become branches grafted onto Christ, the vine. "By the participation of the Spirit, we become communicants in the divine nature. Those in whom the Spirit dwells are divinized." (St. Athanasius)

Conversion (1989)

The first effect of justification is conversion. "Repent, for the kingdom of heaven is at hand." (Mt. 4:17) Turning away from sin, man accepts God's forgiveness and righteousness. "Besides remission of sins, justification is also the sanctification and renewal of the interior man." (Council of Trent – 1547)

A Free Gift (1990-1991)

Justification is God's free gift which detaches man from enslavement to sin and reconciles him to God. Justification is also our acceptance of God's righteousness. In this gift, faith, hope, charity and obedience to God's will are given to us.

Gained By the Cross (1992)

Justification was merited for us by Christ's death on the cross and is given to us in Baptism. We are conformed to God's righteousness so that we can gain eternal life. Paul says, "But now the righteousness of God has been manifested apart from the law. Since all have sinned and fall short of the glory of God, they are justified by his grace as a gift. God justifies him who has faith in Jesus." (Rom. 3: 21-26)

Man's Free Response (1993)

Justification establishes cooperation between God's grace and man's freedom. Man assents to God's Word by the Holy Spirit (who precedes and preserves this assent). "When God touches man's heart, man himself is not inactive since he could reject it. However, without God's grace, man cannot move himself toward God's justice." (Council of Trent 1547)

God's Greatest Work (1994-1995)

Justification is God's most excellent work. "Justification of the wicked is a greater work than the creation of heaven and earth" because "heaven and earth will pass away but the elect will not pass away. He also says that justification is a greater work even than the creation of angels because it witnesses to a greater mercy." (St. Augustine)

Justification is the sanctification of man's whole being. "Yield your members to righteousness for sanctification. The return you get is sanctification and its end, eternal life." (Rom.6:19-22)

GRACE

The Grace of God's Call (1996-1998)

Justification comes from grace (God's free and undeserved help) and is given to us to respond to his call.

By Baptism, the person participates in the life of the three Divine Persons because Christ (the Head of his Body) makes us adopted children of God. We receive the Spirit and henceforth call God "Father"

This call to eternal life is <u>supernatural</u>, coming totally from God's decision and surpassing all power of human intellect and will.

Sanctifying and Actual Grace (1999-2000)

Christ's grace (infused by the Spirit and received in Baptism) is <u>sanctifying</u> and <u>deifying.</u> "Therefore, if any one is in Christ, he is a new creation." (2Cor.5:17)

<u>Sanctifying grace</u> is habitual, the permanent supernatural disposition which perfects the soul. <u>Actual grace</u> is God's intervention, whether at the beginning moment of conversion or in the work of sanctification.

241

Making Us Collaborators (2001-2002)

Only grace can prepare man to collaborate by faith in God's justifying and sanctifying actions. God (who always uses our cooperation) begins "by working so that we might will it." (St. Augustine) "We are only collaborating with God, for his mercy has gone before us. It goes before so we may be called. It follows so we may be glorified. Without him we can do nothing." (St. Augustine)

God's free action requires man to respond freely. Only in freedom can a soul enter into God's communion. God has placed within every person a longing for truth and goodness which eternal life fulfills beyond all imagination. "If at the end of your very good works you rested on the seventh day, so we shall also rest in you on the sabbath of eternal life." (St. Augustine)

The Spirit and His Gifts (2003-2004)

Grace includes both the Holy Spirit himself and the Spirit's gifts. There are sacramental graces (given by each sacrament) and charisms (meaning "gratuitous gift"). Whatever their nature (even extraordinary gifts such as miracles or tongues), they are meant to build up the Church.

Graces of state accompany our responsibilities (both in our Christian life and in our work for the Church). "Having gifts that differ according to the grace given to us, let us use them." (Rom. 12:6)

By Faith and By Fruits (2005)

Because grace is not an object of experience but is known by faith, we cannot rely on our feelings or our works to conclude that we are justified and saved. (Council of Trent 1547) However, God's blessing in our lives shows that grace is at work. Asked about being in the state of grace, Joan of Arc responded at her trial, "If I am not, may it please God to put me in it; if I am, may it please God to keep me there."

MERIT

Right To Recompense (2006-2007)
"In crowning their merits, you are crowning your own gifts" (Preface of saints)

Merit is recompense owed by society to an individual for some action (good or bad) which deserves a reward or a punishment according to the principle of equality.

Man has no strict right to any merit with God. An immeasurable inequality exists between man and God because man has received everything from his Creator.

Yet True Merit (2008-2010)
However, God has freely chosen to have men work with him. Therefore, merit belongs primarily to God's grace and secondarily to man's good actions.

True merit results because God adopted man and made him a "co-heir" with Christ, worthy to obtain the promised inheritance of eternal life." (Council of Trent - 1547) "Our merits are God's gifts." (St. Augustine)

Therefore, no one merits the first grace of forgiveness and justification. However, by the Spirit, we can merit (for ourselves and others) the graces needed for sanctification. Even temporal goods (the objects of our prayers) can be merited in God's wisdom.

Totally A Gift (2011)
Christ's love ensures the supernatural quality and the merit of our actions. The saints knew that their merits were totally a gift. "In the evening of this life, I shall appear before you with empty hands. I wish, then, to be clothed in your own justice and to receive the eternal possession of yourself." (St. Therese of Lisieux)

CHRISTIAN HOLINESS

God's Three Steps (2012-2013)
Paul explains the three steps of God's plan: "Those whom he predestined he also called; those whom he called he also justified; those whom he justified, he also glorified." (Rom.8: 28-30)

243

All Christians are called to this perfection of charity. "Be perfect, as your heavenly Father is perfect." (Mt. 5:48) "In order to reach this perfection the faithful should use the strength given them by Christ's gift. Thus the holiness of the People of God will grow in fruitful abundance." (Second Vatican Council)

Mystical Union (2014-2015)

Spiritual progress which leads to union with God is called mystical. God calls all to this intimate union. Some receive extraordinary mystical signs which manifest the gift which is given to all.

Holiness comes only by the way of the cross. Progress comes through discipline and mortification which lead to peace and joy. "He who climbs never stops going from beginning to beginning, through beginnings that have no end. (St. Gregory of Nyssa)

Final Perseverance (2016)

The Church's children rightly hope for the grace of final perseverance and recompense from God. (Council of Trent - 1547) Believers share in the "blessed hope" that they will be gathered into "the holy city, the new Jerusalem, coming down out of heaven." (Rev. 21:2)

In Brief - 2017 - 2029

THE CHURCH – MOTHER AND TEACHER

A Moral Life In the Church (2030-2031)

In the Church, the Christian
1. receives the Word of God and the sacraments
2. learns the examples of the saints and their spiritual traditions
3. celebrates the holy mysteries in the liturgical year

By a moral life, believers present their "bodies as a living sacrifice, holy and acceptable to God." (Rom.12:1) Moral life finds its summit in the sacraments (especially the Eucharist) where prayer, teaching and grace enlighten and nourish Christian activity.

The Church's Right To Teach (2032-2033)

Because Christ gave to the Church the command "to announce the saving truth" (Second Vatican Council) she has the right to announce moral principles (even in the social order) and to make judgments when needed for "the fundamental rights of the human person and the salvation of souls." (Canon 747, #2)

By catechesis and preaching, the Church's Magisterium (aided by theologians and spiritual authors) pass on to each generation the deposit of Christian moral teaching through the Creed, the Our Father and the Ten Commandments. The Church provides a body of rules, commandments and virtues which come from her faith in Christ.

The Church's Teachers (2034-2037)

The Pope and bishops are the authentic teachers who have Christ's authority. By the ordinary and universal Magisterium they teach people the truths to believe, the charity to practice and the eternal life to hope for.

By infallibility, the Pope and bishops share (to the highest degree) in Christ's authority. This infallibility extends to the entire deposit of God's revelation and to those doctrines (including moral ones) which are needed to preserve and explain the divine teachings.

The Church's Magisterium must extend also to natural law precepts because observing them is necessary for eternal life. By explaining natural law, the church reminds men how they should be before God.

The faithful have a right to be instructed in God's saving law which will purify their judgment and heal wounded reason. They also have a duty to observe the decrees of the Church (even if these concern only Church discipline).

All Can Instruct (2038)

The Holy Spirit uses everyone (pastors, theologians and every dedicated Christian) to teach and apply Christian morality. Believers must experience a life in Christ. In this task, God uses the most humble and the most learned.

Making Decisions With the Church (2039-2040)

A person's conscience should not focus upon his own acts. In making moral judgments, the person should consider the good of all as expressed in the moral law, in Church law and in Church teaching. Personal conscience and reason should not oppose the moral law or the Church's teaching.

Baptismal grace should bring forth a filial spirit toward the Church because the Church has brought us God's mercy, God's Word, and our Eucharistic nourishment.

The Church's Six Precepts (2041-2043)

Six Church precepts oblige Catholics to fulfill the indispensable minimum in prayer and moral effort. Catholics must:

1. Attend Mass on Sundays and holydays of obligation.
2. Confess their sins at least once a year.
3. Receive Holy Communion during the Easter season
4. Keep the holy days of obligation.
5. Observe the prescribed fasting and abstinence.
6. Provide for the material needs of the Church according to their ability.

Witnessing By Goodness Of Life (2044-2046)

The Christian must be morally faithful so that the Church can fulfill her mission in the world. "Good works have great power to draw men to faith and to God."

By their constant convictions and their moral living, Christians build up the Church, which grows until "all attain to mature manhood, the stature of the fullness of Christ." (Eph.4:13)

Christians who live with Christ's mind hasten the coming of God's kingdom. At the same time they fulfill their earthly tasks.

In Brief - 2047 - 2051

Quotes to Remember

Justification is God's most excellent work.

....

30
The Ten Commandments (2052-2082)

Two Texts
The Old Testament gives the Ten Commandments twice, in Exodus and Deuteronomy. (Citations are from both sources.)

1. "I am the Lord your God you shall not have strange Gods before me." (Ex. 20: 2-6; Dt. 5:6-10)
2. "You shall not take the name of the Lord your God in vain." (Ex.20:7-8; Dt. 5:11-12)
3. "Remember to keep holy the Lord's Day." (Ex. 20:8-11; Dt. 5:12-15)
4. "Honor your father and your mother." (Ex. 20:12; Dt. 5:16)
5. "You shall not kill." (Ex. 20:13; Dt. 5:17)
6. "You shall not commit adultery." (Ex. 20:14; Dt.5:18)
7. "You shall not steal." (Ex. 20:15; Dt. 5:19)
8. "You shall not bear false witness against your neighbor." (Ex. 20:16; Dt. 5:20)
9. "You shall not covet your neighbor's wife." (Ex.20:17; Dt.5:21)
10. "You shall not covet your neighbor's goods." (Ex.20:17; Dt.5:21)

The Rich Young Man (2052-2053)
"Teacher what must I do to gain eternal life"? (Mt.19:16; Luke10:25)

Jesus told the young man to recognize the "One who is good." Then, Jesus cited those commandments that concern others. The man was told not to kill, not to commit adultery, not to steal, not to bear false witness, nor to dishonor his parents. Jesus summed up these commands, "You shall love your neighbor as yourself." (Mt. 19: 16-19)

Jesus then invited him to sell all, to give to the poor and follow him. (Mt. 19:21) This second invitation did not abolish the commandments. Instead, the man was invited to rediscover the fullness of these commandments by following Jesus. Besides asking obedience to the law, Jesus also invited his disciples to poverty and chastity. The evangelical counsels are inseparable from the commandments.

A Greater Righteousness (2054)

While acknowledging the Ten Commandments, Jesus preached a "righteousness which exceeds that of the scribes and Pharisees" (Mt. 5:20) and "of the Gentiles." (Mt. 5: 46-47) He reveals the fullness of the demands, saying for example that anyone angry "with his brother shall be liable to judgment." (Mt.5: 21-22)

Two Parts (2055)

Jesus sets forth his commandment of love in two parts, a complete love for God and a love for neighbor as we love ourselves. "These commandments concerning others are summed up by, "You shall love your neighbor as yourself. Love is the fulfilling of the law" (Rom. 13: 9-10)

IN SACRED SCRIPTURE

Written By God's Finger (2056)

God revealed the Decalogue (literally "ten words"). They are unlike any other commandments of Moses because they were written "with the finger of God." (Ex.31:18) Originally given in the book of Exodus (C.20) and Deuteronomy (C.5), their full meaning is revealed in Jesus.

Conditions Needed To Be Free (2057)

Given to the Jews as they left Egypt, these Ten Commandments show the conditions needed for a life freed from sin. Moses promised the people that they "shall live and multiply." (Dt. 30:16) God mentions his liberating power in the commandment on the Sabbath rest. "You shall remember that you were a servant in Egypt and the Lord your God brought you out of there." (Dt.5:15)

Ten Words (2058 -2059)

These "ten words" sum up God's law. Moses said, "He wrote them upon two tables of stone and gave them to me" (Dt.5:22) These two tables are called "the testimony", the terms of the covenant between God and Israel which were to be placed in the Ark of the Covenant (Ex.25: 16)

God spoke these "ten words" amid a divine revelation. He spoke to Moses "face to face on the mountain, out of the midst of the fire." (Dt.5:4)

Part Of A Covenant (2060-2061)

The commandments are part of the Covenant and were given before the covenant was concluded. The Israelites agreed to obey them. "All that the Lord has said, we will heed and do." (Ex.24:7) The Ten Commandments are always connected with the covenant.

These commandments and man's moral life have their full meaning in the covenant. "I am the Lord your God who brought you out of the land of Egypt" show God's love for the people. "In punishment for sin, there was a passing from the paradise of freedom to the slavery of sin. Therefore God said, 'I brought you out of the house of slavery'." (Origen)

Our Response To the Covenant (2062-2063)

The actual ten commands express the implications of belonging to God. By a moral life, man responds to God's covenant and cooperates with God's plan in history.

The opening words show that the covenant is personal. "I am the Lord your God." The singular "you", shows that the recipient is every individual person. Although meant for the whole world, the commandments are given to each person. "Through the Decalogue God prepared man to become his friend and to live in harmony with his neighbor." (St. Irenaeus)

IN CHURCH TRADITION

Core of Church's Moral Teaching (2064-2065)

The Church remains faithful to the scriptures and to Jesus by always teaching the importance of the Ten Commandments.

Since St. Augustine, they have had an important place in the preparation of baptismal candidates and the faithful. In the fifteenth century, they were put in rhymed formulas for easy memorizing. Christian catechisms structured moral teaching around them.

The Numbering (2066-2067)

Their division and numbering have varied. The Catholic Church (and Lutheran confessions) follow the order set by St. Augustine. The Orthodox Churches and reformed communities follow the order set by the Greek Fathers.

The first three commandments concern love of God and the other seven love of neighbor. "As charity comprises the two great commandments, so the Ten Commandments themselves were given on two tablets." (St. Augustine)

Obligatory For All (2068)

The Ten Commandments are obligatory for all Christians and the justified man must keep them. (Council of Trent) "All men may attain salvation through faith, Baptism and the observance of the commandments." (Second Vatican Council)

Their Unity (2069)

The Ten Commandments have a unity. The two tables enlighten each other and form an organic unity. Transgressing one command infringes on the others, while honoring another person honors God. Thus, man's religious and social life come into unity.

NATURAL LAW

Already Written On Man's Heart (2070-2071)

Although revealed by God, these commandments show the essential duties and fundamental rights inherent in human nature. They are a privileged expression of the natural law. "God planted the precepts of the natural law in the heart of man and then reminded him of them through the Decalogue." (St. Irenaeus)

Sinful humanity (although capable of discovering them) needed this help to realize all the requirements of natural law. "A full explanation was necessary because the light of reason was obscured and the will had gone astray." (St. Bonaventure) We know God's commandments by the Church's teaching and by the voice of moral conscience.

Obliging Everyone Everywhere (2072-2073)

Because the commandments express fundamental duties (to God and neighbor) they reveal obligations which are grave, fundamentally immutable and obliging always and everywhere. No one can dispense them because God engraved them on the human heart.

Sometimes the obligations involve matter which are light.

Jesus' Power Within (2074)

"He who abides in me bears much fruit." (Jn.15:5) When we believe in Jesus, he himself becomes the living, interior rule of our activity. "This is my commandment, that you love one another as I have loved you." (Jn. 15:12)

In Brief - 2075 - 2082

Quotes to Remember

The Ten Commandments are unlike any other commandments because written by "the finger of God". (Ex.31:18)

God spoke these Ten Commandments to Moses, "face to face on the mountain, out of the midst of fire". (Dt.5:4)

No one can dispense these commandments because God engraved them on the human heart.

The commandments have always enjoyed a special place in teaching Baptismal candidates and the faithful.

By his moral life, man responds to God's covenant.

31
The First Commandment (2083-2141)

God reminded Israel that he brought them out of Egypt and that they must have no other gods, no graven images of any heavenly or earthly likeness to which they would bow down and adore. (Ex.20:2-5)

Moses and Jesus (2083)

Moses had said "Hear, O Israel, the Lord our God is one Lord." (Dt.6:4) Jesus summed up man's duties. "You shall love the Lord your God with all your heart, and with all your soul and with all your mind." The commandments make explicit man's response to that love.

WORSHIP THE LORD, YOUR GOD

The Liberating God (2084-2085

Jesus said, "You shall worship the Lord your God and him only shall you serve." (Mt.4:10)

God recalls his liberating action, "I brought you out of the land of Egypt." Then, he says, "You shall fear the Lord your God, you shall serve him. You shall not go after other gods." (Ex.20:2-5) God demands that man accept him totally and worship him.

Man's vocation is linked to God revealing himself because Man is called to manifest God's likeness. "There will never be another God and there has been no other since the world began. (St. Justin)

Our Hope In His Faithfulness (2086)

God is an unchangeable being, faithful and just, without any evil. We should hope in him because he is almighty and infinitely beneficent. God begins and ends the Ten Commandments by saying, "I am the Lord." (Roman Catechism)

252

Our Owed Obedience (2087)

Our moral life is based upon our belief in God, to whom we owe an "obedience of faith." (Rom.1:5) Paul condemned the "ignorance of God" as the cause of moral deviations. (Rom. 1:18-32)

Sins Against Faith (2088-2089)

We must protect faith by vigilance and reject everything opposed to it. The sins against faith are:

1. Voluntary doubt – refusing to hold as true what God revealed and the Church teaches (Doubt is involuntary when the person hesitates to believe or cannot overcome objections to faith.)
2. Incredulity – neglect or outright refusal to assent to a revealed truth.
3. Heresy – denial of a truth that must be believed with divine and catholic faith.
4. Apostasy – total repudiation of the Catholic faith.
5. Schism – refusal to submit to the Pope or to accept communion with the Church.

Need For Hope (2090)

Because man cannot fully respond to God's love, he must hope that God will give him the capacity to live according to the commandments. Hope is the confident expectation of God's blessings of this life and of eternal life. Therefore, hope fears to offend God and incur punishment.

Sins Against Hope (2091-2092)

Two sins against hope are:

1. Despair – the person loses all hope of God's forgiveness or his help in getting to heaven. This is against God's goodness, justice and mercy.
2. Presumption is committed by someone who trusts in his own power to save himself; or who presumes on God's forgiveness without any need for repentance and good works.

Sins Against Charity (2093-2094)
Sins against charity are:
1. Indifference – which does not think about God's love and even denies its power
2. Ingratitude – which refuses to acknowledge God's goodness
3. Lukewarmness – which neglects to respond to God's love
4. Spiritual sloth (acedia) - which refuses to delight in God
5. Hatred of God – which presumes to curse God who forbids sin and inflicts punishment

SERVING GOD ALONE

Religion (2095)
By the virtue of religion we have an attitude of charity and render to God what we, as creatures, owe him.

Adoring By Acknowledging (2096-2097)
By adoration (the first act of religion) man acknowledges God as Creator and Master of all that exists. Jesus said "You shall worship the Lord your God, and him only shall you serve." (Lk.4:8)

In adoring God, we acknowledge the "nothingness of the creature". Worshipping God saves the person from self-centeredness, from slavery to sin and from idolatry of the world.

Need For Prayer (2098)
By prayer (a lifting up of our mind to God) we accomplish the needed acts of faith, hope and love. Without prayer we cannot obey God's commands. We must "pray and not lose heart." (Lk.18:1)

Adoring God By Sacrifices (2099-2100)
Sacrifice is a sign of adoration "Every action done so as to cling to God in holiness is a true sacrifice." (St. Augustine)

Outward sacrifices must express a true inner spirit of sacrifice. The prophets denounced sacrifices not given from the heart. Jesus quoted Hosea "I desire mercy and not sacrifice." (Mt. 9:13)

Promises and Vows (2101 – 2102)

Promises are made to God in Baptism, Confirmation, Matrimony and Holy Orders. A person can also promise God some action (prayer, almsgiving, pilgrimage, etc). Fulfilling these promises shows respect for God's majesty.

A vow is a deliberate, free promise concerning a higher good which must be fulfilled. (Canon 1191, #1) By this act of devotion the Christian dedicates his life or promises some action, e.g. St. Paul cut his hair because of a vow. (Acts 18:18)

Evangelical Counsels (2103)

Especially important to the Church are vows concerning the evangelical counsels (poverty, chastity and obedience). Mother Church rejoices in the many men and women who "go beyond what is of precept" (Second Vatican Council). For proportionate reasons, the Church can dispense from vows and promises. (Canon 692; 1196-1197)

SOCIAL DUTY AND RELIGIOUS FREEDOM

Seeking Truth (2104)

The person must seek the truth concerning God and the Church. This search does not contradict a "sincere respect" for various religions nor the need to have love for all who are in error concerning faith.

Offering Genuine Worship (2105)

Man must offer genuine worship both individually and socially. Evangelized by the Church, believers must infuse society with Christian laws and structures. Christians must awaken everyone to the true religion which subsists in the Catholic Church. By being the light of the world, Christians manifest Christ's kingship over human societies. (Pope Leo XIII)

Engaging Religious Freedom (2106-2107)

Nobody can be forced to act against his conscience nor be restrained from acting according to his conscience (within due limits). This right is based upon the person's duty to assent freely to divine truth. This right exists even in those who do not seek the truth or adhere to it.

Even if a constitution grants special civil recognition to one religion, all citizens must enjoy religious freedom.

Limits To Liberty (2108-2109)

Religious liberty is neither a moral license to err nor a right to error. It is a civil liberty granted to every human person who must have immunity (within just limits) from external coercion. This natural right must be acknowledged in civil law.

This right to religious liberty is not unlimited. "Due limits" are determined by political prudence required for the common good according to just legal principles.

NO OTHER GODS

Superstition and Irreligion (2110-2111)

The first commandment (forbidding worship of false gods) prohibits superstition (a perverse excess of religion) and irreligion (a defect of religion).

Superstition is a deviation of religious feeling and of religious practices. Even in true worship, a person can attribute some magical importance to certain prayers or stress the external performance of prayers without interior dispositions.

Idolatry (2112-2114)

Man must not believe in or worship many gods (polytheism). Also, scripture constantly rejects idols made by hand. "They have mouths and they do not speak. Those worshippers who make them are like them." (Ps.115:4-5) Only the true God gives life and intervenes in history.

Idolatry is not just pagan worship. It also consists of honoring a creature who is not God. This could be demons (Satanism), power, pleasure, money, etc. "You cannot serve God and mammon." (Mt.6:24) Martyrs died for not adoring "the Beast." (Rev:13-14) Idolatry always rejects the Lordship of God.

Adoring the true God gives unity to life, while idolatry is a perversion of man's religious sense, "transferring man's indestructible notion of God, to anything other than God." (Origen)

Seven Forms of Divination (2115-2116)

Certainly God can reveal the future to believers. However, man should not be curious about the future.

All forms of divination (false attempts to know the future) must be rejected:

1. recourse to demons
2. conjuring up the devil
3. horoscopes
4. astrology
5. palm reading
6. clairvoyance
7. mediums

These conceal a desire for power over history and other human beings.

Magic, Sorcery and Spiritism (2117)

Magic and sorcery, (the attempts to tame the occult to gain supernatural powers) are against the virtue of religion, even when used for good purposes. These acts are especially evil when they involve recourse to demons. The Church also warns against Spiritism or seeking cures by invoking evil powers.

Three Forms Of Irreligion (2118)

The first commandment condemns:

1 tempting God
2 sacrilege
3 simony

Tempting God (2119)

Tempting God means to put his goodness to a test by word or deed, e.g. Satan asked Jesus to throw himself from the Temple (supposedly to force God to save him). Jesus said "You shall not put your God to the test." (Dt.6:16) This tempting wounds the respect we owe to God and shows doubts about his providence.

Sacrilege (2120)

Sacrilege is to treat unworthily the sacraments, liturgical actions or consecrated persons, places or things. Sacrilege is a grave sin, especially when committed against the Eucharist.

Simony (2121)

Simony is the buying or selling of spiritual things. Simon the magician wanted to buy the spiritual powers of Saint Peter. (Acts 8: 18-24) Concerning spiritual powers Jesus said "Without cost you have received; without cost you are to give." (Mt. 10:8) God, not the human person, is the owner of spiritual gifts.

Money and Sacraments (2122)

No one should be deprived of the sacraments because of poverty. Certainly, competent authority can determine appropriate "offerings."

ATHEISM AND AGNOSTICISM

Three Forms Of Atheism (2123 – 2124)

Atheists either do not perceive man's vital bond to God or they explicitly reject it.

Atheism takes many forms:

1. Practical materialism which restricts man's hopes to his life on earth.
2. Atheistic humanism which sees man as having supreme control of history
3. Contemporary atheism which sees man being liberated by economics. It claims that religion thwarts emancipation because it turns man's hopes to a future life and discourages earthly progress.

Sources of Atheism (2125-2126)

By rejecting or denying God's existence, atheism sins against the virtue of religion. Believers often contribute to atheism by not knowing their faith, by presenting it falsely or by failing to live a life which truly reveals God to others.

Atheism is founded on a false idea of human autonomy which rejects any dependence on God. Acknowledging God does not oppose man's dignity, and is in harmony with man's own desires.

Forms of Agnosticism (2127-2128)

Agnosticism (the belief that God's existence cannot be known) takes many forms.

1. Accepting the existence of a transcendent being who cannot reveal himself and about whom, nothing can be said.
2. Declaring the impossibility of proving, affirming or denying that God exists.

Agnosticism (while sometimes including a search for God) often shows a flight from this ultimate question and a certain moral sluggishness (practical atheism).

God Is Greater Than Images (2129-2130)

God said to Israel "You act corruptly by making a graven image for yourselves, in the form of any figure." (Dt.4:15-16) God revealed himself to Israel, yet he is "greater than all his works" (Sir. 43: 27-28)

Even in the Old Testament, God ordered or allowed the making of the bronze serpent, the Ark of the Covenant and the cherubim.

Christ – A New Era (2131-2132)

Christ introduced a new "economy" of images. The Church has felt justified in making icons of Christ, Mary, angels and saints.(Nicaea II – 787)

The Christian veneration of images is permitted because the honor given to an image passes to its prototype. "Whoever venerates an image venerates the person portrayed in it." (St. Basil) "Religious worship is not directed to the images in themselves, but toward that whose image it is." (St. Thomas Aquinas)

In Brief - 2133 - 2141

Quotes to Remember

Our moral life is based upon our belief on God, to whom we own an "obedience of faith". (Rom.1:5)

All citizens must enjoy religious liberty.

32
The Second Commandment

"You shall not take the name of the Lord your God in vain."
(Ex. 20:7)

HOLY IS HIS NAME

Uniqueness Of God's Name (2142-2143)
The second commandment (also belonging to the virtue of religion) prescribes respect for the Lord's name and governs the use of speech in sacred matters.

God's name is a unique word. Because God confides his name in trust and intimacy, we must not abuse this name or use it in speech except to bless and praise God.

The Mystery Of God (2144-2146)
Respect for his name shows a respect for the mystery of God himself. "There is a class of feelings which we should have to an intense degree as if we literally had the sight of Almighty God." (John Cardinal Newman)

Believers must witness to God's name without fear. Respect for Jesus' name should permeate preaching and catechizing.

The second commandment forbids the abuse of God's name and also of the names of Jesus, Mary and the saints.

Promises (2147)
Promises made in God's name must be respected in justice, so that God is not made a liar.

Five Forms of Blasphemy (2148)
Blasphemy has many forms:
1. words spoken (inwardly or outwardly) of hatred, abuse or defiance of God.
2. failing to respect God in speech
3. misusing God's name
4. language against Christ's Church, saints or sacred things
5. using God's name to cover up criminal practices
6. Seriously harming people in God's name

In itself, blasphemy is a grave sin.

260

Other Sins (2149)

Other sins include:

1. oaths, which misuse God's name and show disrespect
2. magical use of God's name

"God's name is holy when said with veneration." (St. Augustine)

Rejecting False Oaths (2150-2151)

By an oath, someone asks God to witness what is affirmed. God is used as a pledge of one's own truthfulness.

All false oaths must be rejected because God is the norm of all truth. A true oath highlights this relationship of human speech with God's truth. A false oath asks God to be a witness to a lie.

Types of Perjury (2152)

Other sins include:

1. Perjury - making a promise with no intention to keep it
2. Promising under oath to commit an evil deed.

Jesus' Teaching (2153-2154)

Jesus said, "Do not swear at all. Let what you say be simply 'Yes' or 'No'." (Mt.5:34) He wants an awareness that God's presence and truth be honored in all speech. Great discretion must be shown in calling upon his name. Jesus' words do not exclude oaths made for grave and right reasons (as in court). (cf. 2Cor.1:23; Gal.1:20) An oath can be taken only "in truth, in judgment and in justice." (Canon 1199)

Other Circumstances Of Refusing An Oath (2155)

An oath in trivial matters or in certain circumstances must not be taken. Oaths can be refused when asked by a illegitimate civil authority, and must be refused when contrary to the dignity of persons or the Church.

THE CHRISTIAN NAME

The Holiness Of A Christian Name (2156-2158)

A person receives his/her Christian name at Baptism. This should be the name of a saint, of a Christian mystery or of a virtue. A baptismal name should not be "foreign to Christian sentiment." (Canon 855)

To dedicate each day to God's glory, the Christian should begin his morning with the sign of the cross which invokes the name of the Father, Son and Holy Spirit.

God calls everyone by name because a person's name is holy, an icon of the person himself.

Jesus And Your New Name (2159)

The person's name is for eternity, marking each person's uniqueness in the kingdom. Jesus says, "I will give a white stone, with a new name written on the stone." (Rev. 2:17) The elect have Jesus' name and the Father's name "written on their foreheads." (Rev. 14:1)

In Brief – 2160 - 2167

Quotes to Remember

God confided his name to us in trust. We must not abuse this confidence.

....

Do not swear at all. Let what you say be simply "yes" or "no". (Mt.5:34)

....

Believers must witness to God's name without fear.

....

God calls everyone by name. A person's name is holy, an icon of the person himself.

....

Promises made in God's name must be respected in justice.

....

33
The Third Commandment (2168-2195)

"Remember the Sabbath day, to keep it holy" (Ex.20:8)

The Sabbath – Rest and Liberation (2168-2170)

The third commandment says, "The seventh day is a Sabbath of solemn rest, holy to the Lord." (Ex.31:15) Scripture recalls that God created in six days and "rested the seventh day", thus blessing "the sabbath day." (Ex.20:11)

Keeping the Sabbath is Israel's way of remembering their liberation from Egypt, "The Lord your God brought you out. Therefore, he commanded you to keep the Sabbath day." (Dt.5:15)

Sign of the Covenant (2171-2172)

Israel was to keep the Sabbath as a sign of the irrevocable covenant to recall both God's creation and his saving actions for Israel.

The Sabbath is God's model for human activity for he "stopped working and rested." (Ex.31:17) It is a protest against the servitude of work and the worship of money.

Jesus' Interpretation (2173)

Jesus always respected the Sabbath, giving the law its authentic interpretation. "The Sabbath was made for man." (Mk.2:27) The Sabbath is meant "to do good" and "to save life." (Mk.3:4) Jesus is "lord even of the Sabbath." (Mk.2:28)

THE LORD'S DAY

The First and the Eighth (2174)

Jesus rose "on the first day of the week." (Mk.16:2) This "first day" recalls the first creation. As an "eighth day", it symbolizes the new creation begun by Christ's Resurrection. For Christians, Sunday has become the first of all days, the Lord's Day. "We gather on the day of the sun, for it is the first day when God made the world; on this same day Jesus Christ our Savior rose from the dead." (St. Justin)

A New Hope – A New Day (2175-2176)

Sunday replaces the Sabbath for Christians because Christ's Passover fulfills the truth of the Jewish Sabbath. The Old Law worship prepared for the mystery of Christ. "We have come to a new hope, no longer keeping the sabbath, but the Lord's Day." (St. Ignatius of Antioch)

Observing Sunday fulfills the moral command inscribed in man's heart to render public and regular worship to God "as a sign of his universal beneficence to all." (St. Thomas Aquinas) Sunday worship fulfills the Old Law by a weekly celebration of the Creator and Redeemer.

Six Holy Days of Obligation (2177)

The Sunday Eucharistic celebration of the Lord's Day is at the heart of Church life, "the foremost holy day of obligation in the universal Church." Canon 1246 also lists six other days as holydays of obligation which have been accepted by the United States bishops:

1. Christmas,
2. Mary, Mother of God (New Year's),
3. the Ascension,
4. the Assumption (August 15th),
5. All Saints (November 1st)
6. the Immaculate Conception (December 8th)

The Weekly Parish Gathering (2178-2179)

The practice of the weekly Christian assembly comes from the apostolic age. "Do not neglect to meet together but encourage one another." (Heb.10:25) "Come to Church early, approach the Lord and confess your sins, repent in prayer. Be present at the sacred and divine liturgy, conclude its prayer and do not leave before the dismissal." (Sermon on the Lord's Day)

For Eucharist, the faithful gather at the parish (a stable community entrusted to a priest by the diocesan bishop). The parish initiates Christians, gathers them for celebration, teaches Christ's doctrines and shows charity in good works. "You cannot pray at home as at Church where there are great multitudes crying out as from one great heart. In Church, there is the union of minds, the accord of souls and the prayers of the priest." (St. John Chrysostom)

A Grave Obligation (2180-2182)

"On Sundays and holydays the faithful are bound to participate in the Mass." (Canon 1247) This is satisfied in any Catholic rite on the day or the evening before. (Canon 1248)

Under obligation of grave sin, the faithful are bound to attend Mass unless excused for a serious reason (e.g. illness, care of infants) or dispensed by their pastor. (Canon 1245)

By Sunday participation the faithful witness to their belonging to the Church, to their communion in charity and to their hope of salvation.

When No Priest (2183)

If a sacred minister is not available, the faithful should gather in the Church for the Liturgy of the Word, or set aside time with the family or with groups of families for an appropriate period of time. (cf. C1248 #2)

GRACE AND REST

Sunday Priorities (2184)

Human life should have a rhythm of work and rest. By keeping the Lord's day, the faithful cultivate their social and religious lives.

The faithful must not engage in works that hinder the worship due to God, the needed works of mercy or the appropriate relaxation of mind and body. Family needs or social services can legitimately excuse but should not lead to habits that harm religion or family life. "The charity of truth seeks holy leisure; while the necessity of charity accepts just work." (St. Augustine)

Christians with leisure should use the day to help the sick and the elderly. Believers should devote this time to their families, and to prayer to grow in the interior life.

A Common Effort Needed (2187-2188)

Sanctifying Sundays requires a common effort. Christians should not make excessive demands on others. Although traditional activities require some to work, everyone should still set aside some time. Public authorities and employers should ensure citizens and employees a time for rest.

Christians should seek recognition of Sundays and holydays as legal holidays. By defending this Sunday tradition, they will contribute to public life. Even if a country's laws require Sunday to be a "work day", Christians should celebrate it as a festal "day of deliverance."

In Brief - 2189 - 2195

Quotes to Remember

Jesus always respected the Sabbath

·····················

Sunday, as the eighth day, symbolizes the new creation begun by Christ.

·····················

The Sunday Eucharist is at the heart of Church life.

·····················

Come to the Church early. Be present at the sacred and divine liturgy, conclude its prayers and do not leave before the dismissal. (Sermon on the Lord's Day)

·····················

You cannot pray at home as you do at Church. In Church, there is the union of minds, the accord of souls, and the prayers of the priest. (St. John Chrysostom)

·····················

Keeping the Sabbath was Israel's way of remembering their liberation from Egypt.

·····················

Sunday replaces the Sabbath because Christ's Passover fulfills the truth of the Jewish Sabbath.

·····················

34
Fourth Commandment (2196-2257)

"Honor your father and your mother" (Ex.20:12; Dt.5:16)

Fulfilling The Two Commands (2196)
Jesus gave two commandments – to love God with all our heart and soul and mind and strength and to love our neighbor as ourselves. "There is no other commandment greater than these." (Mk.12:29) "The commandments are summed up in this sentence, 'You shall love your neighbor as yourself.'" (Rom.13:8-10)

Positive Duties In Correct Order (2197-2198)
This commandment begins the second table of the Ten Commandments and shows the correct order of charity. After God, we owe honor first to our parents who have given us life. We must also obey those to whom God has given his authority.

This commandment speaks of positive duties, introduces the other commandments (which regard specific duties), and constitutes the foundation of the Church's social doctrine.

To Children and To Others (2199)
The commandment speaks first to children concerning their parents (the most universal relationship), but also requires honor toward elders and ancestors. The commandment extends to pupils, employees, and citizens in their relationships to authority. The commandment presupposes the responsibilities of those in authority (parents, teachers, leaders).

A Promised Reward (2200)
God promises a reward – long life in the land your God gives you." (Ex.20:12) Honoring authority does result in peace and prosperity. Failure to obey harms the family and community.

THE FAMILY IN GOD'S PLAN

Goals of the Family (2201-2203)
The family (created by the consent of the spouses) is meant for their personal good, and for the procreation and education of

children. By the spouses' love and begetting of children, family relationships and responsibilities are created.

The institution of the family (a man, woman and their children) is prior to any recognition by public authority (which has an obligation to recognize it). The husband, wife and their children are the normal reference point to evaluate different forms of family relationships.

God instituted the family when he created man and woman. All the family members are persons equal in dignity. The family has manifold rights and responsibilities.

The Family Of Singular Importance (2204-2206)

The Christian family is "the domestic church." The New Testament shows that it has singular importance in the Church, cf. Eph. 5:21 to 6:4.

The Christian family is a sign of the communion of the Trinity. In procreating and educating children the family reflects the Father's work of creation. The family must pray together, read God's word and evangelize.

Within the family, an affinity of feelings and interests arise from the mutual respect of each other. The family is a "privileged community" in which the spouses share their thoughts and cooperate in their children's upbringing.

The Basic Cell of Society (2207-2208)

The family is the original cell of social life. The stability of family relationships constitute the foundations of a society. The family is the community where children learn moral values and a correct use of their freedom. This initiates them into society.

Family members should take care of the young, old, sick and poor. If the family cannot do this, then other families (or society) must help. "To visit orphans and widows in their affliction is religion pure and undefiled." (Jas.1:27)

Obligations Towards Families (2209-2210)

Appropriate social measures must help those families which cannot fulfill their responsibilities. However, larger communities must not usurp the family's prerogatives or interfere in its life.

Because of the family's overwhelming importance, society must strengthen marriage and family. Civil authorities have a grave duty "to acknowledge the true nature of marriage and the family and to promote domestic prosperity." (Second Vatican Council)

Duties of the Political Community (2211)
The political community must ensure especially:
1. the freedom to establish a family, have children and bring them up with moral and religious convictions
2. the protection of the marriage bond
3. the freedom to profess one's faith and hand it on to the children
4. the right to private property, work, housing and to emigration
5. the right to medical care, family benefits and old age assistance
6. protection from the dangers of drugs, pornography, alcoholism, etc.
7. the freedom to form associations with other families

Touching All Relationships (2212-2213)
This commandment illuminates all human relationships between brothers, sisters, cousins, fellow citizens and the baptized. Every person is seen as a son or daughter of the heavenly Father. The neighbor is a "person" not a "unit." He is a "someone" who deserves respect.

Because human communities are made up of persons, a government must do more than merely guarantee rights. Society must foster a good will based upon the dignity of the person so that right relationships (employer/employee; government/citizens) flourish.

DUTIES OF FAMILY MEMBERS

Honor Coming From Gratitude (2214 - 2215)
Children (whether minors or adults) must honor their parents because of God's fatherhood. This respect must be nourished by a natural affection born from their common bond.

This filial piety derives from gratitude toward those who have enabled the children to grow up in wisdom and grace. "With all your heart honor your father and do not forget the birth pangs of your mother." (Sir.7:27)

Respect By Obedience (2216)

This respect is shown by obedience. "My son, keep your father's commandment, and forsake not your mother's teaching." (Prov.6:20) "A wise son hears his father's instruction, but a scoffer does not listen to rebuke." (Prov.13:1) A child should obey his parents in all that they ask. Pupils should obey the directions of their teachers and others entrusted with their care. A child should not obey a particular order which he is convinced in conscience is morally wrong.

Role Of Grown Children (2217-2218)

Grown children must give parents whatever material and moral support they need in their old age and illness. "Whoever honors his father atones for his sins, and whoever glorifies his mother lays up treasure. Whoever honors his father, will be gladdened by his own children, and when he prays, he will be heard." (Sir.3:3-5)

Other Family Members (2219-2220)

Respect promotes total family harmony between siblings and toward the elderly. "Grandchildren are the crown of the aged." (Prov.17:6)

Christians owe special thanks to those (parents, grandparents, pastors, teachers) who have given them the life of faith. "I am reminded of your sincere faith, a faith that dwelt first in your grandmother Lois and your mother Eunice." (2Tim.1:5)

The Primordial Parental Responsibility (2221-2222)

The procreation of children brings about the duty of their moral and spiritual formation. Therefore, the parents' right and duty to educate children is primordial and inalienable. Parents must see their children as children of God and educate them in God's law.

How They Fulfill (2223-2224)

Parents fulfill this duty by creating a home filled with tenderness, respect and fidelity, in which the virtues of self-denial and sound judgment are taught. Parents (primarily by their own good example) must teach their children to subordinate material desires to spiritual ones. "He who loves his son will not spare the rod." (Sir.30:1) "Fathers, bring your children up in the discipline and instruction of the Lord." (Eph.6:4)

In the home, parents must teach communal responsibilities, turning their children away from degrading influences that ruin society.

Grace From the Sacrament (2225-2226)

By the sacrament of marriage, parents receive the grace to evangelize their children. They must initiate them into the mysteries of faith and associate them with the life of the Church. A good family supports the children's faith throughout their life.

Parents must begin this education in faith in the earliest years. Family catechesis must precede and accompany other forms of instruction. The parish is the privileged place for the family's liturgical life and catechesis (for children and parents).

Contribution By the Children (2227-2228)

Children contribute to their parents' growth and holiness. All must love one another and forgive one another.

At first, parents take care of the physical and spiritual needs of young children. Later, the parents must educate them to the right use of reason and freedom.

Rights of Parents (2229)

Parents have a fundamental right to choose their children's school according to their convictions. They should choose those schools that help them as Christian educators. Public authorities must guarantee this parental right.

Rights of Grown Children (2230-2231)

As adults, children have a right to choose their profession in life. In this choice, they should trust their parents and seek their advice. Parents must not pressure their children into a choice of a profession or of a spouse. They should, however, give judicious advice in these questions.

Those who forgo marriage to help parents or to follow their profession contribute greatly to the human family.

A Person's First Responsibility (2231-2233)

Although important, family ties are not absolute. God calls each person to a vocation and parents must respect this call. "He

271

who loves father or mother more than me is not worthy of me." (Mt.10:37)

Being Jesus' disciple means belonging to God's family and doing God's will. "For whoever does the will of my Father in heaven is my brother and sister and mother." (Mt.12:49) Parents should welcome their child's call to the priesthood or to virginity for the sake of the kingdom.

AUTHORITIES IN CIVIL SOCIETY

Public Authority (2234)

We must honor those who have received public authority from God. The fourth commandment clarifies these duties of government authority and of citizens.

Three Duties of Government (2235-2237)

Authority must be <u>exercised</u> <u>as</u> a <u>service.</u> It is judged by its divine origin, its reasonable motive and its specific object. No authority can command anything which violates the dignity of the person or the natural law.

Authority must <u>express</u> a <u>hierarchy</u> <u>of</u> <u>values</u> which facilitate the exercise of freedom and responsibility. Authority must practice distributive justice which takes into account the needs of all and the contribution of each. These regulations must not satisfy personal interest over the community's interest.

Political authorities must <u>respect</u> <u>the</u> <u>fundamental</u> <u>rights</u> of human persons and dispense justice humanely (especially toward families and the disadvantaged). The political rights attached to citizenship must be granted for the common good and cannot be suspended without legitimate reasons. Citizens must use these political rights for the common good.

Duties of Citizens (2238 – 2240)

Citizens should see authority figures as representatives of God. Loyal cooperation, however, includes the right to voice just criticism against what is harmful to persons or to the community.

Citizens must also <u>contribute</u> <u>to</u> <u>the</u> <u>common</u> <u>good.</u> This common good requires that a citizen fulfill his role in the community's political life.

This co-responsibility means citizens must <u>pay</u> <u>taxes,</u> <u>vote</u> and <u>defend</u> <u>one's</u> <u>country.</u> "Pay to all of them their dues, taxes to whom taxes are due, revenue to whom revenue is due, respect to whom respect is due, honor to whom honor is due." (Rom.13:7) "Christians obey the established laws and their way of life surpasses the laws." (Letter to Diogneties)

Accepting Immigrants (2241)

To the extent that they are able, more prosperous nations must welcome foreigners (who cannot find work in their own country). These foreigners must be safeguarded from harm.

Authorities are able to make this right to immigrate subject to various juridical conditions concerning the immigrant's duties toward the host country. Immigrants must obey laws and contribute to their new country's well being.

Times To Refuse Obedience (2242)

Citizens must refuse to obey directions of civil authorities which are against the moral order, the fundamental rights of persons or the gospel teachings. By refusing obedience, the person correctly serves God and not the political community. A distinction exists between what "is rendered to Caesar" and what "is rendered to God." (Mt.22:21) "We must obey God rather than men." (Acts 5:29)

ARMED RESISTANCE

Conditions For Armed Resistance To Oppression (2343)

Even when public authority oppresses them, citizens should still do what is required by the common good. However, they can defend their own and others' rights within the limits of the natural law and the Gospel.

Armed resistance to political oppression is legitimate only if the following conditions are met:
1. there is a certain, grave and prolonged violation of fundamental rights
2. all other means have been exhausted
3. this resistance will not provoke worse disorders
4. there is a well-founded hope for success
5. no better solution is reasonably possible

THE CHURCH'S VISION

A Society With God's Vision (2244)

Every institution is based upon a vision of man. This vision brings about a hierarchy of values in which most societies recognize the preeminence of man over things. Only divinely revealed religions recognize God as man's origin and destiny.

The Church sees man in relationship to God and invites authorities to adapt a similar viewpoint.

Many societies claim independence from God and create their own goals or borrow them from an ideology. Rejecting any objective criterion of good and evil, they claim a totalitarian power over man.

The Church And the Political Community (2245-2246)

The Church (by her commission and power) is not to be confused with the political community. She teaches the transcendental value of the human person and encourages every citizen's freedom and responsibility.

The Church passes moral judgment in political matters when fundamental rights and the salvation of souls requires. She seeks the good of all by means in accord with the gospel.

In Brief - 2247 - 2257

Quotes to Remember

The family is the original cell of social life.

Because of the family's overwhelming importance, society must strengthen marriages.

Parents must choose those schools which help them as Christian educators.

35
The Fifth Commandment (2258-2330)

"You shall not kill" (Ex.20:13)

Why Life Is Sacred (2258)
Human life is sacred because it is created by God and is meant for an everlasting relationship with God. God is the Lord of life (from beginning to end) and no one has the right to destroy an innocent human being. (Gift of Life – Congregation For the Doctrine of Faith)

RESPECTING HUMAN LIFE

A History Of Violence (2259-2260)
Cain killing his brother Abel reveals the anger and envy which come from original sin. Man has become the enemy of his fellow man. God said, "the voice of your brother's blood is crying to me from the ground." (Gen.4:8-12)

Scripture frequently reminds us of God's gift (human life) and of man's violence. "Whoever sheds the blood of man, by man shall his blood be shed; for God made man in his own image." (Gen.9:6) The Old Testament considered blood as a sign of life, (a teaching which is always necessary).

Biblical Directive (2261-2262)
Scripture specifically says: "Do not slay the innocent and the righteous." (Ex.23:7) The deliberate murder of an innocent person is gravely contrary to man's dignity, to the golden rule and to the holiness of God. This law is universally valid, obliging everyone at all times and all places.

In his Sermon on the Mount, Jesus went further. He prohibited anger, hatred and vengeance. Later, he asked his disciples to love their enemies. In his Passion, he did not defend himself and he told Peter to put away his sword.

Self Defense – The Principle of Double Effect (2263-2264)
The act of self-defense is not an exception to this prohibition. "The act of self-defense can have a double effect: the preservation

275

of one's own life and the killing of an aggressor. The one is intended, the other is not." (St. Thomas Aquinas)

Love for oneself is a fundamental principle of morality and defending one's life is not murder even if it results in the death of another.

"If a man, in self-defense, uses more than necessary violence, it is unlawful, whereas if he repels force with moderation, his defense will be lawful." (St. Thomas Aquinas)

The Duty Of Self-Defense (2265-2266)

Legitimate defense can be a grave duty for those responsible for the lives of others. Because the unjust aggressor against the common good must be made harmless, legitimate authority has the right to use arms to repel aggressors.

Because the state must curb harmful activity legitimate authority has the right and duty to inflict punishment proportionate to the offense. This punishment has two effects, primarily to redress the disorder and secondarily to bring about the correction of the guilty party.

OTHER ISSUES

The Death Penalty (2267)

If the guilty party's identity and responsibility are clearly determined, the Church's traditional teaching does not forbid the use of the death penalty if this is the only possible way of defending human lives against the unjust aggressor. If non-lethal means can be used to protect people's safety, then authority must use these means. In fact, today the state has so many possibilities to make the aggressor incapable of future harm without taking away his life that the cases in which execution is an absolute necessity "are very rare, if not practically non-existent." (Pope John Paul II)

Direct Killing (2268)

Direct and intentional killing are gravely sinful. Both the murderer and those who voluntarily cooperate commit a sin which cries to heaven for vengeance. Infanticide, fratricide, parricide and killing of a spouse (because these involve natural bonds) are especially grave crimes. Concern for eugenics or public health cannot justify any murder even if commanded by public authority.

Other Forbidden Acts (2269)

The fifth commandment also forbids

1. doing anything with the intention of indirectly causing a person's death
2. exposing oneself to mortal danger
3. refusing assistance to a person in danger

Society's acceptance of <u>murderous famines</u> is a grave offense. Those who by their <u>avarice</u> and <u>usury</u> bring about the deaths of others indirectly commit imputable homicide.

Unintentional killing is not imputable. However, there is a grave offense if the person acted without a proportionate reason and brought about a death they did not intend.

ABORTION

Respect For Life From Moment of Conception (2270)

Human life must be respected and absolutely protected from the first moment of conception. The rights of the human person (especially the right to live) must be recognized from the first moment of existence. "Before I formed you in the womb I knew you. Before you were born, I consecrated you." (Jer.1:5)

First Century Teaching (2271)

From the first century, the Church has taught the unchangeable truth that every procured abortion is evil. Direct abortion (willed as an end or a means) is gravely contrary to the moral law. "You shall not kill the embryo by abortion and shall not cause the newborn to perish." (Didache – First Century) "Life must be protected with utmost care from the first moment of conception: abortion and infanticide are abominable crimes." (Second Vatican Council)

Excommunication For Formal Cooperation (2272)

Formal cooperation in an abortion is a grave offense to which the Church attaches an excommunication "by the very commission of the offense." (C 1398 and 1314) By this excommunication, the Church wants to make clear the gravity of the crime and of the irreparable harm to the innocent person, to the parents and to society.

Right To Life – Inherent In the Person (2773)

The inalienable right to life of every innocent person is a constitutive element of society. Every person's right to life and physical integrity from the moment of conception until death does not depend on parents, or the state. They are inherent in the person. (Gift of Life) Legal protection must be given to the unborn child from the moment of conception. These laws must have appropriate penal sanctions for every deliberate violation of the child's rights." (Gift of Life)

Care For Embryo (2274-2275)

The embryo must be defended, cared for and healed (like any other human being). Prenatal diagnosis is licit if it seeks to safeguard and heal the human fetus. It is gravely wrong if it is done to induce an abortion (depending on the results). "A diagnosis must not become a death sentence." (Gift of Life)

Procedures which seek the embryo's health or survival and do not involve disproportionate risks are morally licit. Producing embryos for exploitation or disposable biological material is immoral. Attempts to influence chromosomal or genetic inheritance aimed at sex selection or other predetermined qualities are contrary to the unique dignity of the human person. (Gift of Life)

Euthanasia (2276-2277)

The sick deserve special help so they can lead normal lives. Direct euthanasia (ending the lives of handicapped, sick or dying) is morally unacceptable no matter what the means or the motives.

An act of omission which (by itself or by intention) causes death to eliminate human suffering is murder and is gravely contrary to human dignity. An error in judgment (even in good faith) does not change the nature of the murderous act (which must always be forbidden).

Legitimate Practices (2278 - 2279)

Discontinuing burdensome, dangerous, extraordinary medical procedures or those disproportionate to the expected outcome is legitimate. In this refusal of "over-zealous" treatment, death is not intended but merely accepted. This decision should be made by the patient (if competent) or by those legally entitled to act for the patient (whose will and legitimate interests must be respected).

Ordinary care should not be interrupted even if death is imminent. Painkillers (even at the risk of shortening life) can be used as long as an earlier death is only tolerated as inevitable. Palliative care is also encouraged.

Suicide (2280 - 2281)

We are responsible to preserve our own life for God's honor and our salvation. We are stewards, not owners and life is not ours to dispose of.

Suicide contradicts the human tendency to preserve life. It is gravely contrary to a love of self, a love of neighbor (because it breaks ties of family and friends) and love for God.

Other Issues (2282-2283)

If suicide is committed to set an example (especially to the young) the act assumes the gravity of scandal. No one can voluntarily cooperate in another's suicide. Grave psychological disturbances, anguish, grave fear of hardship, suffering or torture can diminish responsibility.

Because God can always provide an opportunity for repentance, we should not despair of the salvation of the person. The Church prays for those who have committed suicide.

RESPECT FOR OTHERS AND SELF

Scandal – Harm Done To Others (2284-2285)

Scandal is an attitude or behavior which leads another to do evil. Sometimes this even leads to his spiritual death. Scandal is grave if the other is led to a grave offense.

Scandal is graver if committed by those in authority or is done to those who are especially weak. Jesus condemned those who gave scandal to "the little ones", saying it would be better if they were "drowned in the depth of the sea." (Mt.18:6) Scandal coming from those who have the office of teacher is grave. Jesus called the Pharisees "wolves in sheep's clothing." (Mt.7:15)

Scandals From Society (2286-2287)

Scandal comes from laws, institutions, fashions and public opinion. Scandal is committed by "those who establish laws leading to the decline of morals or to social conditions that make obedience to the Commandments practically impossible." (Pope Pius XII) Also accountable are business leaders who encourage fraud and those who manipulate public opinion against moral values.

All who use their power to lead others astray are guilty. "Woe to him by whom scandal comes." (Lk.17:1)

Caring For Our Health (2288-2289)

We must take reasonable care of life and health. Society must provide those living conditions which promote health: education, employment, housing, health care and social assistance. While caring for health, we must reject a cult of the body which idolizes physical perfection. Preferring the strong over the weak is a perversion of human relationships.

Alcohol and Tobacco (2290)

Temperance disposes people to avoid excesses in the use of alcohol, tobacco or medicines. Anyone who endangers their own life and the lives of others by drunk driving (or by high speeds) incurs grave guilt.

Drugs (2291)

The use of drugs inflicts serious harm. Their use (except for therapeutic reasons) is a grave offense. Selling drugs is a scandal, a serious offense and a direct cooperation in the evil of another.

SCIENCE

Scientific Research And the Dignity Of the Person (2292-2293)

Medical or psychological experiments on human beings can promote public health. Although scientific research is an aspect of man's domination over creation, technology must be placed at the service of man. Scientific research finds both its purpose and its limits in the person and in his moral values.

Incorrect Sources Of Morality (2294-2295)

This research is not morally neutral and cannot be judged by its usefulness to some people at the expense of others. The morality of research cannot come from a prevailing ideology.

Research must unconditionally respect moral criteria, which correspond to man's inalienable rights and God's plan.

Research cannot legitimate those acts which are against the person or against the moral law. Even the person's potential consent does not justify such acts. Experimentation is not legitimate if the person is exposed to disproportionate or avoidable risks. Experimentation demands the consent of the person or those who legitimately speak for him.

Proportionate Risks (2296)

Organ transplants demand prior informed consent from the donor or those who legitimately speak for him. They are legitimate if the risks involved are proportionate to the recipient's good. It is morally wrong to directly cause disabling mutilation or death of a person even to delay the death of another person.

Sins Against Bodily Integrity (2297 - 2298)

The following are morally wrong:
1. kidnapping and taking hostage which cause a reign of terror (especially for the victims).
2. terrorism which threatens, wounds or kills indiscriminately
3. torture which uses physical or moral violence to punish or extract confessions
4. directly intended amputations, mutilations and sterilization of innocent persons (except for medical reasons)

In the past, cruel practices were used by governments to maintain order (often without protest from the Church's pastors). Although the past is regrettable, the Church has always taught clemency and mercy. In recent times, these practices have been seen as not necessary and not in conformity with human dignity.

Care For the Deceased Body (2299-2301)

The dying should be cared for in their final moments. Relatives must see that they receive the sacraments.

The bodies of the dead are temples of the Holy Spirit and must be buried with respect (a corporal work of mercy).

Autopsies for legal and scientific purposes are legitimate. Organ donation after death is meritorious. Cremation is permitted if this act does not demonstrate a denial of faith in the body's resurrection. (Canon 1176)

Anger – Revenge – Hatred (2302-2303)

Jesus denounced murderous <u>anger</u> and <u>hatred</u>. When anger is a desire for revenge, it is illicit. However, restitution can be imposed "to correct vices and to maintain order." (St. Thomas Aquinas) Anger is grave when it becomes a desire to kill or seriously wound another. "Anyone who is angry with his brother, shall be liable to judgment." (Mt.5:22)

<u>Hatred</u> is sinful when the person deliberately wills harm to another. The sin is grave when the person desires grave harm. "Love your enemies and pray for those who persecute you." (Mt.5:44)

Varied Aspects Of Peace (2304-2305)

Human life requires peace which is not just an absence of war or a balance of power. Peace demands safeguarding the goods of persons, the freedom of communication, and respect for the personal dignity. Peace is the "tranquility of order" (St. Augustine), the work of justice and the effect of charity.

Earthly peace comes from Christ, the "Prince of Peace." (Is.9:5) By his death, Jesus reconciled man to God and made his Church the sacrament of unity. "Blessed are the peacemakers." (Mt.5:9)

Special Witness To Gospel (2306)

Those who renounce violence bear witness to the gospel, provided they do no harm to the rights and obligations of others. They also bear witness to the grave risks of recourse to violence (with its destruction and death).

Avoiding War (2307-2308)

The fifth commandment forbids the intentional destruction of human life. Because of war's destructive power, the Church prays that God would free the human race from this ancient bondage.

All citizens and governments must work to avoid war. However, "as long as the danger of war persists and no competent international authority exists, governments have the right to lawful self-defense, once all peace efforts have failed." (Second Vatican Council)

Four Conditions For A Just War (2309-2310)

The decision to make a legitimate defense by military force is so serious that the following conditions must be rigorously applied:

1. The damage inflicted by the aggressor on the nation (or community of nations) must be lasting, grave and certain.
2. All other means (to end the aggression) must be shown to be impractical or ineffective.
3. There must be serious prospects of success.
4. Using arms must not cause graver evils or disorders. Today, the power of modern means of mass destruction demands serious evaluation of this condition.

The above four elements constitute what is called the traditional "just war" doctrine. The prudential judgment in evaluating these conditions lies with those having responsibility for the common good.

Under these four conditions, public authorities have the right and duty to impose on their citizens the obligations necessary for national defense. Armed Forces personnel are the servants of national defense and contribute to the common good.

Conscientious Objectors (2311)

Public Authorities must make equitable provision for those who refuse to bear arms because of reasons of conscience. These should serve the community in some other way.

Moral Law In Waging War (2312-2313)

The Church and human reason teach that during armed conflicts the moral law has permanent validity. Therefore, every act between the warring parties is not necessarily licit.

There must be respect for the non-combatants, the wounded and prisoners of war. Actions against the law of nations and against moral principles are crimes. Blind obedience does not excuse those who follow orders.

The extermination of a nation or an ethnic minority is a mortal sin. Soldiers are morally bound to resist such orders.

283

Modern Means Of Mass Destruction (2314)

Indiscriminate destruction of whole cities or vast areas is a crime against both God and man, and deserves unequivocal condemnation. (Second Vatican Council) Unfortunately modern weapons (atomic, biological and chemical) present the opportunity to cause indiscriminate destruction.

Deterrence And the Arms Race (2315)

The accumulation of arms seems to be a paradoxical way to assure peace. This method of deterrence gives rise to strong moral reservations. The "arms race" aggravates the causes of war by spending enormous sums that could be used for the development of peoples. "Over-armament" increases the danger of escalation.

Arms Sales (2316)

Public authorities must regulate the production and sale of arms. Private or collective interests cannot make licit those undertakings which promote violence among nations and compromise the international political order.

Overcoming the Causes Of War (2317)

Injustice, social inequities and envy constantly threaten peace and cause wars. Overcoming these disorders builds up the peace. "Insofar as men are sinners, the threat of war hangs over them. If sin can be vanquished, violence itself will be vanquished. "Nations shall not lift up sword against nation, neither shall they learn war any more.." (Second Vatican Council)

In Brief - 2318 - 2330

Quotes to Remember

Legal protection must be given to the unborn child from the moment of conception.

....

The cases in which the death penalty is an absolute necessity "are very rare, if not practically non-existent." (Pope John Paul II)

....

36
The Sixth Commandment (2331-2400)

"You shall not commit adultery." (Ex.20:14)

Male and Female – A Capacity For Oneness (2331)
God lives in a communion of persons. Man and woman (made in God's image) also have a capacity for love and communion.

Scripture says "God created man in his own image ... male and female he created them." God blessed them and said, "Be fruitful and multiply", (Gen.1:27-28)

Sexuality affects all the aspects of the human person – his affectivity and his capacity to love, to procreate and to bond with others.

Accepting Identity and Dignity (2333-2335)
Every man and woman should accept their sexual identity, knowing that the difference and the complementarity of male/female are oriented to marriage and family life. The harmony of the spouses depends on how this complementarity and mutual support are lived out.

God gave man and woman an equal personal dignity. Man and woman are equally persons, made in the image and likeness of a personal God.

Each sex is an image of God, with equal dignity in a different way. In marriage, the couple imitate in the flesh the Creator's fecundity, because all human generations proceed from spouses "becoming one flesh." (Gen.2:24)

Jesus' Correct Interpretation (2336)
Interpreting this sixth commandment, Jesus said "Everyone who looks at a woman lustfully has already committed adultery with her in his heart" (Mt.5:2728) and "What God has joined together, let no man put asunder." (Mt.19:6) The Church has always taught that this commandment encompasses all of human sexuality.

CALLED TO CHASTITY

Integration of Sexuality Into the Personal (2337)
Chastity is the successful integration of sexuality in the inner union of man's body and soul. Sexuality expresses man's belonging to the bodily and biological world. It becomes truly human when integrated into the relationship of spouses in their lifelong mutual gift to each other. Chastity involves the integrity of the person and the integrality of the gift.

Self-Mastery or Being Dominated (2338-2339)
Chaste persons maintain the integrity of their sexual powers, and insure a unity of the person. Chastity does not tolerate a double life.

Chastity demands an apprenticeship in self-mastery (a training in human freedom). Man either governs his passions or is dominated by them. Freed from slavery to his passions, man gains his dignity and freely chooses the good.

Means To Chastity (2340-2342)
Remaining faithful and resisting temptations require adopting the needed means: self-knowledge, self-discipline, obedience to God's commands, moral virtues and prayer. "By chastity, we are led back to the unity from which we were fragmented into multiplicity." (St. Augustine)

Chastity allows reason to permeate the passions and sensual appetites.

This needed self-mastery is an exacting work requiring efforts at every stage of life, especially in childhood and adolescence.

Growing In Chastity (2343-2345)
Chastity has laws of growth with stages marked by imperfection and even by sin. Man accomplishes moral good by many free decisions made in these stages of growth.

Because personal betterment and the improvement of society are interdependent, chastity requires a cultural effort. The person has a right to an education which respects the spiritual values of human life.

Besides being a moral virtue, chastity is also a fruit of the Spirit who enables man to be pure.

286

Chastity Expressed In Friendship (2346-2347)

Chastity brings about self-mastery, (the gift of an ordered self) and bears witness of God's loving-kindness.

Chastity blossoms into friendship, allows the person to imitate Christ and to share in his divine life. Chastity is a promise of immortality.

Chastity is expressed notably in friendship with others (whether of the same or opposite sex).

Various States Of Chastity (2348-2349)

All the baptized are called to chastity according to their state in life.

Those who profess virginity or consecrated celibacy must give themselves to God with an undivided heart. Others (single or married) live chastity by their state. Married people practice conjugal chastity. Single people must practice continence. "There are three forms of chastity – that of the spouses, of the widows and of the virgins. We do not praise one to the exclusion of the others." (St. Ambrose)

Chastity of the Engaged (2350)

The engaged must live chastity in continence, seeing their engagement as a time of mutual respect and fidelity. They should help each other in chastity and reserve for marriage those expressions of love which belong to married couples.

Six Sins Against Chastity (2351-2356)

Lust is a disordered desire or an inordinate enjoyment of sexual pleasure. Sexual pleasure is morally disordered when sought for itself or isolated from its procreative and unitive purposes.

Masturbation is the deliberate stimulation of the genital organs to derive sexual pleasure. Masturbation is an intrinsically and gravely disordered action because sexual pleasure is sought outside the context of marriage. An equitable judgment about the person's moral responsibility must take account of the person's affective immaturity, the force of acquired habit, conditions of anxiety, and other emotional or social factors that lessen and even extenuate moral culpability.

Fornication (a carnal union between an unmarried man and woman) is gravely contrary to human sexuality (which exists for the good of spouses and procreation of children). A grave scandal exists when the young are corrupted in this matter.

Pornography displays real or simulated sexual acts to a third party, thus perverting the conjugal act. It gravely harms those who pose for pornography and those who distribute and sell (vendors). All those involved are immersed in a fantasy world. It is a grave offense. Civil authorities should prevent the production and sale of pornography.

Prostitution reduces the person to an instrument of sexual pleasure. The person sins gravely against his own body (a temple of the Spirit). Unfortunately, prostitution is a social scourge which even involves children and adolescents (the sin of scandal). While always gravely sinful, imputability can be attenuated by destitution, blackmail or social pressure.

Rape (the forcible violation of another person's sexual intimacy) deeply wounds the victim's freedom. It often marks the victim for life. Rape is always an intrinsically evil act. Even more grave is incest (the rape of children by parents or by those to whom they are entrusted).

HOMOSEXUALITY

Catholic Tradition (2357)
Homosexuality refers to relations between men or between women who experience sexual attraction to others of the same sex. Although homosexuality has taken many forms, its psychological source remains largely unexplained. Catholic tradition (based on biblical texts) has always taught that "homosexual acts are intrinsically disordered." (Congregation for Doctrine of Faith) They are against the natural law, are closed to the gift of life and do not proceed from a genuine sexual complementarity. Under no circumstances can they be approved.

Called To Chastity (2358-2359)
The number of persons with homosexual tendencies is not negligible. They did not choose their condition and they must be accepted with respect. All unjust discrimination must be avoided.

They are called to do God's will and to unite their sacrifices to the Lord's sacrifice on the cross.

Homosexual persons are called to chastity, and to a self-mastery to gain inner freedom. If supported by disinterested friendship, prayer and the sacraments they can approach Christian perfection.

MARITAL LOVE

Correct Ordering Of Sexuality (2360-2362)

Sexuality is ordered to the conjugal love of man and woman. When the spouses are both baptized, their marriage bonds are sanctified by the sacrament.

The sexual act of spouses is not just biological, but touches their innermost beings. Sexual acts are realized in a truly human way only when the man and woman have committed themselves totally to each other for their whole life.

On his wedding night, Tobias prayed with Sarah "I am now taking this kinswoman of mine not because of lust but with sincerity. Grant that she and I many grow old together. They both said 'Amen' and went to sleep for the night." (Tob.8:4-9)

Two Goals of the Sexual Act (2363)

Sexual acts "are truly noble and honorable. They enrich the spouses in joy and gratitude." (Second Vatican Council) "The Creator himself established that the spouses should experience pleasure and enjoyment of body and spirit. Therefore, the spouses do nothing evil in seeking this pleasure and enjoyment." (Pope Pius XII)

The spouses' union achieves the two goals of marriage – the good of the spouses and the transmission of life. These two meanings cannot be separated without compromising the good of marriage and of the family. Conjugal love has the twofold obligation of fidelity and fecundity.

Fidelity To Each Other (2364)

By their irrevocable personal consent, the married couple form an intimate partnership which is governed by God's laws. They give themselves to each other definitively and totally (forming one flesh). They must preserve their covenant as unique and

289

indissoluble. "What God has joined, let not man put asunder." (Mk.10:9)

Faithful To Christ (2365)

Fidelity means constancy in keeping one's word. Matrimony enables the couple to be faithful as Christ is faithful to his Church. "Young husbands should say to their wives, 'I have taken you in my arms and I prefer you to my life itself. My most ardent dream is to spend my life with you so we are not separated in heaven.'" (St. John Chrysostom)

Open To Transmitting Life (2366-2367)

Conjugal love is meant to be fruitful. The child is not "added on" to the couple's mutual giving but "springs from the heart". Therefore, "each and every marriage act must remain open to the transmission of life." (Pope Paul VI – Humanae Vitae) This constant Church teaching "is based on the inseparable connection, established by God, which man on his own initiative may not break, between the unitive significance and the procreative significance which are both inherent to the marriage act." (Pope Paul VI)

Called to give life, spouses share in God's fatherhood and creative power. The transmission of life and education of children are the mission of parents who are cooperators in the Creator's love.

Regulation of Births (2368 - 2369)

Concerning the regulation of births, couples may wish (for a just reason) to space the births of children. This desire must not come from selfishness but must conform to the generosity appropriate with responsible parenthood. Also, their behavior must conform with the objective moral criteria.

"This morality does not depend on a sincere intention or evaluation of motives alone but upon objective criteria drawn from the nature of the person and his acts. These criteria must respect the total meaning of mutual self-giving and human procreation. This is possible only with married chastity practiced with sincerity." (Second Vatican Council)

"By safeguarding the unitive and procreative aspects, the conjugal act preserves its fullness of true marital love." (Pope Paul VI)

Periodic Continence (2370)
Periodic continence (the method of birth regulation based upon the use of the infertile period) is in conformity with the objective moral criteria. These methods respect the spouses' bodies, and encourage tenderness. In contrast "Every action which whether in anticipation of the conjugal act, or in its accomplishment, or in the development of its natural consequences, proposes, whether as an end or a means, to render procreation impossible, is intrinsically evil." (Pope Paul VI)

Contraception (2371)
By contraception, the self-giving of husband and wife is overlaid with contradictory language, namely of not giving oneself totally to the other. This falsifies the inner truth of conjugal love. The difference between contraception and natural family planning involves two irreconcilable concepts of the person and sexuality. (Pope John Paul II)

"The duty of transmitting human life is not limited by the horizons of this life but extend to man's eternal destiny." (Second Vatican Council)

Wrong Demographic Regulation (2372)
The state has the legitimate responsibility to orient the demography of the population, using objective and respectful information but not coercive measures. The state cannot usurp the rights of spouses (who have primary responsibility for procreation). Demographic regulation cannot use means contrary to the moral law.

THE GIFT OF A CHILD

Large Families (2373 – 2375)
Sacred Scripture and the Church see large families as a sign of God's blessings and parental generosity. Childless couples (Like Abraham/Sarah and Jacob/Rachel) often suffer greatly.

Research to reduce human sterility must be "at the service of the person, of his inalienable rights and his integral good in God's plan." (Gift of Life)

Gravely Immoral Techniques (2376 2377)

Any techniques (such as donation of sperm or ovum, surrogate uterus) that entails a disassociation of the spouses by the intrusion of a third party are gravely immoral. These techniques (heterologous artificial insemination and fertilization) infringe on the child's rights to know who his mother and father are. Couples have a "right to become a father and a mother only through each other." (Gift of Life)

Techniques involving only the couple themselves (homologous artificial insemination and fertilization) are less reprehensible yet morally unacceptable because they disassociate procreation from the sexual act. These methods entrust the life and identity of the embryo into the hands of doctors. They place the power of technology over the origin and destiny of the human person. This domination is contrary to that dignity which belongs to both parents and children. Procreation is deprived of its perfection when it is not the fruit of a specific sexual act of the spouses' union. (Gift of Life)

No "Right" To A Child (2378-2379)

Every child is a gift, not a piece of property. He/she is not owed to anyone. No one has "a right to a child." Only the child has genuine rights. The child must be "the fruit of a specific act of the conjugal love of his parents" and to "be respected as a person from the first moment of conception." (Gift of Life)

The gospel shows that physical sterility is not an evil. After exhausting legitimate medical means, a childless couple should unite with Jesus' cross. They can adopt children or perform demanding service for other.

SINS AGAINST MARRIAGE

Adultery (2380 - 2381)

Adultery is committed when sexual relations take place between two people, at least one of whom is married to another. The New Testament and the sixth commandment absolutely forbid adultery. Christ condemned even adultery in desire.

292

Adultery is an injustice, transgressing the rights of the spouse(s), and undermining the institution of marriage. The adulterer also hurts the children who need their parents' stable union.

Divorce (2382)

Jesus insisted that marriage must be indissoluble (God's original plan). He abrogated accommodations that had compromised the sixth commandment. Therefore, between a baptized man and woman "a ratified and consummated marriage cannot be dissolved by any human power or for any reason other than death." (Canon 1141)

Separation (2383)

While maintaining the marriage bond, Canon law does provide for the legitimate separation of spouses (C. 1151-1155). There is no moral offense if a civil divorce is the only way to safeguard children and legal rights.

Contracting Another Marriage (2384)

Divorce is a grave offense against the natural law because it claims to break a freely chosen contract which really lasts until death. Contracting another marriage (even though recognized by civil law) adds to the gravity of sin, because the remarried spouse is in a situation of public and permanent adultery.

"If a husband approaches another woman he is an adulterer because he makes that woman commit adultery. The woman is an adulteress because she has attracted another's husband." (St. Basil)

Reasons Why Wrong (2385)

Divorce is immoral because:
1. It introduces a disorder which harms the deserted spouse
2. It traumatizes children (who are torn between parents).
3. It has a contagious effect upon society.

An abandoned spouse (who has tried to be faithful) has not broken the moral law. The one who destroys a canonically valid marriage commits a grave fault.

Other Offenses Against Marriage (2386 – 2391)

Polygamy radically contradicts God's plan because it contradicts the equal dignity of man and woman. A convert coming from a life of polygamy has an understandable predicament. He must put aside one or more wife and must also honor any obligations he has to them.

Incest is sexual relations between relatives (or in-laws) within a degree that prohibits marriage between them. Paul writes against a "man lying with his father's wife." (1Cor.5:1-5) Incest corrupts family life and regresses toward animality.

Sexual abuse of children by adults who have care for them is a serious offense and a violation of the adult's responsibility. It is compounded by the harm done to the young (who will be scarred all their life).

In a "free union" the couple refuses to give public form to their sexual intimacy. This is hardly a "union" when no commitment is made and the person lacks trust in himself, the other and the future.

Free unions include concubinage, rejection of marriage or inability to make long-term commitments. Because sexual acts must take place within marriage, free unions constitute a grave sin and exclude from Holy Communion because they destroy the very idea of family.

No one has a right to a "trial marriage" (intending to get married later) because sexual relations are legitimate only for men and women in an established marriage. Experience shows that trial marriages do not insure fidelity and security.

In Brief - 2392 – 2400

Quotes to Remember

Chastity does not tolerate a double life.

Man either governs his passions or is governed by them.

37
The Seventh Commandment (2401- 2463))

"You shall not steal"

Unjust Taking or Keeping (2401)
Unjustly taking or keeping a neighbor's goods (or wronging a neighbor concerning his goods) violates the seventh commandment. This commandment also requires justice and charity concerning man's labors. There must be an understanding that all goods are destined for the good of all, and, at the same time, a respect for private property.

MEANT FOR ALL – YET PRIVATE OWNERSHIP

Creation Is For Everyone (2402-2403)
In the beginning, God wanted all men to master the earth and enjoy its fruits. Creation is for everyone's good. However, the earth is divided up to guarantee man's security (which is now threatened by poverty and violence). This appropriation of property is meant to guarantee personal dignity and the gain of basic needs.

Even with the right to private property (acquired by work or by a gift), the original gift of earth belongs to everyone. This universal destination of goods remains primary, even though the common good demands the right to private property.

Benefiting The Greatest Number (2404-2406)
Men must see that their legitimately owned possessions are not just for themselves but are to benefit all. (Second Vatican Council) The human owner is really God's steward, bringing forth fruit to benefit others (first of all his family).

Material and immaterial goods of production (land, factories, personal skills) must be used to benefit the greatest number. Goods for consumption should be used moderately by their owners so he can help the sick and poor.

Political authority can regulate the right to ownership for the common good.

RESPECTING PERSONS AND THEIR GOODS

Three Virtues (2407)
Economic matters demand:
1. Temperance – which moderates attachments to worldly goods
2. Justice –which preserves the just rights of others
3. solidarity – oneness with the poor

Theft And Unjust Taking (2408)
Theft is the taking of another's goods against the reasonable will of the owner. No theft exists if the owner's consent can be presumed or his will violates reason. At times, stealing provides for an essential need (food, shelter, clothing) and requires the use of other's goods.

Unjustly taking or keeping goods (even when not against the civil law) violates this commandment. Unjust taking includes unjust wages, business fraud, retaining borrowed or lost items and unjust pricing.

Eight Other Sins (2409)
Also morally illicit are:
1. speculation – which manipulates prices
2. corruption – which influences the judgments of authority
3. appropriation of an employer's goods
4. work poorly done
5. income tax evasion
6. forging of checks or invoices
7. excessive expenses and waste
8. destroying public or private property

Promises and Contracts (2410-2411)
Morally just promises and contracts must be kept because social life depends on contracts which are completed in good faith.

Contracts demand commutative justice which safeguards the right of each person. Justice demands that debts and obligations be fulfilled.

Two other forms of commutative justice are:
1. legal justice – what a citizen owes to the community

296

2.   distributive justice – what a community owes its citizens (according to their contributions and their needs)

Need To Restore (2412)

By <u>commutative justice</u>, stolen goods must be returned to the owner. Zacchaeus told Jesus "If I have defrauded anyone, I restore it fourfold." (Lk.19:8)

Whoever has taken goods (directly or indirectly) must restore them or return an equivalent in money.

Those who participate in a theft must make restitution in proportion to their responsibility.

Chance And Gambling (2413)

Games of chance and betting are not contrary to justice unless they deprive someone of what he needs for himself or his family. A gambling addiction can become enslavement. Cheating or unfair betting is a grave sin unless the matter is insignificant.

Enslaving For Profit (2414)

Any acts for whatever reason (selfish or commercial) which lead to the enslavement of human beings (bought and sold like merchandise) are against human dignity. These acts reduce a person by violence to an object. Paul asks Christian masters to treat a slave "as a beloved brother." (Philem. 16)

Stewardship For the Animals (2415-2416)

There must be respect for God's creation (animals, plants and things). Care for these resources is a moral imperative. Man does not have absolute dominion over creation. He must consider his neighbor and the good of generations yet to be born.

God surrounds animals with his special care, for they give him glory. Thus, men owe them kindness according to the model of St. Francis of Assisi and St. Philip Neri.

Right and Wrong Use (2417-2418)

Because man has stewardship of animals, he can use them for food and clothing, for pets or for manual work. Medical experimentation on animals (within reasonable limits) is morally acceptable because it helps human life.

Animals must not be made to suffer or to die needlessly. Also, large amounts of money (that should help poor people) should not be used on animals.

THE CHURCH'S SOCIAL DOCTRINE

Moral Teachings On Social Matters (2419-2420)
From the Gospel, the Church receives wisdom about man's social living. She proclaims man's dignity and the demands of peace and justice.

When human rights or the salvation of souls requires, the Church makes moral judgments on economic and social matters. She has a mission distinct from political authorities. The Church is concerned with temporal goods because they are ordered to man's salvation. She tries to inspire right attitudes to goods and economic relationships.

Catholic Social Teaching (2421-2422)
The Church's social doctrine developed in the nineteenth century when the Gospel confronted the new structures of production, new concepts of the state and new forms of labor and ownership. The Church's tradition has a permanent value which is always living and active.

In this social teaching (which comprises a body of doctrine), the Church interprets events in light of Christ's teachings. As Catholics follow this teaching, others will also accept it.

Three Doctrines (2423-2424)
This doctrine proposes the following:
1. Any system determined entirely by economic factors is contrary to the human person.
2. Any theory which makes profit the exclusive and ultimate end of economic activity is morally unacceptable. It produces perverse effects and leads to conflicts.
3. Any system which subordinates the basic rights of persons and groups to the collective organization is contrary to human dignity. Reducing persons to merely means of profit is enslavement.

Law Of the Marketplace (2425)

Although rejecting "communism" and "socialism", the Church has also refused to accept the absolute primacy of the law of the marketplace. There must be reasonable regulation of economic initiatives. Regulation solely by the "law of the marketplace" fails social justice.

ECONOMY AND SOCIAL JUSTICE

Economy Within God's Moral Order (2426)

Economic activity is meant to serve the needs of the human person. Its goal is not merely to multiply goods or increase profit. Economic activity must operate within the moral order by a social justice according to God's plan.

Work As A Duty (2427-2428)

Human work comes from God's call to prolong his original work of creation. Therefore, work is a duty. "If anyone will not work, let him not eat." (2Thes.3:10) By enduring work, man shares in Christ's cross and redemption.

By work, man fulfills the potential inscribed in his nature. Work is for man, not man for work. Man is both the author and the beneficiary of his work, which should supply what he needs and also benefits the community.

Needed Regulations (2429-2430)

Everyone has a right to use their talents to benefit themselves and others. All have a duty to observe legitimate authority's regulations for the common good.

Economic life involves diverse interests which often lead to conflict. These conflicts should be reduced by negotiations involving owners, workers and public authorities.

Importance Of Public Authority (2431)

Economic activity requires individual freedom, private property, stable currency and efficient public service. Public authority, therefore, must guarantee this security so man can be encouraged to honest work. The state must also oversee the exercise of human rights, (even though this task belongs primarily to individuals and their associations).

299

Duties Of Owners (2432)

Owners are responsible for the economic and ecological effects of their businesses. Although profits are needed to guarantee employment, owners must consider the good of persons and not just their own profits.

Just Wage (2433-2434)

Everyone must have access to employment without discrimination (men and women, healthy and sick; natives and immigrants). Society should help citizens to find work.

To refuse a just wage or to withhold it is a grave injustice. This just wage is determined by the person's contribution and need, as well as the nature of the business and the common good. An agreement between the parties does not morally justify an unjust wage.

Some Moral Questions (2435-2436)

A strike is morally legitimate when it cannot be avoided or is needed to gain a proportionate good. Violence is never morally acceptable. A strike which seeks objectives not linked to work or against the common good is not justified.

Unemployment always wounds the person and entails risks for his family.

SOLIDARITY AMONG NATIONS

International Inequality (2437)

Due to an inequality of resources and economic capability, a real gap exists between nations. Some nations develop means of growth while others accumulate debts.

Serious International Problems (2438)

This question demands solidarity among nations. There must be a dismantling of those perverse mechanisms which impede the development of the poor nations. There must be an end to the abusive, (sometimes usurious) financial systems, sinful commercial relationships and the arms race. Nations must redefine their values and mobilize resources toward moral and economic development according to a hierarchy of values.

International Financial Reform (2439-2441)

Rich nations have a grave moral responsibility to ensure economic development in poorer nations. The rich nations have a duty in justice to pay a fair price for the resources gained from poorer countries.

Direct aid to needy countries (given for immediate extraordinary needs) does not provide any lasting solutions. The real need is to reform international financial institutions to promote more equitable relationships with poor countries. Efforts of poor countries to attain growth and liberation (especially in the area of farm labor) must be supported. Third World peasants form the overwhelming majority of the poor.

An increased sense of God and of self demands development of every society. This development multiplies material goods and puts them at the service of persons. In this way, dire poverty and exploitation are reduced.

THE POOR

Duty Of Lay Faithful (2442)

The Church's pastors are not called to intervene in this restructuring of political and economic life. The lay faithful must act for social reform. They must "animate temporal realities" and be "witnesses of peace and justice." (Second Vatican Council)

Blessing The Poor (2443-2444)

God blesses those who help the poor and rebukes those who do not. Jesus will recognize his chosen ones by what they have done for the poor. (Mt.25: 31-36)

The Church's love for the poor is part of a constant tradition. The duty of work flows from love for the poor because the worker can "give to those in need" both materially, culturally and religiously.

Selfish Use Of Riches (2445-2446)

Love for the poor is incompatible with the selfish use of riches. "Come now, you rich, weep and howl for the miseries that are coming upon you. Your gold and silver have rusted and their rust will be evidence against you and will eat your flesh like fire. The wages of the laborers which you kept back by fraud, cry out, and the cries of harvesters have reached the ears of the Lord of hosts." (Jas. 5:1-6)

"Not to enable the poor to share in our goods is to steal from them. The goods we possess are not ours, but theirs." (St. John Chrysostom) "When we attend to the needs of those in want, we give them what is theirs, not ours." (St. Gregory the Great)

Almsgiving – Pleasing To God (2447)

There are spiritual works of mercy (instructing, comforting, forgiving, bearing wrongs patiently) and corporal works of mercy (taking care of the hungry, the homeless, the sick, the imprisoned and burying the dead). Among these works, alms to the poor is most important and pleasing to God. "Give alms and everything will be clean for you." (Lk.11:41) James rebuked any Christian who saw a person in need "without giving them the things needed for the body." (Jas.2:16)

Human misery in its various forms (deprivation, oppression, illness and death) show man's inherited condition of frailty. This human misery always elicited the compassion of Christ and the Church has a preferential love for those in need. In spite of many failings, she must always work for the relief of those in need.

Measures To Help The Poor (2449)

The Old Testament contains many juridical measures to aid the poor (jubilee forgiveness of debts, tithing, daily payment of day laborers, the poors' right to glean the fields). "You shall open wide your hand to your brother, to the needy and to the poor." (Deut. 15:11) Amos spoke vehemently about "buying the needy for a pair of sandals." (8:6) Jesus asks us to recognize his own presence in the poor. "We must not fail to help our neighbors, because in them we serve Jesus" (St. Rose of Lima explaining to her mother why she helped the poor).

In Brief (2450 – 2463)

Quotes to Remember

Creation is for everyone's good. Earth is divided up to guarantee man's security (which is always threatened by poverty and violence).

....

38
The Eighth Commandment (2464-2513)

"You shall not bear false witness against your neighbor."
(Ex.20:16)

Witness To The Truth (2464)
Holy people are called to witness to God who is truth. Therefore, a person cannot misrepresent the truth to others. Offenses against truth (in word or deed) show a lack of commitment to moral uprightness.   Lies are fundamental infidelities to God which undermine his covenant.

LIVING IN THE TRUTH

The Scriptures (2465 – 2466)
The Old Testament teaches that God is the source of all truth and that God's people are called to truth.

Jesus Christ is "full of grace and truth." (Jn.1:14) He is "the truth." (Jn.14:6) Jesus wants his disciples to be consecrated "by means of the truth." (Jn.17:17) He promises that "the truth will make you free." (Jn.8:28) The Holy Spirit will lead the disciples "into all the truth." (Jn.16:13)

Seeking The Truth (2467-2468)
Man must tend toward the truth and witness to the truth. "Persons have a moral obligation to seek truth (especially religious truth) to adhere to the truth and to direct their lives according to the demands of truth." (Second Vatican Council)

Truthfulness consists in showing oneself true in deeds and in words and in avoiding duplicity, dissimulation and hypocrisy.

Discretion and Honesty (2469-2470)
"Men could not live with one another if they were not truthful to one another." (St. Thomas Aquinas)

Truthfulness entails honesty and discretion, realizing what must be expressed and what must be kept secret. "As a matter of honor, one man owes it to another to manifest the truth." (St. Thomas Aquinas)

By a simplicity of lifestyle, Christ's disciple "lives in the truth." We cannot have fellowship with Jesus if "we lie and do not live according to the truth." (1Jn.1:6)

Christian Witness (2471-2472)

Christ proclaimed to Pilate that he had come "to bear witness to the truth. (Jn.18:37) Christians must not be "ashamed of testifying to our Lord." (2Tim.1:8) They must have "a clear conscience toward God and toward men." (Acts 24:16)

Christians must witness to the Gospel by transmitting their faith in words and deeds. All Christians have an obligation by their lives to manifest their Baptism and to reveal the Holy Spirit who strengthened them in Confirmation. (Second Vatican Council)

Martyrs For The Truth (2473-2474)

By martyrdom, a Christian gives supreme witness to Christ and to Christian doctrine. "Let me become the food of the beasts, through whom it will be given me to reach God." (St. Ignatius of Antioch)

The Church collects the acts and words of the martyrs whose witness is written in letters of blood. "It is better for me to die in order to unite myself to Christ Jesus than to reign over the ends of the earth. My birth is approaching." (St. Ignatius of Antioch) "I bless you for having judged me worthy from this day and this hour to be counted among your martyrs." (St. Polycarp)

SINS AGAINST THE TRUTH

Public Statements Against Truth (2475-2476)

Christ's disciples are to "put away all malice and all guile and insincerity and envy and all slander." (1Pet.2:1)

A public statement contrary to the truth has particular gravity. In court, this is false witness. When made under oath it is perjury. Because these acts can condemn the innocent or exonerate the guilty, they compromise the justice needed in judicial decisions.

Inflicting Unjust Injury (2477-2479)

Respect for the reputation of others forbids every attitude or words which inflict unjust injury. These include:

1. <u>rash judgment</u> – which assumes as true the moral fault of another without sufficient evidence
2. <u>detraction</u> – which discloses a person's faults to another without any valid reason
3. <u>calumny (slander)</u> – which harms another's reputation by saying what is not true

A disciple avoids rash judgment by being careful in interpreting the deeds of another. "Every good Christian must be more ready to give a favorable interpretation to a person's words than to condemn them." (St. Ignatius of Loyola)

Everyone has a right to their good name. Therefore, <u>detraction</u> and <u>calumny</u> (which destroy that reputation) are sins against justice and charity.

Offenses Against The Truth (2480-2481)

Every word or attitude (<u>adulation, flattery</u>) which encourages or confirms a person in their evil deeds is forbidden. This <u>adulation</u> is grave if it makes someone an accomplice in a grave matter. Adulation is venial if done to be agreeable or to meet a need. Friendship (or any other reason) never justifies duplicitous speech.

<u>Boasting</u> and <u>bragging</u> offend truth. <u>Irony</u> (aimed to hurt another by maliciously caricaturing them) also offends truth.

The Lie – Direct Offense Against Truth (2482-2484)

A <u>lie</u> is a falsehood spoken with the intent to deceive. Jesus denounces lying as the work of the devil. "He is a liar and the father of lies." (Jn.8:44)

Lying (the attempt to lead into error someone who has the right to know the truth) is the most direct offense against the truth. Lies injure man's relation to the truth, to his neighbor and to the Lord.

The <u>gravity of a lie</u> depends upon the truth which it deforms, and upon the circumstances, the intentions and the harm suffered by the victims. A lie is usually venial and becomes mortal when it does grave injury.

Effects Of Lying (2485-2486)

Lying is condemned because it profanes speech which is meant to communicate truth. The culpability is greater if the lie entails the risk of serious consequences for those who are led astray.

Lying does violence to the other person by affecting his ability to know (a condition for every decision). It sows discord, destroys society, undermines trust and tears apart social relationships.

Reparation For Lying (2487)

The person who lied must make reparation, even if this can only be done secretly. The victim must be compensated, or (if that is impossible) be given moral satisfaction. The reparation of harm or of a good reputation must be judged according to the extent of the damage inflicted.

Truth – A Correct Response (2488-2489)

The right to be told the truth is not unconditional. The person must judge if it is appropriate to reveal the truth.

Both truth and charity dictate the correct response to someone seeking information. Some reasons (safety, privacy, the common good) allow silence or discreet language. Avoiding scandal demands great discretion. The truth need not be revealed to someone who has no right to know.

Special Cases (2490-2491)

The priest cannot violate the secret of the sacrament of Reconciliation. "The sacramental seal is inviolable. It is a crime for a confessor in any way to betray a penitent by word or any other manner for any reason." (Canon 983)

Professional secrets (known to office holders, doctors, lawyers, etc.) or confidential information given under secrecy must be kept secret unless grave harm to the person, to the confidant, or to a third part can be avoided only by divulging the truth. Private information prejudicial to another (even when not given under secrecy) cannot be divulged without a serious and proportionate reason.

MEANS OF SOCIAL COMMUNICATIONS

Media and Peoples' Private Lives (2492)

There should be an appropriate reserve concerning peoples' private lives. The media should maintain a balance between the common good (the right to know) and the individual (the right to privacy). Interfering in the private lives of public persons must be condemned if it infringes on their privacy and freedom.

Media – Serving Society (2493-2494)

The media plays a major role in information and formation. Due to technological progress, the media's role in influencing public opinion is constantly increasing.

Media information must be at the service of society (which has a right to information based on truth and justice). "The context of the communication must be true and communicated honestly and properly. In gathering news, the moral law and the rights of man must be upheld." (Second Vatican Council)

News Media – Justice, Yet Charity (2495-2497)

News must help to form and transmit sound public opinion. Solidarity results from a free flow of ideas that further knowledge and respect for others.

The mass media causes a certain passivity. Both listener and viewer must use discipline to form correct consciences and to combat unwholesome influences.

Journalists must serve the truth with charity. They must respect both the facts and the limits of critical judgments concerning individuals. They must not stoop to defamation.

Manipulating Public Opinion (2498-2499)

Public authorities must defend a true freedom of information. By legislation, they must safeguard public morality and social progress. They must punish those in the media who violate the reputation and privacy of others. They must respond to the well-founded concerns of the people about the use of media. Nothing can justify disinformation or manipulation of public opinion. Public intervention must not injure the freedom of the person or the group.

Totalitarian states must be condemned for exercising political control of the media, of manipulating trials and of repressing what they see as "thought crimes."

Truth In The Beauty Of Art (2500)

Truth carries the joy and splendor of spiritual beauty. Truth is found in forms beyond words which touch the human heart. Before revealing through words, God revealed himself by the beauty of all creation, (which is understood by children and by scientists). From creation, man can perceive "the author of beauty." (Wis.13:5) "Wisdom is a reflection of eternal light, a spotless mirror of the working of God and an image of his goodness. I became enamored of her beauty." (Wis.7:25-26)

The Mystery OF God (2501-2503)

Man expresses his relationship to God by the beauty of artistic works. Art (a distinctly human form of expression) comes from the person's inner riches and gives a form to truth. Art bears a likeness to God in his creating activity. However, art is not an absolute goal and must be ordered to man's ultimate goal. (Pope Pius XII)

Sacred art glorifies the mystery of God in his invisible beauty and in the visible love of Christ, in whom the "fullness of God dwells bodily." (Col.2:9) God's beauty is also reflected in the Virgin Mary, the angels and saints.

Bishops must promote sacred art (old and new) in all its forms. They must also remove from the liturgy and from places of worship whatever does not conform to the truth of faith and to authentic beauty.

In Brief - 2504 - 2513

Quotes to Remember

God's people are called to truth. The media, in gathering news must communicate it honestly and properly.

39
The Ninth Commandment (2514 – 2533)

"You shall not covet your neighbor's wife." (Ex. 20:17)

Three Types of Illicit Desires (2514)
Everyone who looks at a woman lustfully has already committed adultery with her in his heart" (Mt.5:28)

St. John lists three types of concupiscence, lust of the flesh, lust of the eyes and the pride of life. (Jn.2:16)   In Catholic tradition,   the   ninth   commandment   forbids   lust   (carnal concupiscence).

Defining "Concupiscence" (2515)
"Concupiscence" refers to any intense form of human desire. In Christian theology, concupiscence means a movement of the sensitive appetite which is against human reason.   Paul calls it a rebellion of the flesh against the spirit.   Concupiscence (which comes from original sin) unsettles man's moral powers and inclines him to sin (although not itself being a sin).

The Flesh Wars Against The Spirit (2516)
Because man is a composite being (spirit and body) a certain tension exists.   There is a struggle of tendencies between "spirit" and "flesh."   This struggle comes from the consequences of sin.

St. Paul did not condemn the body.   Rather he was concerned with the body's good works which come from submission to the Spirit or its bad works which come from resistance to the Spirit (Pope John Paul II).

PURIFYING THE HEART

Jesus Stresses the Heart (2517-2519)
Jesus said that evil acts come "out of the heart." (Mt.15:19) The struggle against carnal covetousness entails purifying the heart (the seat of moral personality).   "Be like little children who do not know the evil that destroys man's life." (Shepherd of the Hermas)

"Blessed are the pure in heart for they shall see God." (Mt.5:8)   "Pure of heart" means attuning the will and intellect to God's will, especially concerning charity, chastity and the truths of faith. "Christians must believe the Creed so that by believing they may obey God, by obeying they may live well, and by living well they may purify their hearts. With pure hearts they can understand what they believe." (St. Augustine)

Being pure in heart is a condition of seeing God in heaven. On earth, this purity helps us to see according to God, to perceive the human body (our own and our neighbor's) as a temple of the Holy Spirit.

Four Victories In The Struggle (2520)

Although Baptism purifies from all sin, the struggle against disordered desires continues. The person will prevail by:

1. chastity by which the person can love with an undivided heart.
2. purity of intention – by which the baptized seeks the right goals and fulfills God's will in everything.
3. purity of vision by which the person rejects impure sights and thoughts
4. prayer – by which the person seeks God's help.

"I thought continence arose from my own powers. Yet no one can be continent unless you (God) grant it. You would surely have granted it if my inner-groaning had reached your ears." (St. Augustine)

Modesty Protects The Mystery (2521-2524)

Purity requires modesty (keeping veiled what should remain hidden). Modesty guards our looks towards others and behaves toward them according to their human dignity.

Modesty encourages moderation in loving relationships. It protects the mystery of the person and demands a definitive commitment between man and woman. Modesty is decency, both in choosing clothing and in keeping silence in the face of unhealthy curiosity.

A modesty of feelings protests voyeuristic advertisements and a media which goes too far in exhibiting the human body. Modesty resists the allurements of fashions and the pressure of prevailing customs.

Modesty is an intuition of man's spiritual dignity which results when the person becomes aware of being a human subject.

Modesty awakens (in both children and adolescents) a respect for the human person.

Purifying Our Society (2525-2527)
The social climate and the media must be purified. Only purity of heart brings a freedom from widespread eroticism and avoids voyeuristic entertainment.

Moral permissiveness is based on a false idea of human freedom. Educators must teach the truth about the human heart and the spiritual dignity of man.

The Gospel of Christ always renews a culture and removes evil present through sin. The Gospel elevates modesty and causes the gifts in every culture to blossom. (Second Vatican Council)

In Brief (2528 – 2533)

Quotes to Remember

Everyone who looks at a woman lustfully has already committed adultery with her in his heart. (Mt. 5:28)

St. Paul did not condemn the body.

The body's good works come from submission to the Spirit. The bad works come from the body's resistance to the Spirit.

Be like little children who do not know the evil that destroys. (Shepherd of Hermas)

The social climate and the media must be purified.

40
The Tenth Commandment (2534-2557)

"You shall not covet anything that is your neighbor's. "
(Ex.20:17)
"Where your treasure is, there your heart will be. " (Mt.6:21)

Relationship To Ninth (2534)
By forbidding us to covet a neighbor's goods, the tenth commandment completes the ninth commandment. It also completes the seventh commandment because theft, robbery and fraud are rooted in covetousness.

COVETOUS DESIRES

A Disordered Seeking (2535)
By the sensitive appetite, man desires what he does not have. These desires (although good in themselves) can exceed the limits of reason and lead us to covet what belongs to or is owed to another.

Sins (2536)
This commandment forbids:
1. greed – the desire to amass unlimited earthly wealth
2. avarice – a passion for riches and the power that comes from them
3. any desires which involve unjust harm to our neighbor's goods
"We should banish our desires for whatever does not belong to us. Our immense thirst for goods is never quenched. As it is written 'He who loves money never has enough'." (Roman Catechism) It is not sinful to desire to gain a neighbor's goods by just means.

Difficult Struggle (2537)
Some people "have a harder struggle against their criminal desires." Among these, the Roman Catechism mentions:
1. merchants – who in scarcity can charge high prices
2. friends – who can take advantage of impoverished neighbors

3.   lawyers – who are eager for important cases

Envy (2538-2540)

Envy must be banished. Nathan told King David the parable of the rich man (with many sheep) who envied and stole the poor man's one sheep. (1Kings 1:1-29)

"Envy arms us against one another. We are engaged in making Christ's Body a corpse. We devour one another like beasts." (St. John Chrysostom)

Envy (sadness at another's goods and the desire to acquire them even unjustly) is a mortal sin when it wishes grave harm to another.   "Envy is the diabolical sin." (St. Augustine)   "From envy are born hatred, calumny, joy at a neighbor's misfortune and sadness at his prosperity." (St. Gregory the Great)

Envy (a form of sadness) comes from lack of charity. "Rejoice in your brother's progress and you will immediately give glory to God. Conquer envy by rejoicing in the merits of others." (St. John Chrysostom)

DESIRES OF THE HOLY SPIRIT

Failure Of Israel's Law (2541-2542)

God warned man about seduction. Unfortunately, Eve saw the forbidden fruit as "good for food, and a delight to the eyes." (Gen.3:6)

Israel's Law never justified and even became an instrument of "lust." (Rom.7:7) Paul saw the conflict between God's law and the "law of sin which dwells in my members." (Rom.7:23)

Now – God's Righteousness (2543)

But now "the righteousness of God has been manifested apart from the law ... through faith in Jesus Christ for all who believe." (Rom.3:21-22) Crucified in the flesh, believers should "be led by the Spirit and follow the desires of the Spirit." (Gal.5:24)

Jesus' Teaching (2544-2545)

Jesus asked his disciples to "renounce all that they have for his sake" (Lk.14:33) and taught that detachment from riches was needed to enter the kingdom.

313

The faithful must rightly direct their desires so they are not hindered by use of worldly things or their adherence to riches. (Second Vatican Council)

Poor And Rich (2546-2547)

The Beatitudes reveal an order of happiness and peace, and celebrate the joy of the poor. "The Word speaks of voluntary humility as 'poverty of spirit.'" (St. Gregory of Nyssa)

Jesus grieved over the rich because only abandonment to God frees us from anxiety about tomorrow. "The proud seek and love earthly kingdoms, for the poor their kingdom is heaven." (St. Augustine)

Seeking God (2548-2550)

Desiring the vision of God frees man from his inordinate attachment to this world's goods. "To see is to possess. Whoever sees God has obtained every conceivable good." (St. Gregory of Nyssa)

Holy people mortify their cravings and prevail over the seductions of pleasure to gain all of God's promises.

"In heaven there will be true glory and true honor. There true peace will reign. God himself will be virtue's reward. God will be all in all. We shall love God without surfeit. This state, like eternal life itself, will be common to all." (St. Augustine)

In Brief - 2551 - 2557

Quotes to Remember

We should banish our desires for whatever does not belong to us, because our immense thirst for goods is never quenched. He who loves money, never has enough. (Roman Catechism)

....

Conquer envy by rejoicing in your brother's prosperity. (St. John Chrysostom)

....

PART FOUR
CHRISTIAN
PRAYER
(2558-2865)

41
Prayer In the Christian Life (2558-2649)

A Personal Relationship With God (2558)

The Church professes faith in the <u>Apostles Creed</u> (Part One) and celebrates faith in <u>sacramental liturgy</u> (Part Two) so the faithful might conform to God's will in the <u>Ten Commandments</u> (Part Three). To believe, celebrate and live this mystery demands a personal relationship with the living God through prayer (Part Four). "Prayer is a surge of the heart, a simple look toward heaven, a cry of recognition and of love, embracing both trial and joy." (St. Therese of Lisieux)

Begging Before God (2559)

"Prayer is the raising of one's mind and heart to God or the requesting of good things from God." (St. John Damascene) "We do not know how to pray as we ought." (Rom. 8:26) "Man is a beggar before God." (St. Augustine)

God's Thirst For Us (2560-2561)

Jesus said to the Samaritan woman "If you knew the gift of God." (Jn.4:10) At the well of prayer, Jesus meets every human being. Jesus' thirst is his desire for us. In prayer we encounter of God's thirst for us so we may thirst for him.

Our asking corresponds to God's plea. "They have forsaken me, the fountain of living waters and have hewn out broken cisterns which hold no water." (Jer.2:13) Prayer is a response to God's promise of salvation.

The Prayer of The Whole Person (2562-2563)
Prayer must come from the whole person. Scripture speaks of prayer coming from man's soul, spirit and his heart (over 1000 times). If our heart is far from God, our prayer is in vain.

The heart is man's hidden center, (beyond the grasp of reason) which only God's Spirit can fully know. The heart is the place of decision where we choose life or death. It is a place of our encounter and our covenant with God.

From The Covenant With The Trinity (2564-2565)
Christian prayer is a covenant relationship in Christ, springing from the Spirit and ourselves and directed toward the Father in union with Christ's human will.

Prayer is the living relationship of the children with the Father, Son and Spirit. The Kingdom is "the union of the entire Holy Trinity with the whole human spirit." (St. Gregory of Nazeanzus) Prayer is the habit of being in the presence of the Trinity.

God Tirelessly Calls All To Prayer (2566-2567)
By creation, God gave existence to every being. However, only man and angels can acknowledge the majesty of God. Even after sin, man remained in God's image and retained a desire for God. All religions show man's search for God.

God tirelessly calls man to an encounter (called prayer) even though man forgets God, hides from God or accuses God of abandonment. In prayer, God acts first and man responds. Prayer is a reciprocal call, a covenant drama which engages man's heart.

THE OLD TESTAMENT

Meeting God In History (2568)
God's first call was to our first parents after they sinned. "Where are you? What is this you have done"? (Gen.3: 9,13) Jesus responded to this question, "I have come to do your will, O God" (Heb.5-7). Prayer is man's encounter with God within history

316

Abel – Noah – Abraham (2569)

In the Bible's first nine chapters, prayer deals with the offering of creation. Abel offered the firstling of his flock (Gen.4:4) and Noah offered holocausts of the clean animals and clean birds (Gen.8:20). God blessed all creation in Noah's offering. (Gen.9:1-17) The special revelation of prayer begins with Abraham.

Abraham's Tested Faith (2570-2572)

The Lord directed Abraham. (Gen.12:4) His heart was submissive. At first, he prayed in deeds (building altars at each stage). Later, Abraham spoke to God of seemingly unfulfilled promises. (Gen.15:2) Prayer always involved a faith which was tested.

At Mamre, Abraham welcomed a mysterious guest into his tent. (Gen.18:1-15) Once he received God's plan, Abraham realized God's compassion and interceded more boldly.

Abraham's final purification of faith involved the sacrifice of his son Isaac. Abraham believed that God could provide a sacrifice (Gen. 22:8) and "was able to raise men even from the dead" (Heb.11:19). So, Abraham was conformed to God.

Jacob (2573)

God renewed his promise to Jacob (the ancestor of Israel's twelve tribes) when he wrestled a mysterious figure. In this story, the Church sees prayer as a battle of faith and a triumph of perseverance.

Intercession of Moses (2574-2575)

The prayer of Moses became the most striking example of intercession, ultimately fulfilled in the "one mediator ... the man Christ Jesus. (1Tim.2:5)

God called Moses from the burning bush. (Ex. 3:1-10) In this primordial image of prayer, the living God revealed himself and made Moses his messenger to save his people. Only after long debate did Moses attune his will to God.

Face To Face (2576)

"The Lord used to speak to Moses face to face, as a man speaks to his friend" (Ex.33:11). With this contemplative prayer,

Moses remained faithful to his mission, conversing at length with God. God spoke "clearly, not in riddles" and Moses was more humble "than anyone else on the face of the earth."
(Num.12:3, 7-8)

Bold In Intercession (2577)

Seeing that God was slow to anger and abounding in love, Moses grew determined in his intercession. He interceded during the Amalek battle (Ex.17:8-12) and asked that Miriam be healed. (Num.12:13-14) After the Israelite apostasy, Moses stood "in the breach before God to save the people. (Ex.32:1-34:9) Moses' arguments have emboldened intercessors of the Old and the New Covenant who saw that God will not forsake his people.

Samuel – David – Solomon (2578-2580)

The leaders and the prophets taught Israel to pray. The infant Samuel learned from his mother Hannah, how "to stand before the Lord", and from the priest Eli, how to listen to the Lord. (1Sam.3:9-10)

David, was a model of prayer in his submission to God's will. In the Psalms, David is the prophet of both Jewish and Christian prayer.

At the dedication of the temple, Solomon's prayer relied on God's promises and recalled his mighty deeds. The king begged for the peoples' daily needs, so that the nations would know God.

Temple Ritualism (2581)

The temple was the place for education in prayer. Pilgrimages, feasts and sacrifices (signs of holiness) were really ways of prayer. Because ritualism encouraged an excessively external worship, the prophets had to call for a conversion of heart.

Elijah (2582-2584)

Elijah taught the widow of Zarephath to believe in God's word and confirmed her faith by bringing her child to life. At Mount Carmel, Elijah prayed "Answer me, O Lord, answer me." This was the decisive test for the people's faith.

Elijah, like Moses, hid himself in the cleft of God's holy mountain until God's presence passed by. Only at the

318

Transfiguration, did Moses and Elijah see the unveiled "face of Christ". (Lk.9:30-35)

The prophets received strength from their encounters with God. They did not fly from the world but were attentive to God's word.

A Deepening – The Psalms (2585-2586)

The Psalms are the Old Testament's masterwork of prayer. They nourished and expressed the prayer of God's people. The Psalms embrace all creation. They recall the past and extend to the future. They commemorate God's promises and look for the Messiah. Prayed by Christ himself, they remain essential to the Church's prayer.

God's Words (2587-2588)

In the Psalms, God's words became man's prayer. The Psalms whether individual or communal, lamentation or thanksgiving, are a reflection of the Psalmist's experiences. Every psalm can be prayed in truth by everyone.

Blessings On Our Lips (2589)

The Psalms have the characteristics of simplicity, spontaneity, and a desire for God. They portray distraught persons who still believe in God and submit to his will. Collected for the assembly's praise, they sing "Alleluia" ("Praise the Lord"). "What is more pleasing than a psalm? A psalm is a blessing on the lips of the people, is the voice of the Church and a confession of faith in song." (St. Ambrose)

In Brief (2590 – 2597)

The Fullness of Jesus' Prayer (2598)

The full drama of prayer is revealed in Jesus. We must approach Jesus contemplating him and asking him to teach us to pray.

A Filial Prayer (2599)

In his human heart Jesus learned to pray from his mother, from the synagogue and the Jerusalem temple. At 12, Jesus said "I must be in my Father's house." (Lk.2:49) This reveals a filial prayer which the Father wants from his children.

Prayer At Three Decisive Moments (2600)

Before his three decisive moments (Baptism, Transfiguration and Passion) Jesus prayed. He also prayed before three other decisive moments involving the apostles (his choosing them, his commissioning Peter and his prayer that Peter's faith would not fail).

Jesus At Prayer (2601-2602)

Jesus prayed in solitude, preferably at night. He prayed for all men, and by his prayer shared in all their human experiences. His words and work manifest the prayers which he said in secret.

Two Special Moments (2603-2604)

Two other gospel texts preserve explicit prayers of Jesus. In the first prayer Jesus blesses the Father and thanks him for revealing "to the childlike." Jesus exclaimed "Yes, Father!" which prefigured his prayer in the garden, ("Thy will be done").

In his second prayer Jesus prayed "Father, I thank you for having heard me. I know that you always hear me." This implies that the Father answers Jesus' petitions and that Jesus is always asking. Another prayer of Jesus' (his priestly prayer in John 17 is closely linked with the Our Father.

Selfless Prayer (2605)

Jesus' total selflessness is shown by his prayer in the Garden ("Not my will be done, but yours" (Lk22:42) and by his final seven words on the cross:
1. "Father, forgive them, for they know not what they do." (Lk.23:34)
2. "Today, you will be with me in paradise." (Lk.23,43)

3. "Woman, behold your son." "Behold your mother."(Jn.19:26-27)
4. "I thirst." (Jn.19:28)
5. "My God, my God, why have your forsaken me?" (Mk.15:34)
6. "It is finished." (Jn.19:30)
7. "Father, into your hands, I commit my spirit." (Lk.23:46)

Conclusion Of The Prayer Drama (2606)

Jesus sums up all the troubles of enslaved humanity. "My God, my God, why have you forsaken me? (Mk.15:37) When the Father accepted these prayers and raised Jesus, the drama of prayer was brought to completion. Psalm 2 gives the key to Christ's prayer. "You are my Son, today (the resurrection day) I have begotten you. Ask of me and I will make the nations your heritage." (V.7-8)

While Jesus was "in the flesh" he offered prayers which were heard by the Father. By obedience, he was made perfect and "became the source of eternal salvation to all who obey him." (Heb.5:7-9)

THE TEACHING OF JESUS

Conversion and Faith (2607-2609)

Jesus also gave explicit teaching on prayer. First, Jesus revealed the newness of the coming kingdom in parables. Then he spoke clearly to the disciples of the Father and the Holy Spirit.

Jesus insisted on conversion of heart, reconciliation with brothers and love for enemies. We should pray in secret without multiplying words, and seek first the kingdom in a filial conversion to the Father.

This conversion leads to faith, an adherence to the Father to whom we have access through the Son.

Boldness And Watchfulness (2610-2612)

Jesus taught filial boldness. "Whatever you ask in prayer, believe that you receive it, and you will." (Mk.11:24) Jesus was saddened by "lack of faith", but was heartened by the great faith of the Centurion (Mt.8:10) and the Canaanite woman. (Mt.15:28)

Prayer in faith consists not in saying "Lord, Lord" but in doing the Father's will.

Prayer is a watchfulness, in memory of Jesus' first coming and in hope of Jesus' second coming. Prayer is always a battle, much needed to avoid falling into temptation.

Three Parables (2613)

St. Luke gives the three parables on prayer:

1. The man who borrowed loaves from his friend late at night. (Lk.11:5-13) This shows the Father will give the Holy Spirit to all who ask.
2. The widow who wanted justice from the judge. (Lk.18:1-8) This teaches us to pray without ceasing.
3. The tax collector's prayer in the temple. (Lk.18:9-14) This shows the need for humility.

Prayer After Jesus' Ascension (2614-2615)

Jesus revealed a new way to pray. We must "ask in his name" because through Jesus we have access to the Father. In this new covenant, we have certitude in our petitions.

When our prayer is united to Jesus, the Father gives us "another Paraclete, the "Spirit of truth." (Jn.14:16-17) In his final discourse, Jesus stressed this new dimension of prayer. "Hitherto, you have asked nothing in my name." (Jn.16:24)

Jesus Responds To Prayer (2616)

In his earthly ministry, Jesus answered prayers of <u>faith expressed in words</u> (as the leper, Jairus, the Canaanite woman, the good thief) and the prayer of faith made in silence (the woman with the hemorrhage, the bearers of the paralytic, the woman who anointed his feet). The urgent prayer of the blind man (Mt.9:27) has become the <u>Jesus Prayer</u> "Lord, Jesus Christ, Son of God, have mercy on me, a sinner." Jesus always responded to faith. "Jesus prays for us as our priest, prays in us as our Head, and is prayed to by us as our God." (St. Augustine)

THE PRAYER OF MARY

Mary's Cooperative Prayer (2617)

At the Annunciation, Mary's prayer cooperated in Christ's conception. At Pentecost Mary's prayer cooperated in forming the Church, Christ's Body. God found in Mary the acceptance he had always wanted. "Let it be done to me according to your word." (Lk.1:38)

Her Prayer of Intercession (2618)

Mary's prayer of intercession was revealed at a wedding feast. This prefigured the wedding banquet of the Lamb, when Jesus gave his body and blood for his bride, the Church. At the foot of the cross, Mary became the "mother of all the living." (Gen.3:20)

Her Maternal Prayer (2619)

Mary's Magnificat is a song of the Mother of God and of the Church. It is a song of Zion and of the new People of God; a song "of the poor" who hope in the fulfillment of God's promises.

In Brief - 2620 - 2622

PRAYER IN THE AGE OF THE CHURCH

Prayer After Pentecost (2623-2624)

After Pentecost, the Spirit formed the Church in prayer. The early believers "devoted themselves to the apostles' teaching and fellowship, to the breaking of bread and the prayers." (Acts 2:42)

Spirit-Led Formulations (2625)

The prayers of Scripture, especially the Psalms, are fulfilled in Christ. Also, the Spirit leads to new formulations of prayer in the Church's liturgical and spiritual traditions. The prayer forms revealed in the apostolic and canonical Scriptures remain normative.

Ascent and Descent (2626-2628)

The two fundamental forms of prayer are an <u>ascent</u> in the Spirit through Christ to the Father (our blessing of God) and a descent of the Spirit's gift through Christ from the Father (his blessing of us).

By adoration man exalts the greatness of the Creator and the power of the Savior. Adoration gives homage to the "King of Glory" (Ps.24: 9-10) by silence in his all-holy presence.

PETITION AND INTERCESSION

Types of Petition (2629-2630)

The New Testament has a rich vocabulary, is rich in shades of meaning (ask, beseech, invoke, entreat, cry out). By petition, we admit that we do not have control of our lives. We are sinners who, by asking, turn back to God.

The New Testament lacks the prayers of lamentation (so frequent in the Old Testament) because the Church is buoyed with hope in Christ's resurrection. Christian petition is a "groaning", a "labor pain" while we "await the redemption of our bodies." (Rm.8:22-24) Our prayer is in the Holy Spirit who "intercedes for us with sighs too deep for words." (Rom.8:26)

Three Kinds Of Petition (2631-2633)

Our first petition must be for the forgiveness of sins. "God be merciful to me a sinner." (Lk.18:13) This petition brings us back into communion with God and one another.

Christian petition must center on the kingdom to come. We pray for the kingdom and whatever is necessary to cooperate with its coming. Paul showed a solitude for all the churches in his prayer.

Every need is an object of petition. Christ is glorified by what we ask for in his name. (Jn.14:13) James and Paul tell us to pray always.

Interceding For Others (2634-2636)

We imitate Jesus who "always lives to make intercession." (Heb.7:25) The Spirit "himself intercedes for the saints according to God's will." (Rom.8:26-27)

Interceding for others (as Abraham did) shows a heart attuned to God's mercy. Christians participate in Christ's intercession by praying for the interests of others, even of enemies.

324

Paul asked the Ephesian community to "pray at every opportunity in the Spirit" and to make "supplications for all the holy ones." (Eph.6:18) He asked for intercession, "for all men, for kings, and all in high positions." (1Tim.2:1)

THANKSGIVING AND PRAISE

Always Giving Thanks (2637-2638)
Thanksgiving characterizes the prayer of the Church because Christ has consecrated all creation to the Father.

Every event and need is an occasion for thanksgiving, "Give thanks in all circumstances." (1Thess.5:18)

Praise of God (2639)
Of all prayer forms, praise recognizes most immediately that God is God and gives him glory simply because He is. By praise, we testify that we are children of God adopted in Christ. Praise embraces other prayer forms and carries them to God.

Praise Of Early Church (2640-2641)
The Acts of the Apostles often expresses the people's wonder and awe at Christ's mighty works. The early community was often "praising God." (Acts2:47)

The earlier believers addressed "one another in psalms and hymns and spiritual songs." (Eph.5:19) They composed their own hymns glorifying all that God did in Christ. These extended hymns of praise are called doxologies. (cf. Eph.1:3-14; Rom.16:25-27; Eph.3:20-21; Jude 24-25)

Heavenly Praise (2642-2643)
The book of Revelation has the songs of the heavenly liturgy and the intercession of the martyrs. The church sings with these saints, giving thanks to the "Father of lights" from whom "every perfect gift" comes. (Jas.1:17)

In Brief - 2644 – 2649

42
The Tradition of Prayer (2650 – 2696)

Having A Will To Learn (2650-2651)
Prayer is not just a spontaneous interior outpouring. A will to pray is required. Knowing what Scripture says about prayer is not enough. The believer learns how to pray from the Spirit according to the Church's living traditions. By this Christian prayer tradition, faith is shaped and grows.

THE WELLSPRINGS OF PRAYER

The Living Water (2652)
The Spirit is the living water who leads us to Christ. The Christian life has several wellsprings of the Spirit.

Praying the Scriptures (2653 – 2654)
We gain "the surpassing knowledge of Jesus Christ" (Phil 3:8) by reading the Scriptures. Prayer must accompany this reading. "We speak to him when we pray. We listen to him when we read." (St. Ambrose)

"Seek in reading and you will find in meditating; knock in mental prayer and it will be opened to you by contemplation." (Grugo the Canthusian)

Assimilating Liturgical Prayer (2655)
The sacramental liturgy makes present the mystery of salvation. The celebration continues in the heart that prays. The heart assimilates the liturgy before and after the celebration.

Faith, Hope and Love (2656-2658)
We enter into prayer by the narrow gate of faith for we seek the face of the Lord.

By hope, we celebrate the liturgy in expectation of Christ's return Prayer nourishes that hope. "I waited patiently for the Lord and he heard my cry." (Ps.40:2) Hope leads to love. "Hope does not disappoint us because God's love has been poured into our hearts." (Rom.5:5)

Prayer draws everything into Christ's <u>love.</u> "My God, if my tongue cannot say in every moment that I love you, I want my heart to repeat it to you as often as I draw breath." (Cure of Ars)

Praying For Today (2659-2660)
The Spirit is given in every event of the day. Jesus always spoke about today. (Mt.6:11 and 34) We encounter God <u>today</u>, not yesterday or tomorrow "O that today you would hear his voice." (Ps.95:7) To pray amid daily events is a secret revealed to the children. We must pray that the kingdom influence every day events.

In Brief - 2661 –2662

THE WAY OF PRAYER

Prayer Of the Local Church (2663)
Each local Church (according to its history and culture) proposes a language of prayer (words, melodies, works of art). The Church's Magisterium discerns if these prayer forms are in accord with apostolic tradition. Pastors and catechists should explain these forms in relationship to Jesus Christ.

Access To the Father (2664)
Our prayer (communal or personal) has access to the Father only "in the name' of Jesus. Jesus' sacred humanity is the way by which the Spirit teaches us to pray to the Father.

Praying to Jesus (2665)
We also pray to the Lord Jesus. Although Church prayer is said to the Father, certain psalms and the New Testament engrave in our hearts invitations to Christ. They call him by many names (Word of God, Son of God, Lord, Savior, Lamb of God, King, Beloved Son, Son of the Virgin, Good Shepherd, Life, Light, Hope, our Resurrection and Friend of Mankind).

Jesus – The Special Name (2666-2669)
However, one name, "<u>Jesus</u>" (meaning <u>Yahweh saves</u>), contains everything. His name has been given to us. This name alone contains God's work of salvation. To invoke "Jesus" is to welcome God's only begotten Son.

The invocation "Lord Jesus Christ, Son of God, have mercy on us sinners" combines the Philippian hymn (2:6-11) with the prayer of the publican and the blind man.

To pray always the person need only invoke the holy name, "Jesus." This prayer is possible at all times and has one preoccupation, to love God as Jesus did.

The Church venerates the heart of Jesus and adores the Incarnate Word in his heart which was pierced for everyone. Thus, Christian prayer walks the way of the cross.

Invoking The Holy Spirit (2670-2672)

Only by the Spirit can we say, "Jesus is Lord" only by the Holy Spirit. (1Cor.12:3) Therefore, we should also call upon the Spirit. "If the Spirit should not be worshipped, how can he divinize me through Baptism?" (St. Gregory of Nazeanzus)

Traditionally, we ask the Father, through Christ, to give us the Spirit. The traditional prayer is "Come Holy Spirit, fill the hearts of your faithful and enkindle in them the fire of your love." The sequence of Pentecost asks the Spirit to "come dwell in us, cleanse and save us."

The Holy Spirit is the Master of Christian prayer. In every path of prayer, the same Spirit acts. All Christian prayer is in communion of the Holy Spirit.

PRAYER WITH MARY

Mary's Universal Motherhood (2673-2674)

Through Jesus' glorified humanity, our prayer unites us with his mother. (cf Acts 1:14)

Her consent of faith (given at the Annunciation) perdured to the cross of Jesus. Jesus, the only mediator, is the way of our prayer. Mary shows us to the way.

Two Distinct Movements (2675)

The Church developed prayers to the Mother of God which show two distinct movements. The first magnifies God for his great deeds toward Mary. The second entrusts our petitions to Mary (who knows Jesus' humanity so well).

The Hail Mary expresses these two movements. "Hail Mary" is God's greeting, showing God's high regard for her lowliness. "Full of grace, the Lord is with thee" reveals two truths. First, Mary is filled with grace because the Lord is with her. She is "the Ark of the Covenant, the dwelling of God with men." (Rev.21:3) Second, as "full of grace" she gives herself totally to Jesus whom she will give to the world.

Elizabeth's Words (2676)

"Blessed art thou among women and blessed is the fruit of thy womb, Jesus." Elizabeth said these words when she "was filled with the Holy Spirit." Mary was blessed because she "believed that the Lord's word would be fulfilled." (Lk.1:42-45) Mary became the mother of believers who will receive the fruit of her womb.

"Holy Mary, Mother Of God" (2677)

Because she gave us Jesus, Mary is the Mother of God and our mother. Her prayer for us is "Let it be done according to your word." (Lk.1:38)

"Pray for us sinners, now and at the hour of our death." By asking her prayers, we entrust ourselves to her both today and at "the hour of death."

The Rosary (2678-2679)

Medieval piety developed the rosary in place of the Liturgy of the Hours. In the East, the Marian litany stayed closer to the Byzantine choral office. Other traditions (Armenian, Coptic, Syriac) developed popular hymns to Mary.

Mary is the perfect pray-er, and when we pray to her we adhere to the Father's plan.

In Brief - 2680 – 2682

329

GUIDES FOR PRAYER

The Saints (2683)
The saints by their example, their writings and their prayers are part of the Church's prayer tradition. When the saints entered heaven, they were "put in charge of many things." (Mt.25:21) They intercede for us and we should seek that intercession.

Various Spiritualities (2684)
Many "spiritualities" have developed within the Church through personal charisms, as followers shared in the charism of another (as Elisha shared in Elijah's charism). A spirituality also arises through convergence of liturgy and theology (an integration of faith in a given historical environment). These distinct schools of Christian spirituality are essential guides to the faithful. "The saints are for the Spirit a place where he dwells as in his own home." (St. Basil)

Helpers In Prayer (2685-2686)
Education in prayer takes place primarily in the Christian family (the "domestic Church") where young children are awakened to the Spirit by daily family prayer.

Ordained ministers are responsible for forming people in prayer by leading them to God's Word, the liturgy and a theological understanding.

Consecrated To Prayer (2687)
Hermits, monks and nuns devote themselves to praising God and interceding. This consecrated life cannot be sustained or spread without prayer.

Personal Prayer (2688)
Catechesis must teach people to meditate on the Word of God and to practice personal piety. Prayers should be memorized and savored for their inner meaning.

Prayer Groups (2689)
The rise of prayer groups is a driving force for prayer renewal. These groups must drink from authentic wellsprings and always have a concern for ecclesial communion.

Spiritual Directors (2690)

The Holy Spirit gives wisdom so that some persons might become spiritual directors and true servants of the prayer tradition. Each person must "take care into whose hands he entrusts himself" because "in addition to being learned and discreet, a director should be experienced." (St. John of the Cross)

Five Places of Prayer (2691)

The parish church is the proper place for liturgical prayer and exposition of the Blessed Sacrament. A "prayer corner" (with the Scriptures and icon) fosters individual and family prayer. Monasteries help the faithful participate in liturgy and provide needed solitude. Pilgrimages can help a renewal in prayer. Shrines are special places for Christian prayer.

In Brief 2692 – 2696

Quotes to Remember

Knowing what Scripture says about prayer is not enough.
A will to pray is required.

....

Our prayer has access to the Father, only
"in the name" of Jesus.

....

The Holy Spirit is the Master of Christian prayer.

....

Medieval piety developed the rosary in place of the
Liturgy of the Hours.

....

When we pray to Mary, we adhere to the Father's plan.

....

43

The Life of Prayer (2697 - 2758)

Forgetting To Pray (2697-2698)

We tend to forget to pray. The spiritual fathers (Deuteronomy and the prophets) teach that prayer must be awakened by the heart's memory. "We must remember God more often than we draw breath." (St. Gregory of Nazeanzus) To pray "at all times" we must pray at specific times.

The Church proposes rhythms to nourish continual prayer. Prayers are said daily, morning and evening, before and after meals and at the Liturgy of the Hours. We pray at the Eucharist on Sunday and the great feasts.

EXPRESSIONS OF PRAYER

Three Major Expressions (2699)

Each believer responds to God's promptings according to his own prayer expression. There are three major expressions of prayer; vocal, meditative and contemplative. All three are based upon vigilance in dwelling in God's Word and Presence.

Need For Words (2700 - 2702)

God speaks to us by his Word and our prayer takes flesh by words (vocal or mental). Most importantly, our prayer being heard depends "on the fervor of our souls." (St. John Chrysostom)

Vocal prayer is essential. Jesus prayed aloud in the synagogue and (as the Gospels show) he raised his voice in blessing and even in his agony.

Even interior prayer must involve the senses. We need to express our feelings externally and have our whole being participate in prayer.

Words – Beginning of Contemplation (2703-2704)

God wants worshippers in Spirit and in Truth, i.e. prayer rising from the soul's depths and expressed by the body. Vocal prayer (being external and so human) is readily accessible to groups. However, even personal prayer needs vocal prayer. We must be aware of him "to whom we speak" (St. Teresa of Jesus). Vocal prayer can become an initial form of contemplative prayer.

Meditation (2705 – 2706)

By meditation the believer seeks to understand so he can respond to the Lord. Attentiveness is often difficult and we can be helped by books (Bible, Gospel, spiritual books, the book of creation and the today book of history).

As meditation confronts us, we discover the movements in our hearts. We then ask, "Lord, what do you want me to do?"

The Fruits Of Meditation (2707-2708)

Christians have a duty to meditate regularly so they will be good soil for God's Word. Meditation mobilizes our inner faculties and deepens our faith to bring about conversion. Believers must meditate on the mysteries of Christ (as in the rosary) and then go further to a union with Jesus.

Contemplative Prayer (2709 – 2719)

Contemplative prayer is a "close sharing between friends, taking time frequently to be alone with him whom we know loves us." (St. Teresa of Jesus)

In contemplation, we seek Jesus in a pure faith and live in him. Although still meditating, we fix our gaze on the Lord.

Determination To Pray (2711-2712)

By a determined will, we choose the time and duration of prayer, not giving up prayer during trials and darkness. The believer can always enter into this inner prayer, independent of conditions (internal or external) and of emotional states.

Contemplative prayer is a "gathering up", a recollection brought about by the Spirit. By this awakening we enter into the presence of the ever-awaiting Lord. We give our hearts to the Lord to be purified and transformed.

The Child and The Sinner (2713 - 2714)

Contemplation is the prayer of the child and of the forgiven sinner who welcomes and responds to God's love. The believer returns the love given by the Spirit (for all is grace from God).

Contemplation is a humble surrender to the Father's will in union with Jesus.

Contemplative prayer must be accepted in poverty. It is a covenant relationship, a communion in which the Trinity conforms the believer to God's image.

The Gaze Of Contemplation (2715-2716)

In the intense moments of contemplative prayer, the Father strengthens us so "Christ may dwell in our hearts through faith." (Eph.3:16)

"I look at him and he looks at me" (a peasant at Ars) This gaze is a renunciation of self. It purifies us and teaches us to see everything in the light of truth. Contemplation turns our gaze to the "mysteries of Christ." It gives interior knowledge, "the more to love him and follow him." (St. Ignatius of Loyola)

Various Aspects (2717-2718)

Contemplative prayer is an active hearing and an unconditional acceptance of the Word of God. We participate in the "Yes" of Jesus and the "Let it be" of Mary.

It is "silent love" (John of the Cross). In this silence, the Father speaks his Word and the Spirit helps us to pray as Jesus did.

This prayer is one with Christ's prayer. Through it, the believer participates in Christ's mystery which is celebrated in the Eucharist and is made alive by contemplation.

Night Of Faith (2719)

Contemplative prayer, if it abides in the night of faith, becomes a communion of love.

It passes through the agony, death and tomb of Jesus' Passion. We must "keep watch with him one hour." (Mt.26:40)

In Brief - 2720 – 2724

THE BATTLE OF PRAYER

Responding to the Gift (2725)

Prayer is a gift to which we must respond. This presupposes effort. All the great scriptural figures (including Christ himself) show that prayer is a battle, both against ourselves and against Satan the tempter. We pray as we live because we live as we pray. Therefore, we must habitually live by the Spirit so we can pray in the Spirit.

Four False Ideas (2726)

There are some erroneous notions of prayer:
1. Prayer is a psychological activity
2. Prayer is concentration to reach a mental world
3. Prayer is mere ritual.
4. Prayer is an occupation for which the believer "does not have time."

Discouragement comes about because people do not realize that true prayer comes from the Spirit not from ourselves.

Four Wrong Attitudes (2727)

There are wrong attitudes (coming from the mentality of this present world) which believes that:
1. Only what can be verified by science is true. Prayer deals with mysteries.
2. Only producing is important. Prayer is unproductive.
3. Only sensuality and comfort are exalted. Prayer involves being caught up in the glory of God.
4. Life means activism. Prayer seems to be a withdrawal from the world.

Four Problems In Failure (2728)

There are four failures in prayer:
1. discouragement from dryness
2. sadness caused by material attachments
3. disappointment over not being heard
4. refusal to accept prayer as an unmerited gift

All these lead to the conclusion "What good is it to pray?" Three virtues are needed – humility, trust and perseverance.

Distractions (2729-2730)

<u>Distractions</u> in prayer are an habitual difficulty. The secret is to turn our heart away from their causes (our attachments). We must have a preferential love for the Lord. This leads us to a purified heart and a choice to serve the right master.

This battle demands <u>vigilance</u> (a sobriety of the heart). Jesus spoke of his own coming, each day and on the final day. Even if the bridegroom comes at midnight, our lights must be lit. "Come, seek his face." (Ps.27:8)

Dryness In Prayer (2731)

The problem of <u>dryness</u> belongs to contemplative prayer when the person has no taste for thoughts and feelings even spiritual ones. In this moment of <u>sheer faith</u> the person must cling to Jesus. If this dryness comes from "lack of roots", the battle requires a conversion.

Lack Of Faith (2732)

<u>The most common temptation is a lack of faith</u> which comes from the thousand cares which vie for priority in our life. What is our real love? Do we really believe in the Lord? Do we really believe his words "Apart from me, you can do nothing."

Spiritual Sloth (2733)

Presumption can lead to <u>acedia (spiritual sloth)</u>, a depression coming from lax ascetical practices and decreased vigilance. Discouragement, although painful, is the reverse of presumption. For the humble, this distress can lead to greater constancy in prayer.

WHY PRAYER IS NOT HEARD

Need For Trust (2734)

Filial trust proves itself in tribulation. The person should ask, "Why do I feel that way?" and "How is my prayer heard?"

Not Being Heard (2735 –2736)

We don't worry if our prayers are acceptable to God, but we demand to see results from our petitions. Is God just an instrument to be used?

We must be convinced that "We do not know how to pray as we ought." (Rom.8:26) The Father knows what we need and (respecting the dignity of our human freedom) he gives us the Spirit to ask for what he wants.

Problems Listed By James (2737)

St. James (4:1-10) notes many problems in prayer:
1. We ask wrongly, to spend it on our passions. (4:3)
2. We are "adulterers", asking with divided hearts. (4:4)
3. We don't realize that God jealously yearns for our spirit (4:5) and we will only be heard if we have the Spirit's desires.

"Don't be troubled if you do not immediately receive. God desires to do something even greater for you, while you cling to him in prayer. (Evagrius Ponticus) "God wills that we may be able to receive what he is prepared to give." (St. Augustine)

Basing Our Prayer on Jesus' Gift (2738-2739)

From revelation, we know that faith in prayer rests upon what God has already done for us, namely, the supreme gift of Jesus' death and resurrection.

Paul teaches that we must boldly trust the Spirit's prayer (within us) and the Father's love (which has given us Jesus). God's first response to prayer is always to transform our hearts.

Jesus – Praying In and For Us (2740-2741)

Jesus is our prayer model. He prays in us (seeking only the Father's will). Jesus also prays for us, gathering up our and always interceding before the Father. (Heb.7:25) United with Jesus, our prayer will obtain even the Holy Spirit himself who contains all gifts.

Praying Always (2742)

"Pray constantly." (1Thess.5:17) "Pray at all times in the Spirit." (Eph.5:20) "We have not been commanded to work constantly, but it has been laid down that we are to pray without ceasing." (Evagrius Ponticus)

Three Truths From Tireless Fervor (2743-2745)

This tireless fervor opens us to <u>three</u> <u>enlightening</u> <u>facts</u> about prayer.

1. It is always possible to pray because Christ is with us always. "It is possible to offer fervent prayer even while walking in public, while buying or selling, or even while cooking." (St. John Chrysostom)
2. Prayer is a vital necessity. "It is utterly impossible for a man who prays eagerly and invokes God ceaselessly ever to sin." (St. John Chrysostom) "Those who pray are certainly saved. Those who do not pray are certainly damned." (St. Alphonsus Liguori)
3. Prayer and Christian life are inseparable. "He prays without ceasing who unites prayers to works and works to prayer." (Origin)

Jesus' Priestly Prayer (2746-2748)

In John Chapter 17, Jesus prayed to the Father. This is his longest recorded prayer in the gospels. It is Jesus' "priestly prayer", inseparable from his sacrificial death and his going to his Father.

In this prayer, all is recapitulated in Christ (God and the world, the Word and the flesh, eternal life and time, his disciples and those believers who would follow).

Until the End Of Time (2749)

This prayer continues until the end of time, bringing all things toward their consummation. Jesus has given himself back to his Father who had given him everything. The Son who made himself servant is Lord (Pantocrator). He prays in us and is also the God who hears us.

Fulfills the Our Father (2750-2751)

This priestly prayer (Jn. C17) fulfills the great petitions of the Our Father: zeal for the Father's kingdom, accomplishment of his plan, and deliverance from evil.

In this prayer Jesus reveals the very mystery of prayer, the knowledge that he and the Father are inseparably one.

In Brief - 2752 – 2758

44
The Lord's Prayer – "Our Father"
(2759 –2802)

Luke and Matthew's Texts (2759)

When a disciple said "Lord, teach us to pray, as John taught his disciples" (Lk.11:1), Jesus gave us the Our Father. Luke presents a brief text of five petitions (11:2-4) and Matthew gives seven petitions. (6:9-13) The Church's liturgical tradition follows Matthew:

> *Our Father who art in heaven,*
> *hallowed be thy name*
> *Thy kingdom come.*
> *Thy will be done on earth, as it is in heaven*
> *Give us this day our daily bread,*
> *and forgive us our trespasses,*
> *as we forgive those who trespass against us,*
> *and lead us not into temptation,*
> *but deliver us from evil.*

Added Later (2760)

Later, a doxology was added "For yours are the power and the glory forever" (Didache) and "the kingdom." (Apostolic Constitutions)

A SUMMARY OF THE GOSPELS

Summarizing the Gospels (2761)

"The Lord's prayer is truly the summary of the whole gospel. Since everyone has petitions peculiar to his circumstances, the Lord's prayer is said first (before other petitions) as the foundation of further desires." (Tertullian)

At The Heart Of the Scriptures (2762-2763)

"I do not think you will find any holy prayer in Scripture that is not contained and included in the Lord's Prayer." (St. Augustine)

The Good News summarized in the Sermon on the Mount, and this prayer to the Father are at the heart of the gospel proclamation. "The Lord's Prayer is the most perfect of prayers. In it we ask for things in the sequence that they should be desired. It teaches us what to ask for and in what order we should desire them." (St. Thomas Aquinas)

The Sermon on the Mount (2764)

In both the teaching (The Sermon on the Mount) and in the prayer (The Our Father) Jesus gives new forms to our desires. Jesus teaches by his words and then shows us how to ask in prayer. The rightness of our life in Jesus depends on the rightness of our prayer.

Meaning of "Lord's Prayer" (2765-2766)

The expression "The Lord's Prayer" means that Jesus gave us the words that he received from the Father. As Word Incarnate, Jesus knows the needs of his human brothers and sisters and reveals them to us.

Jesus does not give us a mere formula. He gives us the Spirit, by whom these words become "spirit and life." "The Father searches our hearts and the Spirit intercedes for the saints according to God's will." (Rom.9:27)

THE PRAYER OF THE CHURCH

In the Early Church (2767)

This indivisible gift (of Jesus' words and the Spirit himself) was received by the Church from the beginning. The early Church said The Lord's Prayer three times a day (in place of the Jewish "Eighteen Benedictions").

In the Liturgy (2768-2769)

The Lord's Prayer is rooted in liturgical prayer. It is recited at the major hours and in the three initiation sacraments. "Jesus did not say 'my Father' who art in heaven, but 'our' Father, thus offering petitions for the Church." (St. John Chrysostom)

The Lord's Prayer shows the new birth in Baptism and Confirmation. Those "born anew" learn to invoke God as Father (which they can do because they are indelibly sealed by the Spirit).

Most patristic commentaries on this prayer are addressed to catechumens and neophytes.

At Mass, the Lord's Prayer comes between the Eucharistic Prayer and Communion summing up all petitions and knocking at the door of the Messianic banquet (anticipated in Eucharist).

At Eucharist (2770-2771)

The Lord's Prayer is the prayer of the "end time", which began at Pentecost and will be fulfilled when the Lord returns. Quite different from the Old Testament, the petitions of the Our Father are based on the salvation already accomplished in Christ.

The Seven Groanings (2772)

The seven petitions express the groanings of the present age (which is a time of patience and expectation) during which "it does not yet appear what we shall be." (1Jn.3:2) The Eucharist and the Lord's Prayer both await the Lord "until he comes." (1Cor.11:26)

In Brief - 2773 - 2776

OUR FATHER WHO ART IN HEAVEN

We Dare to Say (2777 – 2778)

Both Western and Eastern liturgies tell us to say "Our Father" with filial boldness. In contrast, Moses was told "Do not come near; put off your shoes from your feet." (Ex.3:5) This is because Jesus has crossed over the threshold of holiness, bringing us into the Father's presence. "Here am I, and the children God has given me." (Heb.1:13) "When would a mortal dare call God 'Father' if man were not animated by a power from on high?" (St. Peter Chrysologus)

The liturgies describe this power as "Parrhesia", (meaning filial trust, humble boldness and the certainty of being loved).

A Purified Idea of Father (2779)

We must purify our minds of certain false images stemming from our own experiences and from our culture. Really, "No one knows the Father except the Son and anyone to whom the Son chooses to reveal him", namely, "to little children." (Mt.11:25-27) If we impose our ideas of "father" upon him, we would fabricate an idol. The mystery of the Father is revealed only by the Son. "The expression God the Father had never been revealed to anyone. Now the Father's name has been revealed to us in the Son, for the name 'Son' implies the new name 'Father'." (Tertullian)

The Spirit's Help (2780)

Because Jesus revealed this truth, we can invoke God as "Father." Although we cannot even conceive of the Son's relation to the Father, the Spirit enables those who believe in Jesus to participate in that relationship.

Adoring The Father (2781-2782)

In this prayer, we are in communion with the Father and the Son, and recognize the Father with a new sense of wonder. Our prayer is adoration (we recognize him as "Father") and thanksgiving (for having revealed his name and having dwelling within us).

We can adore the Father. He has adopted us in Baptism and has made us other "Christs." "God predestined us to adoption as his sons. You who have become sharers in Christ are appropriately called 'Christs'." (St. Cyril of Jerusalem) "The reborn man says first of all 'Father' because he is now a son." (St. Cyprian)

Self-Revelation (2783)

The Lord's Prayer reveals us to ourselves: "Suddenly your sins have been forgiven. From being a wicked servant you have become a good son. Suddenly you have received the grace of Christ and all your sins have been forgiven. Raise your eyes to the Father and say 'Our Father' so you may merit being his son." (St. Ambrose)

Two Dispositions (2784-2785)

This gift of adoption demands two fundamental dispositions:
1. We must desire to be like the Father because we are restored to his likeness.
   "When we call God 'our Father' we ought to behave as sons of God." (St. Cyprian)

"You cannot call God your Father if you preserve a cruel and inhuman heart." (St. John Chrysostom) We must contemplate the Father's beauty, and adorn our souls accordingly." (St. Gregory of Nyssa)

2. We must "become like children" (Mt.18:3) to receive the Father's revelation. "The soul speaks very familiarly to God as to its own Father." (St. John Cassian) "What would he not give his children who ask, since he has already granted the gift of being his children." (St. Augustine)

Meaning of "Our" (2786-2788)

"Our" does not express our possession of God but a new relationship with him.

"Our" recognizes that in Christ's new eternal covenant, we are "his" people and he is "our" God. We must respond to this "grace and truth" of Christ (Jn. 1:17).

The Our Father is the prayer of the "end time." "Our" shows that we believe that God will say to the victor, "I will be his God and he shall be my son." (Rev.21:7)

Communion Not Division (2789-2790)

By addressing the Father, we do not divide the Godhead. Rather, we confess that the Son is eternally begotten by him and the Spirit proceeds from him. Our communion is with the Father, the Son and the Spirit. When we pray to the Father we glorify the Son and the Spirit.

Obviously the word "our" refers to more than one person. There is only one God, recognized as Father by all the baptized. United with Jesus ("the firstborn among many brethren – Rom. 8:29), the Church is in communion with the Father and the Spirit. "Our" shows that all are "of one heart and soul." (Acts 4:32)

Our Division And Individualism (2791-2793)

Although Christians are divided, "our" shows our common patrimony and summons us to join in Jesus' prayer for unity.

We must leave individualism behind. The "our" and "us" in the four last petitions includes everyone. This prayer demands that we overcome our division.

We must bring everyone to "our" Father. We must be open to all who do not know Christ so that he might "gather into one the children of God." (Jn.11:52)

Who Art in Heaven" (2794)

"In heaven" doesn't mean that God is in a place (space). It expresses God's way of being. He is not "elsewhere." Because he is holy, God is close to the contrite heart. "God is in the hearts of the just as in his holy temple. Those who pray should desire the one they invoke to dwell in them." (St. Augustine) "'Heaven' could also be those who bear the image of the heavenly world." (St. Cyril of Jerusalem)

Our Homeland and Our Goal (2795-2796)

Sin has exiled us but conversion returns us to the Father's house. Christ has "descended" and "ascended" and heaven and earth are reconciled in him.

"Our Father who art in heaven" means we are already seated "with him in the heavenly places in Christ Jesus." (Eph.2:6) Yet we "groan and long to put on our heavenly dwelling. (2Cor.5:2) "Christians spend their lives on earth, but are citizens of heaven." (Letter to Diognetus)

In Brief - 2797- 2802

Quotes to Remember

Because Jesus revealed this truth, we can invoke God as Father. Saying "our" invites us to leave our individualism behind.

The Lord's Prayer is truly a summary of the whole gospel. (Tertullian)

45
The Seven Petitions (2803 – 2865)

Seven Petitions (2803)
The Spirit stirs up seven petitions within us. The <u>first three</u> (more theological) draw us to the Father's glory. The <u>last four</u> (ways toward him) commend our wretchedness to his grace.

First Three (2804).
The first three petitions (thy name, thy kingdom and thy will) carry us to the Father for his own sake. We do not mention ourselves because the three petitions (hallowed be thy name, thy kingdom come, thy will be done) are already answered in Christ's saving sacrifice. This prayer seeks their fulfillment, because God is not yet all in all.

Last Four (2805-2806)
The last four petitions (like the Eucharistic epiclesis) offer up our expectations. They concern this present world. <u>Give us</u> and <u>forgive us</u> concern our need to be fed and healed of sin. <u>Lead us</u> and <u>deliver us</u> concern our battle for the victory of life.

The first three petitions strengthen us in faith, hope and charity. The final four concern our needs asking the Father to accomplish (through Christ and the Spirit) his plan for us and the whole world.

HALLOWED BE THY NAME

Immersion into the Mystery (2807 – 2808)
"To hallow" does not seek to cause God to be holy but recognizes that God is holy (a prayer of adoration). These words begin our immersion into God's innermost mystery and the drama of salvation. "Hallowed be thy name" draws us into God's loving kindness, so we might "be holy and blameless before him in love." (Eph.1:4) God reveals his name by accomplishing. His work is done in us only if his name is hallowed.

Glory of Holiness (2809)

God's holiness is his inaccessible center. Scripture uses the word "glory" to mean the revealing of this holiness. God crowned man "with glory and honor" but, by sin, man fell "short of the glory of God." (Rom.3:23) Since then, God has manifested his holiness by revealing his name.

Revealing His Name (2810-2812)

God did not reveal his name when he made a covenant with Abraham. Gradually he revealed his name to Moses and made his name known clearly when he "triumphed gloriously" over the Egyptians. (Ex.15:1) From the Sinai covenant, they became "his own" people, a "holy (consecrated) nation" (Ex.19:5-6) because his name dwelled with Israel.

Even though God commanded the Israelites to "be holy, for I am holy" and showed patience to them, the people profaned his name among the nations. Therefore, the returned exiles and Old Testament prophets burned passionately for his name.

In Jesus, God's name is the heart of the priestly prayer. "For their sake, I consecrate myself, that they also might be consecrated in truth." (Jn.17:11-19) Having sanctified his own name, Jesus reveals the Father's name. The Father gives Jesus a name above every other name "Jesus Christ is Lord, to the glory of God the Father." (Phil.2:9-11)

The Nations Called To Holiness (2813-2815)

In Baptism we were sanctified in Jesus' name and the Father called us to total holiness. "We ask that we who were sanctified in Baptism may persevere in what we have begun to be, for we need sanctification daily." (St. Cyprian)

His name being holy among the nations depends on our life and prayer. "We ask that this name be hallowed through our actions. For God's name is blessed when we live well and is blasphemed when we live wickedly. (St. Peter Chrysologus) "We ask that his name be hallowed in us and also in others for his precept obliges us to pray for every one, even our enemies." (Tertullian)

This first petition is fulfilled in Christ's priestly prayer, "Holy Father, protect in your name those whom you have given me." (Jn.17:11)

The New Testament (2816)

The New Testament Greek word (basileia) can mean "kingship" (abstract noun), "kingdom" (concrete noun) or "reign" (action noun). Ever since the Last Supper, the Kingdom has been coming and is in our midst through Eucharist. It will come fully when Christ hands over the kingdom to his Father. "The Kingdom of God means Christ himself. As he is our resurrection, so he can also be understood as the Kingdom of God, for in him we shall reign." (St. Cyprian)

The Final Coming (2817-2819)

The Spirit and the Bride cry "Come, Lord Jesus." (Rev.22:20) "The souls of the martyrs cry out 'How long before you judge and avenge our blood on those who dwell on the earth? Indeed, as soon as possible, Lord, may your kingdom come." (Tertullian)

"Thy kingdom come" refers primarily to the final coming of Christ. Desiring this Second Coming does not distract the Church from its earthly mission because the Spirit must "complete his work on earth", (Fourth Eucharistic Prayer)

Since Pentecost, a decisive battle has begun between "the flesh" and the Spirit. "Only a pure soul can boldly say 'Thy kingdom come'. Therefore, let not sin reign in your mortal bodies." (St. Cyril of Jerusalem)

Earthly Progress (2820-2821)

Christians distinguish between the growth of God's reign and cultural progress. However, they do not separate the two. Man's call to eternal life reinforces his duty to use well what God has created to serve justice and peace.

THY WILL BE DONE

Thy Will Be Done on Earth as it is in heaven" (2822 – 2823)

Our Father "desires all men to be saved" (1Tim.2:3), "not wishing that any should perish." (2Pet.3:9) His commandment "Love one another even as I have loved you".

Paul wrote, "He has made known to us the mystery of his will ... to gather up all things in Christ. In him we have also obtained an inheritance." (Eph.1:9-11) Therefore, we ask that this plan be fully realized on earth as in heaven.

Fulfilled In Jesus' Will (2824)

Through Christ's human will, the Father's will has been perfectly fulfilled. Only Jesus can say "I always do what is pleasing to him." (Jn.8:29) Jesus prayed "Not my will but yours be done." (Lk.22;42) He delivered us "from the present evil age, according to the will of the Father." (Gal.1:4) Now, we are sanctified "through the offering of his body." (Heb.10:10)

Surrendering Our Will (2825)

If Jesus "learned obedience through what he suffered" (Heb.5:8) we, (the children of adoption), should also learn obedience. Therefore, we ask that our will be united with Jesus' will for the life of the world. "In committing ourselves to Christ, we can become one spirit with him and thereby accomplish his will." (Origen)

"He teaches us to be humble by making us see that our virtue depends on grace from on high. He commands us to pray for the whole world on earth so that earth will not differ from heaven." (St. John Chrysostom)

Learning God's Will (2826-2827)

Jesus taught that we can only enter heaven by doing "the will of my Father in heaven." (Mt.7:21)

God listens to him who "is devout and does his will." (Jn.9:31) This is the power of the Church's prayer in the Eucharist. The Church also prays with Mary and the saints who have done God's will. "We can understand the words, 'Thy will be done on earth as it is in heaven' to mean 'in the Church as in Our Lord Jesus Christ himself, in the Bride just as in the Bridegroom'." (St. Augustine)

"Give Us This Day" (2828 – 2829)

"Give us" shows a child's trust in the heavenly Father, who gives all "their food in due season." (Ps.104:27) This petition glorifies the Father by acknowledging his goodness.

These words also express a "covenant." The word "us", shows that God is the Father of everyone.

Our Daily Bread (2830)

The Father who gives life also provides nourishment (all the goods and blessings which we need). On the Mount, Jesus demanded a filial trust in God's providence. He invited us to be free from nagging worry. "Since everything belongs to God, he who possesses God wants for nothing, if he himself is not found wanting before God." (St. Cyprian)

The World's Hungry (2831-2834)

The world's hungry provide a profound meaning to this petition. Hunger demands that praying Christians help the hungry. This petition cannot be isolated from Jesus' parables about Lazarus and the Last Judgment.

The whole earth should "rise" in the new leaven of the kingdom. Justice must be established in all relationships (economic, social, international). Just structures can come only from people who want to be just. "Our" bread is one loaf for the many. We must share "our bread" with the "many." Our abundance should remedy the needs of others.

"Pray as if everything depended on God and work as if everything depended on you." (St. Ignatius of Loyola) Even though we attained our food by work, it is still the gift of the Father whom we should thank by grace at meals.

Hunger For God's Word (2835)

"Man does not live by bread alone but by every word that proceeds from the mouth of God." (Mt.4:4) Christians must "proclaim the good news to the poor" because there is a famine on the earth "for hearing the word of the Lord." (Amos 9:11) This petition concerns the Bread of Life, that is, God's Word and the Eucharist.

"This Day" (2836)

"This day" expresses not just mortal time, but the "today" of God. "If you receive the bread each day, each day is today for you. If Christ is yours today, he rises for you every day." (St. Ambrose)

The Daily Eucharist (2837)

Epiousius (Greek for "daily") appears nowhere else in the New Testament. "Daily" shows that good things are needed for day-to-day subsistence. "Daily" refers to the Body of Christ, the "Medicine of immortality." The heavenly meaning of "this day" is evident, the Day of the Lord, the feast anticipated in the Eucharist, the foretaste of the kingdom. Therefore, Eucharist should be celebrated every day. "The Eucharist is our daily bread. Its effect is that we may become what we receive. Our daily bread is also the reading you hear and the hymns you sing in church. All are necessities for our pilgrimage." (St. Augustine)

"The Father urges us children of heaven to ask for the bread of heaven. Christ himself is the bread who furnishes the faithful each day with food from heaven." (St. Peter Chrysologus)

FORGIVE US OUR TRESPASSES

Forgiving and Being Forgiven (2838)

This petition is not listed with the first three because of an astonishing requirement. Our sins won't be forgiven unless we forgive others. Our petition seeks a future good (our forgiveness). However, the word "as" shows that our own forgiving must happen now.

"And forgive us our trespasses ..." (2839)

When we begged that God's name be holy, we also asked that we be made holy. Although clothed in baptismal grace, we do not cease to sin. In this new petition, we are as the prodigal son and the tax collectors. We begin with this confession because in Christ "we have redemption, the forgiveness of our sins" (Col.1:14). In the sacraments, we have the efficacious sign that we received this forgiveness.

350

Forgiving Hearts (2840-2841)

Christ's mercy cannot penetrate our hearts if we have not forgiven those who sinned against us. Love is indivisible. We cannot love God (whom we cannot see) and not love others (whom we do see). By refusing to forgive others, our hearts become hardened to God's mercy. However, confessing our sins opens us to God's grace.

Jesus says explicitly "If you forgive others their transgressions, your heavenly Father will forgive you. But if you do not forgive others, neither will your Father forgive your transgressions." (Mt.6:14-15)

Jesus' Use Of "As" (2842)

Jesus frequently used the word "as." He told us to "Be perfect as your heavenly Father is perfect" (Mt.5:48); to love "as I have loved you" (Jn.13:34); to be merciful "as your Father is merciful." (Lk.6:36) To act as Jesus, the believer must vitally participate in the life and love of God. We must have the mind of Christ "forgiving one another as God in Christ forgave us." (Eph.4:32)

Jesus' Parable (2843)

The Lord ended his parable of the merciless servant by saying "So also my heavenly Father will do to every one of you, if you do not forgive your brother from your heart." (Mt.18:35) Sins are bound and loosed only "in the depths of our heart", where the Holy Spirit can turn injury into compassion and hurt into intercession.

To Enemies (2844)

This forgiveness must extend to enemies. Only hearts attuned to God's compassion can receive the gift of prayer. Forgiveness proclaims to the world that love is stronger than sin. Only by love can men be reconciled with God and with one another.

To Everything (2845)

Divine forgiveness has no limits in forgiving "sins" (Lk.11:4) or "debts" .(Mt.6:12) We are all debtors owing to no one, "except to love one another." (Rom.13:8) "God does not accept the sacrifice of a sower of division, but commands that he depart

351

from the altar so he may first be reconciled with his brother."
(St. Cyprian)

LEAD US NOT INTO TEMPTATION

Blocking Our Way (2846 – 2847)

Sins come from consenting to temptation. We ask God not to lead us into temptation, meaning "do not allow us to enter" or "do not let us yield to" temptation. God cannot be tempted and he tempts no one. This petition asks him to block our way into temptation and to give us the Spirit of discernment.

The Spirit helps us to know the difference between trials (needed for our spiritual growth) and temptations (which lead to death). We also discern between "being tempted" and "consenting to temptation" realizing that some things seem desirable but their fruit is death. "There is a certain usefulness to temptation. We discover our evil inclinations." (Origen)

Serving Which Master? (2848)

"Lead us not into temptation" demands a "decision of the heart". "No one can serve two masters." (Mt.6:24) "If we live by the Spirit, let us also walk by the Spirit. (Gal.5:25) When we are tempted, God will "provide the way of escape, so you may be able to endure it." (1Cor.10:13)

Victory By Prayer (2849)

Jesus overcame his temptations by prayer and our victory is also won by prayer. In this petition, Christ unites us to his battle, urges us to vigilance, and prays to the Father, "Keep them in your name." (Jn.17:11) This petition dramatically asks for final perseverance, "So, I am coming like a thief! Blessed is he who is awake." (Rev.16:15)

DELIVER US FROM EVIL

Delivering All (2850)

This last petition is also included in Jesus' priestly prayer, "I ask you to protect them from the evil one." (Jn.17:15) We must pray for the deliverance of the whole human family. Our interdependence in this battle with sin becomes our solidarity in Christ's Body.

Satan (2851-2852)

This evil is personal (not abstract). It refers to Satan, the angel who opposes God. The devil (dia-bolos) "throws himself across" God's plan and his work of salvation. Satan ("a liar and the father of lies") is the "deceiver of the whole world." (Jn.8:44 and Rev.12:9) Through him, sin and death entered the world. By his definitive defeat all creation will be freed "from the corruption of sin and death." (Eucharistic Prayer IV) "The one begotten by God he protects and the evil one does not touch him. We know that we are of God and the whole world is in the power of the evil one." (1Jn.5:18-19) "The Lord keeps you from the evils of your adversary the devil. One who entrusts himself to God does not dread the devil." (St. Ambrose)

Cast Out (2853)

At his death, Jesus won this victory over the "prince of this world" (Jn.14:30) and Satan "was cast out." (Jn.12:31 and Rev.12:10) Then, Satan pursued the woman but she was preserved from sin (Immaculate Conception) and from death. (Assumption) He was "angry with the woman, and went off to make war on the rest of her offspring." (Rev.12:7) Therefore, we pray "Come, Lord Jesus" (Rev.22:17) since only his coming will deliver us from the Evil One.

From All Evils (2854)

We ask to be freed from all the evils (past, present and future) caused by Satan. In this petition, the Church brings all the distress of the world before the Father and asks for perseverance in awaiting Christ's return. She anticipates the final gathering of everyone in Jesus for he has "the keys of Death and Hades." Jesus is the one who "is and who was and who is to come, the Almighty." (Rev.1:8 and 18) "Deliver us from every evil and grant us peace ... so we might be free from sin and protected from all anxiety" (said at Mass after the Lord's Prayer).

353

"For the kingdom, the power and the glory are yours, now and forever" (2855)

This restates the first three petitions (the glory of God's name; the coming of the Kingdom; the power of his saving will). Satan falsely attributed kingship, power and glory to himself (Lk.4:5-6) but Christ restores these to the Father until he hands over the kingdom to him. Then God will be all in all.

By saying Amen" we ratify all that is contained in the prayer. (St. Cyril of Jerusalem)

In Brief - 2857 – 2865

Quotes to Remember

The first three petitions carry us to the Father for his own sake. The last four petitions offer up our expectations.

....

"Hallowed be thy name" begins our immersion into God's innermost mystery.

....

"Thy Kingdom come" refers primarily to Christ's final coming.

....

We ask that our will be united to Jesus' will for the life of the world.

....

Even though we have obtained our bread by work, it is still a gift of the Father.

....

Our sins won't be forgiven unless we forgive others.

....

We ask to be freed from all the evils caused by Satan.

....

354

SUBJECT INDEX

357

Drugs
2291
Dualism
285
Dying
1681, 1682, 1683
See also: Death
Earth
See: Creation, World
Easter
638, 639, 640, 654, 1169, 1170, 1339,
1363
Eccesaistical provinces
887
Economy
2426. 2429, 2430, 2431, 2432
Economy of salvation
489, 1092, 1095, 1168
Ecumenism
820
Embryo
2274
See also : Matrimony
Emmanuel
712
Emotions
See Passions
Endtime
See Jesus Christ : Second Coming
Enmity
1852
Environment
See : Creation
Envy
1866, 2538, 2539, 2540, 2553
Eparchy
833
Epiclesis
1105, 1106, 1109, 1127
Episcopal conferences
887
Episcopate
See: Bishop
Eremitical life
See: Evangelical counsels, Church,
structure
Eternal life
1020, 1023
See also: Resurrection of the dead
Eucharist
611, 737, 790, 893, 1000, 1099, 1113,
1118, 1210, 1211, 1212, 1322, 1323,
1324, 1324, 1325, 1326, 1327, 1328,
1329, 1329, 1329, 1330, 1331, 1332,
1333, 1334, 1335, 1336, 1337, 1355,
1359, 1365, 1366, 1369, 1370, 1371,
1372, 1373, 1378, 1380, 1382, 1391,
1392, 1393, 1394, 1395, 1396, 1397,
1402, 1403, 1404, 1405, 1406, 1407,
1410, 1411, 1412, 1413, 1414, 1415,
1416, 1417, 1418, 1524, 1566, 1617

1846, 2120, 2643
Eucharistic celebration; Communion; celebration of Mass
893, 903, 1105, 1142, 1244, 1341, 1342,
1343, 1345, 1345, 1346, 1347, 1348,
1349, 1350, 1351, 1352, 1353, 1355,
1356, 1362, 1384, 1385, 1388, 1389,
1390, 1391, 1398, 1399, 1400, 1401,
1408, 1409, 1552, 2042, 2177, 2180, 2770
Eucharistic ministers
1348
Eucharistic prayer
See Eucharistic celebration
Euthanasia
2276, 2277, 2278, 2324
Evangelical counsels
914, 915, 917, 920, 922, 925, 928, 930,
931, 944, 1973, 2053
See also: Poverty, Obedience, Chastity,
Virginity, Church: structure
Evil
309, 310, 311, 312, 385, 401, 403, 412,
671, 677, 684, 998, 1431, 1606, 1607,
1707, 1708, 1755, 2117, 2284
Excommunication
1463
Exorcism
550, 1237,1673
Extravagance; waste
2409
Extreme Unction
See: Anointing of the Sick
Faith
13, 14, 18, 26, 108, 114, 142, 143, 144,
145, 146, 147, 148, 150, 151, 152, 153,
154, 155, 156, 157, 158, 159, 160, 161,
162, 163, 164, 165, 166, 168, 170, 171,
172, 176, 177, 178, 179, 180, 181, 182,
183, 184, 197, 200, 202, 212, 222, 223,
224, 228, 229, 233, 234, 309, 425, 463
487, 494, 573, 846, 1033, 1124, 1813,
2086, 2087, 2088, 2226, 2656
Faith, profession of
167, 185, 186, 189, 190, 191, 192, 193,
194, 195, 199, 202, 512, 815, 816
See also: Creed
Faithful, the; believers
87, 91, 92, 93, 131, 737, 871, 872, 873,
889, 892, 896, 1124, 1141, 2037, 2073
Faithfulness
736, 1832
See: Matrimony;Divorce
Family
1655, 1882, 2201, 2206, 2207, 2208,
2215, 2216, 2217, 2219, 2232, 2385
2685
See also: Parents
Famine
2269
Fasting; Lenten fasting
538, 1434, 1438, 2043, See also: Liturgy

Father
See parents; Trinity; God
Fathers of the Church
8, 688
Fear
1735, 1765
Fear of the Lord
1831
Feast days
See: Holy Days of Obligation
Fertility; infertility
See: Matrimony; purpose
Fertilization
See; Matrimony; purpose
"Filioque"
246, 247, 248
See also: Trinity
Fire
696, 718
Flattery
2480
Force
See; Violence
Forgery
2409
Fornication
1852, 2353
Fortitude
1805, 1808, 1831
Fortune-telling
2116
Fraternal harmony
815, 821, 1939, 2213
Fraud
2409
Freedom
908, 1730, 1731, 1732, 1733, 1734, 1738,
1739, 1740, 1741, 1742, 1744, 1745,
1746, 1747, 1748, 1749, 1861, 2008
Freedom of religion
2108
See also: Society; duties of the state
Friendship
277, 374, 396, 1468, 1939, 2010, 2347
Funerals
1686, 1684, 1686, 1687
Games of chance
2413
Generosity
1832
Genocide
2313
Gentleness
736, 1832
Gluttony
1866
Gnosticism
285
God
1, 33, 35, 39, 48, 62, 64, 74, 105, 203,
205, 206, 209, 210, 213, 214, 218, 231,
268, 269, 271, 272, 275, 277, 295, 300,
301, 302, 303, 304, 307, 308, 309, 314,
370, 385, 395, 410, 412, 422, 431, 733,
1037, 1604, 1718, 1730, 1850, 2012,
2084, 2085, 2115, 2143, 2146, 2149,
2150, 2161, 2164, 2465, 2567, 2782,
2807, 2809, 2810, 2812, 2814
Good
1755
Goodness
736, 1832
Good News
See: Gospel
Gospel
2, 76, 125, 126, 514, 534, 571, 573, 1946,
1963
Grace
35, 153, 654, 678, 824, 1021, 1810, 1987,
1989, 1996, 1997, 1998, 1999, 2000,
2001, 2002, 2003, 2004, 2005, 2010,
2011, 2021, 2022, 2023, 2025
Greed
See Desires, disordered
Habits
1735
Hail Mary
435, 2676
Happiness
1723, 1818
Hatred
1765, 2262, 2303
Health
2288, 2289, 2290, 2291
Heart of Jesus, adoration of
1439, 2669
Heaven
325, 326, 1023
See: World: Creation
Hell
633, 1033, 1035, 1036, 1037, 1861
Heresy
817, 2089
Hierarchy
See: Truth; Dogma, Church: structure
Holiness, sanctity; saints
686, 688, 828, 946, 956, 1717, 2012,
2013, 2015, 2028, 2030, 2030, 2156, 2683
Holy Days of Obligation
2042, 2177, 2180, 2185, 2187, 2192, 2193
Holy Spirit
14, 152, 202, 244, 304, 683, 684, 685,
687, 689, 691, 692, 693, 694, 695, 696,
697, 698, 699, 700, 701, 702, 703, 706,
707, 714, 715, 718, 720, 722, 723, 725,
727, 728, 729, 730, 731, 732, 733, 734,
735, 736, 737, 739, 740, 741, 742, 743,
744, 747, 749, 768, 797, 798, 813, 827,
852, 976, 1091, 1099, 1109, 1266, 1303,
1433, 1508, 1520, 1585, 1699, 1742,
1830, 1831, 1832, 1845, 1864, 2004,
2017, 2652

Holy Water
1668

Homily
2033

Homosexuality
2357, 2359

Honor
2479

Hope
1813, 1817, 1819, 2090, 2091, 2086, 2657

Horoscopes
2116

Hostages, taking of
2297

Humility
724, 525, 559, 2540, 2559, 2628, 2631, 2706, 2713

Hypostatis; hypostatic union
252, 464
See also: Trinity

Icon
1159, 1160, 2141

Idolatry
1852, 2112, 2113

Ignorance
1735

Impurity
1852

Inadvertence
1735

Incarnation
464, 470
See also; Jesus Christ

Incest
2388

Incredulity
2089

Inculturation
854, 1205, 1232

Indifference
2094

Indulgences
1471, 1472, 1498

Infertility
See Matrimony

Ingratitude
2094

Initiation
See: Baptism, Confirmation, Eucharist, Catechumenate

Inspiration
106
See also: Scripture, Sacred

"Intercommunion"
See: Eucharistic celebration, communion

Irony
2481

Irreligion
2110, 2112

Islam
841

Israel; Israelites
62, 203, 218, 238, 287, 348, 401, 431, 433, 436, 441, 522, 539, 576, 579, 674, 708, 711, 716, 751, 759, 839, 1961, 2085, 2573,
See also: Prayer, liturgy

Jealousy
1852

Jesus Christ
3, 102, 126, 160, 202, 209, 211, 272, 280, 305, 312, 331, 349, 359, 411, 422, 426, 427, 429, 430, 432, 434, 435, 436, 437, 439, 440, 441, 443, 444, 446, 450, 452, 453, 454, 455, 456, 457, 458, 459, 460, 461, 463, 465, 469, 470, 471, 472, 473, 475, 476, 477, 479, 480, 481, 483, 504, 514, 516, 517, 518, 520, 522, 523, 525, 527, 531, 532, 533, 534, 535, 538, 541, 542, 544, 546, 547, 549, 550, 551, 554, 555, 556, 557, 559, 561, 563, 564, 565, 566, 567, 568, 569, 570, 572, 574, 575, 576, 577, 580, 581, 583, 585, 587, 588, 589, 590, 591, 592, 593, 594, 595, 597 598, 599, 601, 602, 605, 606, 608, 612, 615, 619, 620, 621, 622, 623, 624, 625, 627, 629, 630, 631, 636, 638, 639, 640, 641, 642, 645, 646, 647, 648, 651, 652, 653, 655, 657, 658, 659, 661, 662, 663, 665, 668, 669, 670, 671, 672, 673, 674, 675, 677, 678, 679, 680, 681, 713, 724 727, 728, 792, 830, 849, 858, 908, 947, 988, 994, 1038, 1040, 1041, 1051, 1060, 1065, 1069, 1084, 1085, 1107, 1115, 1130, 1223, 1503, 1507, 1544, 1612, 1613, 1614, 1618, 1708, 1716, 1741, 1953, 2052, 2173, 2174, 2262, 2305, 2444, 2599, 2600, 2601, 2602, 2603, 2607, 2616, 2746, 2859

Jesus Prayer
2616, 2667

Jews
See; Israel

John the Baptist
523, 535, 608, 696, 717, 718, 719, 720, 1224

Journalists
2497

Joy
301, 523, 736, 1829, 1832
See also: Happiness

Judgment, rash
2477

Justice
1805, 1807, 2411
See also: Virtues, Cardinal virtues

Justification
654, 1266, 1446, 1987, 1989, 1991, 1992, 1993, 1994, 1995, 2018, 2020

Kidnapping
2297

361

Media
2493,   2494, 2496, 2497, 2498
Medical treatment
2278, 2292, 2295, 2296, 2297
Medicine
2290
Meditation
2705
Men
355, 383
See also: man: human sexual identity
Mercy
1829, 2447
Merit
2006, 2007, 2010, 2011, 2023
Messiah
410, 436, 440, 528, 535, 540, 572, 590,
664, 674, 695, 702, 711, 712, 840
Millenarianism
676
Misappropriation of funds
2409
Missions; missionary work
849, 850, 851, 852, 853, 854, 855, 856,
858, 931
Modesty
1832, 2521, 2523, 2522
Monophysitism
467
Morality
407
Mortal sin
See: Sin, mortal sin
Mother
See parents; Church; mary
Murder
See: Killing
Music
1856, 1857, 1858
Muslims
See: Islam
Mutilation
2297
Myron
See Chrism
Mystagogy
1075
Name
2156, 2165
Natural sciences
284
Neighbor, love of
1825, 2179, 2196, 2443, 2488
New Covenant
612, 839, 1965
New Testament
124, 125, 128, 684
Oaths
2150, 2152, 2153, 2154, 2155
Obedience
615, 1900, 2242, 2313

Oikonomia
236
Oil
See: Chrism
Old Covenant
839, 1539, 1961
Old Testament
121, 128, 697, 707, 1093, 1156
Orders, sacrament of Holy
897, 1113, 1119, 1210, 1461, 1536, 1537,
1538, 1539, 1544, 1556, 1557, 1558,
1559, 1562, 1563, 1564, 1567, 1568,
1569, 1570, 1572, 1573, 1575, 1577,
1578, 1579, 1580, 1581, 1582, 1584,
1585, 1587, 1588, 1591, 1593, 1594,
1595, 1596, 1597, 1598, 1599
See also: Priest
Original justice
379
Original sin
See: Sin
Orthodox Churches
838
Our Father
2761, 2765, 2767, 2769, 2770, 2771,
2773, 2774, 2775, 2776, 2803, 2857
Palliative care
2279
Pantheism
285
Parables
546
Paraclete
692
See also: Holy Spirit
Parents; children; childrearing
2197, 2198, 2199, 2200, 2214, 2221,
2222, 2225, 2228, 2229, 2247, 2251
2253, 2373, 2378
Parish
2179
Particular church
814, 833, 834, 835
Passions
1735, 1762, 1763, 1765, 1766, 1767,
1769, 1770, 1771, 1772, 1773, 1775
1860, 2552
Passover of Christ; Paschal mystery
571, 671, 731, 1067, 1164, 2175
See also: Easter
Patience
736, 1832
Patriarch
61, 205, 707
Patriarchate
887
Peace
736, 1832, 1829, 2304, 2305, 2317
Penance
See: Penance, sacrament of; Contrition

364

ABBREVIATIONS

The following abbreviations are used for the books of the Bible cited in the text.

Gen	Genesis	*Sir*	Sirach
Ex	Exodus		(Ecclesiasticus)
Lev	Leviticus	*Bar*	Baruch
Num	Numbers	*1 Esd*	1 Esdras
Deut	Deuteronomy	*2 Esd*	2 Sdras
Josh	Joshua	*Let Jer*	Letter of Jeremiah
Judg	Judges	*Song of Thr*	Prayer of Azariah
Ruth	Ruth	and the Song of the Three Jews	
1 Sam	1 Samuel	*Sus*	Susanna
2 Sam	2 Samuel	*Bel*	Bel and the Dragon
1 Kings	1 Kings	*1 Macc*	1 Maccabees
2 Kings	2 Kings	*2 Macc*	2 Maccabees
1 Chr	1 Chronicles	*3 Macc*	3 Maccabees
2 Chr	2 Chronicles	*4 Macc*	4 Maccabees
Ezra	Ezra	*Pr Man*	Prayer of Manasseh
Neh	Nehemiah	*Mt*	Matthew
Esth	Esther	*Mk*	Mark
Job	Job	Lk	Luke
Ps	Psalms	*Jn*	John
Prov	Proverbs	*Acts*	Acts of the
Eccl	Ecclesiastes	Apostles	
Song	Song of Solomon	*Rom*	Romans
Isa	Isaiah	*1 Cor*	1 Corinthians
Jer	Jeremiah	*2 Cor*	2 Corinthians
Lam	Lamentations	*Gal*	Galatians
Ezek	Ezekiel	*Eph*	Ephesians
Dan	Daniel	*Phil*	Philippians
Hos	Hosea	*Col*	Colossians
Joel	Joel	*1 Thess*	1 Thessalonians
Am	Amos	*2 Thess*	2 Thessalonians
Ob	Obadiah	*1 Tim*	1 Timothy
Jon	Jonah	*2 Tim*	2 Timothy
Mic	Micah	*Titus*	Titus
Nah	Nahum	*Philem*	Philemon
Hab	Habakkuk	*Heb*	Hebrews
Zeph	Zephaniah	Jas	James
Hag	Haggai	*1 Pet*	1 Peter
Zech	Zechariah	*2 Pet*	2 Peter
Mal	Malachi	*1 Jn*	1 John
Tob	Tobit	*2 Jn*	2 John
Jdt	Judith	*3 Jn*	3 John
Add Esth	Additions to Esther	*Jude*	Jude
Wis	Wisdom	*Rev*	Revelation